# From

# SILVER WINGS

# To

# GOLDEN YEARS

# Words to Live By

**Learn and acknowledge your limitations.**

Set goals within your limitations

After choosing attainable goals be determined to be the best. Compete only against yourself. After you have mastered your niches you will be acknowledged, respected and satisfied.

Mark Twain said it best as quoted by Justin Kaplan in his introduction to *Mark Twain's Short Stories:*

**Mark Twain:**

...I have had a 'call' to literature, of a low order—i.e., humorous. It is nothing to be proud of, but it is my strongest suit, & if I were to listen to that maxim of stern duty which says that to do right you must multiply the one or the two or the three talents which the Almighty entrusts to your keeping, I would long ago have ceased to meddle with things for which I was by nature unfitted...

# From
# SILVER WINGS
# To
# GOLDEN YEARS

Greatest Generation Memoir
WWII pilot: Stearman, B-25
Portland: Streetcar/Bus
Long Line Trucker
Photo: Aerial, Weddings,
Beauty Pageants,
Rose Festival Queen,
NW Rodeo,
Portland Boxing Club,
Oregon AOPA
Steens Mountain High Altitude Running Camp

# Charles E. Romans

**ISBN-10:1535410507**

**ISBN-13:978-1535410502**

Library of Congress Control Number: **2016915282**
CreateSpace Independent Publishing Platform, North Charleston, SC

Printed by CreateSpace,
An Amazon. com Company

USA

# Contents

## BOOK 1
## From Baby Shoes to Silver Wings

Henry and Lorene   1
A Family of Orphans   3
The John Daly Farm   4
My World   5
The Lathams  7
Mr. Daly's Woodlot   8

**Life on a Prairie Farm**

Barnyard Drama   9
Planting Corn   10
Train Travel 1930 Style   11
The Galloping Goose   12

**Hartford Grade School**

1931   14
Hazardous Road to Hartford   15
One Strong Father   16
The Good Old Days   17
The Fire – 1934   18
Our Old Kentucky Home   21
Homemakers and /entrepreneurs   21
Miss Artie   22
Lands of Lincoln   22
My Kentucky Land   24
   School Days
1939 – 1940   25

**A Defining Summer**

Muscles   27
Aviation   28
Operating Vehicles   29
Photography   29
Grammar   31
1941   32
1941 – 1942   33
1942   35
1942 – 1943   37
News (Barber Shop)   39
18   40
My Day at Western   42

## BOOK 2
## Silver Wings

The Long Road to Jefferson Barracks    44
The Hinkle Field House    45
The Gymnasium    46
I meet Norma Montague    47
The Meridian Bus    47
San Antonio    49
San Angelo    50
Solo    51
Baby Shoes to Silver Wings    52
Speech    54
Pampa, Texas    55
To San Marcos the Long Way    58
At Home in San Marcos    59

## BOOK 3
## Settling in Oregon

Country Boy Needs a Job    68
Earthquakes    69
Nell Roy's First Oregon Job    70
Milk Man    72

## BOOK 4
## Streetcars and BUSES

Horsecars and a Lost Doll    74
Kentucky Meets Virginia in Oregon    76
Hot Beef Sandwich    77
Sleep    78
Pat Daniels    79
Council Crest    81
Dinty's    83
Our First Auto    84
Vanport Flood    85
I Become a Builder    86
Childbirth 1940s Style    86
Nancy    87
Boogie Woogie and WWII    88
Tricks    89

Electric Buses 91
Our First TV    92
Oysters  93
Gangsters and Small Cars      95
Greco    96
PA    97
His Stamina Dropped   98
Hazards in Uniform      100
Drama on Eighty-Second Avenue    102
Roll up the Wire  104
3-D       105
Back to Flying     106
Weather        106
Huey    107
West to Omaha    108
The Stranger on my Bus    110
The Passenger    110
Minnie Pearl    112
Captain Johann Eloff   113
Me and Joe Louis    114
Ten Dollars and a Bus Ticket     116
Dr. Irwin Ladd    117
Dr. Robert A. Bradley   119
Me and General MacArthur's Aid    119
    Portland by Starlight
Long Pageant of Beauty     120
        By Doug Baker
    Night Flight Over Mount St. Helens    121
Melba and Stubby Staubitz    122
Foggy Flight    122
Conquering Mount Hood  124
Our Mary Worth    125
A Mary Worth Episode by "Auntie"     126
The Sunday Drive    127
Shuttle Across the Pacific from Seattle    128
Dry Dock    130

# BOOK 5
# Photography

James and Jane Caine  132
A Busy Afternoon    133
Me and Charles Morse  133

11 Sisters  135
A Drawer Full of Money and a Glass of Milk  136
Basque Country  137
Harlan and Lou Rice  138
Dee's Distinguished Portraits  139
The Wedding Photographer  139
Ilse's Hollywood Studio  141
Portland Rose Festival  142
Grant High School Wedding  143
The Myna Bird  144
Yuen Lui Studios  144
Bob, Child Photographer Extraordinaire  146
Paul Harvey  147
The Case of the Pancake House  148
Aircraft Owners and Pilots Association  150
Slot Cars  150
Studio Manager  151

# BOOK 6
# Truck Driver

Learning from the Corn Flakers  152
Hired by Exley  154
Cowboys and Indians  156
Martha and Common Sense  157
Cowboy Hats and Asparagus  158
Asleep at the Wheel  159
Kid Talk and Salty Language  160
Boats  160
Pollard Flat  161
Home on the Road  161
Old 97  162
El Camino Real  165
Obituary on the World Wide Web  167
Where are your Big Trees?  167
Casual Driver  170
American Made  171
Wolf Creek Pass  173
1973 USA Trip  177
North Pacific Canners and Packers (Flav-R-Pac Foods)  180
Going Home  180
Blizzard  182
Me and Resers  185

A Cup of Coffee    187
Train to Chicago  188
Dubuque, Iowa Hams and Oregon Strawberries    189
Guns 191
The Spokane World's Fair 192
A Big Bouquet of Roses    193
Star Wars    194
Hold Up in Gary  195
Cancer  196
Trucking – A Job/A Blessing 197
Dr. George Crile, Jr.    199
Unnecessary Radical Practices    200
Mount Vernon    202
A Thread through the Fabric of My Life    203
Oshkosh    204
Divorce    205
35 Years    207

# BOOK 7
## Libby Jane

J. J. Forester  209
Atlasta   212
Los Angeles and San Bernardino    214
I Meet Vivian  216
Melinda    217
Romantic Poets    218
Wedding 1981    220
Our Love Story    221
A Freightliner Built for Two    223
The Hearst Castle    227
Jack London and Me    228

# BOOK  8
## School Buses

Arthur L. Williams    232
School Bus Services 233
Happy Noise   234
Anna – A Little Blind Orphan    234
Heard on the bus    236
Chocolate Cake   237
Bali  238
The Khyber Pass    239

Two Tonys   240
Oregon's Pacific Coast  241
Bus Biz is Born   243
Mt. Hood Ski Trips  244
Mt. Hood Meadows    245
The Basque   246
Faux Greyhound Driver   248
Steens Mountain High Altitude Running Camp   249
History's Black Marks  251
Mountain Storm  253
The Big Day   254
Denio, Nevada   255
Saturday Morning   255
Portland, Oregon to Portland, Maine  256
El Paso, Phoenix and Home   258
A Steens Mountain Farewell  258
Transporting Firefighters  260
SBS to Ryder   264

# BOOK 9
## Back to Kentucky

Our Old Kentucky Home  266
Me and Reeta   268
Eden's Child by Reeta Burden   268
Driving Again – School Buses and Lawn Mowers   270
Digital Photography   272
Indians in Butler County  273
Janie's Ch... Ch... Cha...   275

### Memory and Old Age

Memory Box  276
1914 – 2014   277
Backing Up? Watch Out!  278
The Toughest Job   279
Once Upon a Time – Once   280
Golden Years  282
Veterans Affairs Medical   283
A Visit to the V. A. Nashville  284
Treasures and Memories  286
Tapestry Complete  287
Janie's Country Boy 288
Romans Bluff and Green River   289

## Foreword

I entered the world on August 3, 1925. For the next nine years I would live on this 100 acre farm in central Illinois. After our home burned Dad moved his family back to his boyhood home in Butler County, Kentucky. That was my home for the next nine years.

That hot summer when I was born two threads were formed in St. James, Missouri that would weave through the fabric of my life. Eight year old Libby Jane Forester would take a ride with a barnstormer named Charles A. Lindbergh. One night in 1926 Lindbergh bailed out and crashed his plane 10 miles from where I was sleeping. When I was six I started school wearing a helmet and goggles like hundreds of other little airplane pilot wannabes. In 1945 I became a Second Lieutenant, officer and pilot, after training in B-25s.

In December 1945 I left Pampa, Texas for Oregon with my Texas bride, Nell Roy and her parents.

In 1946 Libby Jane and her husband, Burl Borden became our neighbors in Portland, Oregon where I was operating streetcars. In 1981 the widow Libby Jane became my wife in my second marriage. By marriage I became Uncle to her sister's son, a Flying Tiger in WWII.

I first experienced fatherhood when my daughter, Charla Kay, was born in 1949. I was thoroughly disillusioned by ridiculous rules and arrogant doctors. As I butted heads with the mighty medical establishment I was privileged to meet and work with the two greatest rebel doctors in modern times, Dr. Robert Bradley with the Porter Hospital in Denver and Dr. George Crile, Jr. with the Cleveland Clinic in Ohio.

I acquired a camera and darkroom equipment in 1940. From 1942 I was, besides other trades, a professional photographer. A camera opens doors. I met the retired heavyweight champion, Joe Louis, to complete a thread that began in 1937.

I photographed middle weight champion, Bobo Olsen in action and as he posed with 7' 3" Ewart Potgieter from South Africa.

I photographed the Portland Rose Festival Queen.

As an innovative wedding photographer I recorded ceremonies of Catholic, Protestant, Greek Orthodox and Moslem weddings. At Grant High School where the movie, *Mr. Holland's Opus* was filmed, I recorded a wedding event of grand proportions ending at midnight with a black rum cake in a Haitian moment.

These few threads are typical of the many that have been woven through the fabric of my life to create a tapestry of memories that is beyond anything I could have imagined. The last threads are being woven into the fringe forming the end of my tapestry. Sit by me in the pilot's seat or driver's seat. See what I see through the windshield. See what I see through the eyes of my friends or my Libby Jane as she approaches 100 years of living.

Many of these stories were first published in *The Butler County Banner*, formerly, *The Green River Republican of Morgantown, Kentucky*. I became a regular correspondent with a weekly story accompanied by 1 to 3 photos. This book is mostly those weekly columns, grouped and modified for continuity.

Those of us who served in WWII are said to be the greatest generation. We supposedly saved the world for the next generation. Where is that world now?

This is my life. It is a way of life that is gone forever. I can't save it. I can only save the memory of it. The middle class had many opportunities. Each choice and change I made seemed like a different life, a different existence, a different story, a different *book*. This is my tapestry of memories.

# From

# SILVER WINGS

# To

# GOLDEN YEARS

I left Morgantown, Kentucky in 1943 to enter the United States Army Air Corp. I returned in 1997. Since then a weekly column in the Butler County Banner has carried hundreds of stories of my life in Butler County and beyond. Every story has been accompanied by one to three pictures.

The pictures are a natural contribution. My Great Grandfather, David Coats, was a professional photographer beginning in the late 1800s. My mother left me a shoebox full of Brownie Kodak photos snatched from the fire that burned our Illinois farmhouse in 1934. Photography has been my avocation since 1942.

My 99 year old wife has contributed stories and photos from her rich life and that of her father who was born in 1854.

Much of this volume was gleaned from those Banner stories. It is a story like no other. It is a view of an America that is gone forever.

*Charles E. Romans*

BOOK 1

From
Baby Shoes
To
Silver
Wings

## Henry and Lorene

There were few roads out of Butler County. There were steamboats on Green River; or you could walk. Henry Romans and his pal, Charlie Ingram, got work on the farm of John Robert Vincent. They walked from Butler County to the farm in Muhlenberg County.

After a few weeks of associating with the Vincent family, Henry made up his mind. In Morgantown he bought a ring and prepared to propose to the oldest daughter of Robert and Maude Vincent. When he next arrived at the Vincent's he was too late. Charlie was engaged to Violet. Twenty year old Henry then offered his ring to sixteen year old Opal Lorene, the second oldest Vincent girl.

Henry (no middle initial) Romans, my father, was six years old when his father, Newton Aaron Romans, died. There were no commodities or food banks and Dad said they would have starved to death if there had not been so many fish in Green River that ran along the back of the 60-acre farm. But his mother, Mary, had no grease to fry the fish and no salt to season them. She boiled the fish to make them edible and they were able to survive. When Dad was fourteen his mother could no longer cope so she ended her life. Dad had evidently exhibited a maturity and judgement that impressed his mother. Although he was the middle child of the 5, she left a note asking Dad to take care of his 3 brothers and 1 sister.

Mom, Opal Lorene, was number 2 of what would eventually be 10 children in the Vincent family. If Grandma left for a while she had Lorene take charge. Grandma was going to her in-laws one day so she gave young Lorene her long handled bell she used when teaching school. She told her to ring the bell in case of emergency. She walked past the barn, through the pasture gate and up the steep hill. At the top where the road continued toward Cleaton she turned left where a short road lead to the home of Grandpa's parents. She had just arrived at the top of the hill when the school bell began ringing with an urgency that just wouldn't stop. She ran for home. Mom's younger brother, Elmer, had grabbed the bell and vigorously rang it as Mom chased him around and around the house. When Grandma breathlessly came around the corner Mom had caught him and had him across her lap giving him a spanking he wouldn't soon forget. Grandma saw that the emergency was under control and went back up the hill on her errand.

Although these 2 mature young people, Henry Romans and Lorene Vincent were matched up by a failed strategy it proved to be an excellent match.

The friendship between Charlie Ingram and Henry Romans was even stronger after they had wives who were sisters.

The Romans lived in a small house on 2 acres deeded off the Vincent farm. Their first child was born there. He was named Robert Newton after his two grandfathers, John Robert Vincent and Newton Aaron Romans. Sadly, he died of pneumonia on March 10, 1924 when he was a few weeks old, a common occurrence in those days.

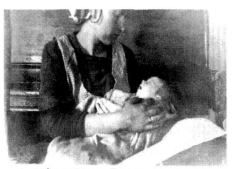

Robert Newton Romans  3-10 1924

## A Family of Orphans

When Arthur Dotson, a WWI veteran, came to Kentucky from Tennessee and married Dad's Sister, Stella, he was marrying into a family of orphans. He took his wife to Illinois, a more prosperous farming land, to seek his fortune. He leased a 300 acre farm from the Hieronymus family and made it prosper. Uncle Dot could neither read nor write and signed his checks with an X. He was good at figures and was a good manager. He was the first in Tazewell County to have rubber tired tractors and farm equipment so he could go on the public roads and do custom work for his neighbors. Uncle Dot became an anchor for his neighborhood and the Romans family.

Dad had not married yet when he checked out Illinois. He got a job in a factory in Peoria and lived in a boarding house. One morning the landlady roared in to where they were eating breakfast at the common table and demanded to know who caused the toilet to overflow all over the bathroom floor. In recounting the incident Dad told me he kept quiet. He had flushed it but he didn't plug it. Years later when I heard Mom sing her version of an Irish song made popular by Bing Crosby it reminded me of Dad's boarding house escapade.

Who threw the overalls in Mrs. Murphy's chowder?
No one answered her at all so she shouted all the louder.

Dad dated a young woman named Dolly but nothing serious developed and he wasn't cut out for factory work so he went back to Kentucky. Later, Dolly and her husband, Morton Meeks would be one of the family friends we visited.

1924

### The John Daly Farm

When the word came that the 100 acre John Daly farm, next one west of the Dotson's 300 acres, was available, Dad and Mom closed their little house and headed north in 1924. The Daly farmhouse was the birthplace of me in 1925, Wanda Nell in 1927 and of Velma Louise in 1930. After it burned in 1934, the twins, Harold Wayne and Henry Duane, were born in the remodeled garage.

Dad always wore a long sleeved blue shirt while working in the sun. They have a saying down south: Horses sweat, men perspire and ladies glow. Perspire is not an adequate word for the way water poured off Dad; he sweated. With plenty of water he could work in the sun on the hottest of days. I inherited that ability from him with an exception; for 80 years I worked in the sun without a shirt.

One hot August day, Dad, with some neighbors was working in the harvest on the Ernest Anderson farm. Someone came running yelling to get Dad's attention. "Hurry home. Your wife is having the baby." Dad hurried across the road and up the lane in time to be with Mom when I was born. Soon Dad used the Model T to pick up Mom's mother and sister Ann at the train station in Atlanta. She wanted to hold her newest grandson.

I wasn't meant to be the oldest in the family of Henry and Lorene Romans. I was left that position by my older brother whom I never knew. Our grandfathers' names went to the grave with Robert Newton so I was named Charles after John Daly's son and Ernest after Ernest Anderson. With Ernest as my middle name the Anderson thread through the pattern of my life is with me to perpetuity.

Ernest Anderson was a relative by marriage. His brother, Richard, was married to Dad's cousin, Leora Pryor. Their daughter, Dorothy, stayed with us for several days when the twins were born. When we moved back to Kentucky in 1934, Richard and Ora, with Dorothy, moved also. Now, eighty years after we moved I attend Sunday meetings in Beaver Dam, Kentucky with Dorothy's son, Harold Austin and his wife Lola while Dorothy lives in a rest home nearby. More about the Andersons later for they are truly one of the beautiful threads through the pattern of my memories.

I was about 5 when we visited Kentucky. I posed with Dad, Grandpa John Vincent and Grandpa's parents. With Great Grandpa

and Great Grandma in the picture we were 4 generations.

## My World

My mind full of curiosity would be fed for the first nine years in this Tazewell County, Hittle Township in Central Illinois. Our house faced west. In the front yard the garage was the end of the lane that went south to our left. Turning left at the end of the lane would take us along the fields of Ernest Anderson and the first lane on the left was to the home and farm buildings of Uncle Dot and Aunt Stella.

But at the end of the lane this time, let us turn right (west). In a few yards we are in front of Irv and Lennie Latham's home where young Gene would become my playmate. The next crossroad intersection was called Center said to be the geographic center of Illinois. Going left takes us past Ross Sellers home. Wanda called him Salt Cellars! It is one mile to Armington, Pop. 500.

Center had a name but it was just an intersection with a rail road crossing. Across the railroad stood a grain elevator on the right and across the lawn was the home of John Gar. His daughter, Eva, stayed with Mom for a few days when I was born. Some 40 years later as I trucked through this area. I would stop to see Eva at the rest home at Lincoln where she lived. The state capitol was at Springfield about 50 miles south of Armington and Lincoln was in between. Eva said that I was coming to see her more often than her son who lived nearby.

A larger town, Minier, was some 5 miles north of Center. We were getting ready to go to Minier in the Model T Ford one day. Mom needed some groceries. Five year old Wanda asked her, "Are we going to Your Neer?"

The first driveway on the left going north was the home of a Dutchman, John Pioneer. He pronounced it 'Pan-near.' The Verry Brothers bank he called the Worry Bank! Dad responded by saying the bank also worried him sometimes.

Dad's youngest brother, Bill, married Oma Berry and lived on the next farm to the Pioneers. Then on the next intersection with Hartford Road we turned right at the home of Homer Holstein. Soon we are in front of Shan Kindred's home. His farm is back to back with Dad's farm. Wanda and I would walk across our pasture, then across the Kindred field and yard, then a mile east to Hartford grade school.

The lane across the road from the school lead to the Burton home back of the Dotson farm. Classmate Dorothy was my age and Marjorie was older.

At the next intersection we go right and we are soon in front of Lyle Rhodes home. I was to be his farm hand in the spring and early summer of 1943. It was then I learned about Uncle John. Dad's second oldest brother, John, was working on this same farm in 1927. At the end of the day he was sweating excessively and feeling weak. He soon died of pneumonia. I was too young to remember Uncle John but he had given me a present, a hollow rubber ball, which I had long enough to remember it.

The summer I worked for Lyle and Ms. Hallie I rode my bicycle down past the Reynolds farm to the next road, turned right past the

Becker's whose daughter had the rhythmic name, Buella Bell Becker, then turned right on uncle Dot's lane ready for a weekend with my cousins.

This was my world for nine years - plus four high school summers.

## The Lathams

In her medicine cabinet Mom had an arsenal of medicines for ailments, cuts and bruises. Among her medications there was Vermifuge for worms, Watkins Liniment for aches and pains, Iodine and Mercurochrome for cuts and bruises, and when we moved to Kentucky, Sassafras Root Tea was added in the Spring - 'it thins the blood.'

When we had a scrape we hated to see Mom coming with the iodine bottle. That stuff could *sting!* Mercurochrome was much milder and supposedly kept down infection as well.

The Model T Ford took money for gasoline so Dad hooked up the 2 horses, Dan (the black one) and Goldie (the white one) to the new buggy to go to Armington on an errand. Wanda and I climbed aboard to go along. After our long lane we turned right. Dad gave the horses their head and we went racing past the Latham home. Lennie called Mom on the phone and asked, "When did Henry get a 2 wheel buggy?" Mom told her we only had the 4 wheeler. We had passed the Latham place so fast she thought she saw only 2 wheels!

Dad made his purchase and we headed home. When we got to Latham's he pulled over and hitched the horses and headed for the barn where he saw Irv. Four-year-old Wanda and I raced into the house where their grown son, Rex, was sitting at the table for a late breakfast. We told him and Lennie that Dad had bought a huge bottle of Mercurochrome, indicating with our hands that it was a tall, long necked bottle that must hold at least a fruit jar full of Mercurochrome. They scoffed at the idea. "It doesn't come in bottles that big."

Wanda and I hurried out to the buggy to get the proof. We came back with the big package. On the table we proceeded to remove the butcher paper and out fell a curry comb for grooming horses! Rex almost turned over his chair he was laughing so hard!

## Mr. Daly's Woodlot

Straps around his hand held a pad in his palm with a claw in the middle. With that Dad could tear the shuck back and snap the ear of corn out and flip it to the high backboard where it fell into the wagon. He often had the next ear in the air before that one was in the wagon.

With the harvest in and winter in the air it was time to get the rest of the winter heating and cooking wood in. Dad removed the extra boards down to the basic bed of the wagon and mounted the spring seat up front and we were ready to haul wood. Our landlord owned a wood lot west of the farm and as tenants we had the use of it.

Dad hitched up the team. We climbed into the seat, went down the lane and turned right. At Center we did not turn left to Armington nor right for Minier. We continued west about another mile and turned left into the lot. After shutting the gate we proceeded to a patch of timber where Dad sawed and chopped and loaded the wagon.

Wood gathering time was fun. Berry vines grew in the open spaces on the Daly woodlot. They called them Dew berries. They were delicious. The Boysenberry jam and jelly we buy now has a similar taste. The Boysenberry and Dew berry are related to the Blackberry. In Oregon they raise a small black raspberry often called blackcaps. They taste much as I remember the dew berry. Their delicious flavor and the memories they evoke make them my favorite berry. On the way back we were caught in a hailstorm. A hailstone pinged me on my right ear. I quickly reached on top of my head and unfastened the straps on my aviation helmet. Soon the flaps were over my ears and the straps fastened firmly under my chin and the goggles over my eyes. That hailstone nailed the memory of that helmet firmly into my brain. When our home burned I lost my Lindbergh inspired, wannabe pilot, school helmet. A decade later I would be wearing a real aviation helmet as I racked up 103 hours of flight time in open cockpit WWI type airplanes.

## Life on a Prairie Farm

### Barnyard Drama

Mom played a trick on that old setting hen. She filled the nest with Guinea eggs. When they hatched the old hen found her out and abandoned the Guinea keets. She laid her own eggs in the hedge row and had the chickens she wanted.

Wanda, in her baby talk, called Linnie Latham 'Guinea'. So when Mom told her these new fowl were Guineas she wouldn't go along with that. "They are Guinea's chickens."

Mom had her 300 egg incubator loaded. From a hayloft nest I had stolen 2 pigeon eggs and added them to the incubator. They hatched in due time and one pigeon was wild from the beginning but Pete stayed around with us but always just out of reach. The baby guineas learned that the old rooster could find and scratch up food as well as a mother hen. Every morning it became a familiar sight: Mr. Rooster leads the parade with a dozen baby guineas following and Pete the pigeon bringing up the rear. If only there had been a camcorder! But that scene is a snapshot of memory I always enjoy.

Mom took a picture of Dad holding 2 year old me. He had to hold me because I didn't want to pose. I wanted to play with my 2 pet pigs. They make good pets.

Another fowl Mom kept was geese. From them we got feather beds and pillows and roast goose. The old gander had a mean streak. Velma would be screaming as he chased her about the yard, nipping at her legs and bottom at every step.

One morning I had left for school when Mom heard frantic bellering from our cow. Mom could imagine her chasing me or stomping me to death as she ran out of the house and looked across the barnyard. The old gander had a hold on the cow's tail and she was like a bull trying to get rid of a tenacious rodeo cowboy.

Dad bought me a retired racehorse but no saddle. I rode him to the end of the lane and he decided to race back to the house. I got a grip on his mane and held on for dear life. I was still on when he stopped at the barnyard gate. My riding career came to an abrupt halt. After that I would only ride a tame, plodding work horse. But being farm kids, my sisters and I never got too sentimental about the animals. We enjoyed the fresh meat with Mom's garden vegetables. We would watch Dad butcher the hogs and we soon had chunks of liver on a stick roasting in the fire where Dad heated water for removing the hair. I don't know how much help we were but we tried. We would use the round scraper with the sharp rim to shave off the hair. That could be tough work. They are not called hog bristles for nothing. We tried to do a good job since we didn't want hair on our bacon.

Farm kids found plenty to do to keep them busy and interested.

Robert Dotson

**Corn Planter**
The farmers check planted their corn. The rows were 3 feet apart and the hills were 3 feet apart. The cultivator could plow between the hills either north and south or east and west.

Uncle Dot was driving to Armington one day. As he turned left at Center there was Ross Sellers sitting on his corn planter. He had just moved the wire over and hooked into the planter and had the horses headed to cross the field. Uncle Dot honked his horn at him. The startled horses leaped ahead and raced across the field as Ross picked himself up where he had toppled backwards off the spring seat. The horses stopped at the far end of the field and everyone agreed; those were the two straightest rows of corn in the field that year!

1928 Charles & Wanda with mother

**Train Travel 1930s Style**

Four hundred miles separated Mom from her folks but trains kept them in touch. Mom's mother, my grandmother from Cleaton, Kentucky soon came to see her latest grandson. Dad probably picked her up at the Atlanta, Illinois train station in his Model T Ford. Mom's shadow shows in the picture as she used her Brownie Kodak to photograph Grandma holding me. Sarah Ann, Mom's youngest sister at that time was with her. Mom's youngest sibling would be born two years later. I would be 2 years older than my youngest Aunt! Sue is my last aunt living at the time of this writing. My 3 year old visit was in 1928 when Wanda was 1 year old.

As I got older I appreciated the trips more. It was an exciting time for us youngsters. I loved those friendly black porters in their snappy uniforms. It was a fine occupation for our African Americans at that time. After several hours of riding we would arrive at Central City where our relatives would meet the train to take us out to Grandpa's farm. Red Cap porters would meet the train to handle our baggage. One went up and down the platform hawking a nearby hotel for those who needed a room. "Hotel Lu Ray across the way." Another was trying to be louder, "Hotel MacDowell, uptown."

In my personal library the Hotel Red Book for 1956 still had the Hotel Lu Ray listed. It also showed that Central City was served by the Illinois Central Railroad.

It was a great era for travel. I am glad I lived it. I became a lifelong railroad fan.

## The Galloping Goose

About a mile west of our home the next section line road ran north and south. A railroad track ran parallel on the far side of the road. A commuter train called The Galloping Goose ran by every day. It usually had the engine and 2 cars. In my small childhood world it came from somewhere up north and went somewhere down south and then back. The most delicious wild strawberries grew on the railroad right of way. Over 80 years later I judge strawberries, "Are they as sweet as the ones by the railroad?"

Mom's sister was visiting and they decided to go pick some berries. I was taken along. Soon we heard a train coming. I asked if I could stand about 6 feet from the track. That seemed safe enough. When the train came thundering by it didn't seem so safe. When the train got by I had backed up several feet!

Mom was driving the Model T Ford to Armington for some groceries. I went along. Down the lane, turn right (west) about a mile then left with the train tracks on our right and we were soon in Armington. When Mom turned right to go into downtown it was just a few feet to the RR Crossing. She looked right. Sure enough, here comes The Galloping Goose. She slammed on the brakes. I had been standing on my feet in the back seat; instantly I was standing on my head in front of the front seat!

Mom was working in the kitchen when she heard the whistle of The Galloping Goose. The sound went persistently on and on. "I wonder if there is something wrong," she thought. "That seems to be coming from Bill's place" She headed for the phone.

Uncle Bill had opened the pasture gate and driven his Model T on the level of the railroad tracks. He went back and secured the gate and started back to the car when he heard the train coming from the south. He tried to move the car but saw that he was too late. I can still remember him telling us about it. "I shut my eyes and thought of death."

The cow catcher on the front of the train slammed under the side of the car booting it upward. Uncle Bill was hurtled through the cloth roof and landed on his feet beside the track!

Dads next Model T was an enclosed 2 door family car. It was the

one that brought us to Butler County, Kentucky in 1934.

Dad still owned their first home and 2 acres in Muhlenberg County. He traded that to Grandma for a 1930 Model A. Mom refused to drive it. She didn't like that newfangled gearshift. Her driving days ended with the Model A. Mine began.

## Hartford Grade School

**1931.**
I turned 6 years old. It was time to start going to school. Hartford Grade School was in the rural of Tazewell, County, Illinois. It was a one and a half mile walk from our farm. There were no school buses. I didn't start school among all strangers. Dad's sister Stella lived on the next farm east of us. She had 3 children in Hartford when I started: Betty, Edna Mae and Buster

Dad's brother Bill had 3 children but they lived west of us in a different school district.

Miss Luella Hainline was our teacher all 4 years I went to Hartford. All eight grades were in one big room. Each class stepped forward and sat in chairs before the teacher to recite our lessons. Anyone making the slightest noise in the big room got their hand spanked with a one foot ruler.

Mom caused me some embarrassment. She sent me to school scrubbed clean and neat. Miss Hainline once sat me on her lap and told all how neat I was and how clean I smelled. But I was not a teacher's pet and I was not a sissy. I didn't like the rough play of some boys so I was often playing with the girls where I early showed my artistic bent by making the prettiest decorated mud pies!

During the second grade we were told we would have a test in the afternoon. I didn't know what a test was but everyone seemed either excited or apprehensive. I was terrified. When the bell rang after lunch everyone went to their seat except me. I hid in the nearby cornfield. The teacher and 2 helpers came looking for me. I finally yielded to the inevitable and gave myself up. We went in and Miss Hainline asked her spies to point out who had misbehaved while she was gone. A few got their hand slapped with the ruler. I was ignored. They just thought I had gotten lost. The test didn't prove to be so bad and never again would I be afraid to face a problem head on. In 1933 my sister Wanda joined me on the walk to school. Betty Dotson had graduated but her little sister Opal had joined us.

I am in the very middle of the 1933 group picture with Buster Dotson on my right and Edna Mae behind me. Opal Dotson, named after my mother, Opal Lorene, is second from the right on the front row and my sister Wanda is first on the left.

Dad's family gave me 9 first cousins, Dotson's had 5, Uncle Bill had 3 and Uncle Vannie Romans in Muhlenberg County, Kentucky had 1.

Mom's 9 brothers and sisters gave me too many cousins to count! In all I had over 30 first cousins. So I could say I had cousins by the dozens!

In 1934 in the middle of the fourth grade, we moved to Kentucky where I finished the fourth grade at Science Hill (Big Hill) school on Logansport Road with Dad's cousin, Miss Bessie Romans as teacher.

I was 40 years old when I saw Miss Hainline one last time. I was on vacation from Portland, Oregon and stopped at a gas station in the edge of Armington. Someone told me Luella Hainline was a block down the street with her family. Her mother had just died. I went to the house and knocked. The door opened and I recognized Miss Hainline sitting across the room. "I am here to see that lady but she probably doesn't know me." I said as I pointed to her.

She amazed me by saying, "You're Charles Romans!"

## Hazardous Road to Hartford
There were no school buses so unless there was a blizzard in progress, school was open. I walked to school and sometimes walked over the fences on the snowdrifts. I would cross our pasture, then cross Shan Kindred's field and barn lot. Then to exit into the driveway I would step up on the cattle's water tank that was in a gap in the fence. A big step to the other rim and I could step down and be across the fence.

One frigid day I slipped on the icy rim and plunged to the bottom through a layer of ice. I climbed out and went to the house. Mrs. Gladys Kindred had a big daughter, Florine and a small son. The only dry clothes she had to fit me were Margie's, the girl my age. No, Thanks! I warmed up and walked the cold trip back home.

Later when the Health Nurse visited our school and I got my checkup in the library Miss Hainline introduced me to the nurse, "This is the young man who fell in the water tank."

"Yep," I said. "My head went up and my speller went down."

That was when they first learned that I had lost my Speller book in the water tank.

Spring could be hazardous, also. One afternoon I was crossing the Kindred's plowed field for home. The old black gumbo soil was wet and sticky. My 4 buckle overshoes were secure but it was all I could do to pull one up and put it in front of the other. A few yards from the home fence I gave up and stood bawling in frustration. Mom finally heard me and came to the rescue. When she was a few feet from me, I mustered up enough strength to walk out.

## One Strong Father

The 100 acre Daly place that we farmed in central Illinois had a 40 acre field on the east side of the lane and a 40 acre field on the west side. The other 20 acres were the yard, the barn yard, garden and truck patch.

Dad walked across the east field to the Dotson farm to see his sister. When he left to come back to our house that afternoon it had started to snow quite hard. He climbed the fence and started west. He was soon in a white out. After several minutes he didn't find the west fence or gate to the house. He kept walking. An hour passed and he still hadn't found a fence. When one is walking blind they tend to walk in circles. He kept walking and hoping, not giving up until he finally bumped into the fence. He had no idea which side of the field he was on but he stayed in touch with the fence until he came to the gate and the home he had feared he would never see again. Others have tired out and frozen to death in like circumstances.

Summer brought another huge problem. A plague of chinch bugs was coming our way from the west. Chinch bugs were native to the American scene, living on grass. When the Midwest farmers raised big fields of grassy plants like wheat and oats and even sweet tender blades of corn they took it to be *their* bounty and proliferated into huge swarms leaving the land bare as they moved across their feeding path.

The farmers tried to fight back. I, little Charles, tagged along and watched as Dad prepared for the onslaught. He had a nice crop of corn coming up in the east 40. Could he save any of it?

First, he plowed a furrow about 3 inches deep around the field. Then about every twenty feet he dug a post hole. Next, he took a 5 gallon pail and put a nail hole in the bottom. Filling that with creosote he removed the nail and walked along the furrow laying a narrow line of creosote between and through the postholes. He kept carrying buckets of this pungent liquid until he had circled the field. Then a puddle of creosote was poured in the bottom of each hole.

Just in time! The ground was black with these little critters as they crossed the lane. Dad had spent a lot on preparing for this but a lot of work and expense on the crop was at stake. In the middle of the furrow the bugs came to the line of creosote and sought a way to the corn on the other side. They followed the line to the post hole where they fell into the puddle in the bottom and died. After some time the bugs would acquire wings but it was hoped that by then the corn would be hardy and a reasonable pay crop would survive.

To get the chinch bugs back to the minor pest they are today, farmers switched to soy beans. That was a necessary thing to do but an odd turn of events. Hardly any Americans would eat soy beans and soy products. Most were sold to the Orient. But now we have learned what they knew; soy beans, tofu, soy milk and other soy products are a delicious and healthy food. With a generous mix of soy bean fields and pesticides, corn and wheat is thriving as never before. Chinch bugs are still with us as a minor nuisance. For a while, Chinch bugs were a plague that gave a father a chance to show his little son how to persevere when the odds looked hopeless.

**The Good Old Days**

The depression was on but for us children, life was great. When the folks bought groceries at Mr. Beasley's in Minier he gave us Milky Way bars. When we bought groceries in Armington we were given 10 cent tickets for the Saturday night movies.

We stopped by to visit with Mrs. Allen until movie time one Saturday evening. Then on Sunday morning we visited again while I read her Sunday funny paper in color. Casually she asked, "What movie did you see last night?" It was about Buffalo Bill. "Oh!" she exclaimed, "I wish I had gone with you. I dated him when I was young."

Mrs. Allen was a fine gracious lady. When her husband, John, died she had given me his safety razor as a gift. It is a prized possession. She had also visited the funeral train of Abraham Lincoln as it came through on its way to his final resting place in Springfield. Truly history was touching me early in life.

My mother was born in 1904 and was 10 years old when WWI started. She was 13 when the US entered the war in 1917. The only thing I remember her saying about the war was that one more call up would have taken her father into the military. It must have been a concern for the family.

Mom liked to sing. She learned lyrics from magazines and tunes and lyrics from the radio. She sung the babies to sleep in the rocking chair and entertained us as we grew older. Her songs included WWI songs.

The old Edison phonograph had records that were cylinders. Our collection included "Over There" and "The Last Long Mile." After I was old enough to use the phonograph I played them over and over until they perished when our home burned in 1934. Fifty years later I wrote a parody with the tune of "The Last Long Mile" for the Steens Mountain High Altitude Running Camp.

In the evenings, Mom read stories and the Bible to us. On Saturday we enjoyed the Saturday Evening Post and listened to Lulu Bell and Scotty on the Chicago station WLS owned by Sears, the World's Largest Store.

Dad's father had 3 brothers. Uncle Walter lived in Bowling Green, Kentucky. Uncle Leslie lived in Morgantown, Kentucky. Uncle Wesley lived nearby in Minier, Illinois. So surrounded by friends and relatives and a prospering farm we enjoyed life.

### The Fire - 1934

I and my 2 sisters, Wanda and Velma had been born in the old Daly farm house. By May the crops were planted and school was still in session. Then one night I awakened and I was in a chair in the front yard. A huge elm and a coffee bean tree were in the front yard. We 3 children had been placed with them between us and the house. The house was ablaze and it was feared that shotgun shells may explode our way.

A fire had started in the kitchen at the east end of the house and when it burned the dining room a chimney fell and woke mom. After securing us children Dad and Mom carried out the family pictures and a few pieces of furniture before the flames drove them back.

The Armington Fire Department circled the section but never found the lane to our house.

The only thing salvaged from the ashes was my Old Dog Tray nut cracker. After new black and red paint it was like new. For weeks I would pedal my tricycle around and around the ash heap that had been our home.

We spent the rest of the night in the chicken house. Dad got a tent for us to live in while the garage was remodeled into a home. With crops in the fields we couldn't move until the harvest was over. A folding bed left more room in the living room. At an auction Dad bought a cook stove for a quarter and was told it wouldn't bake. After he installed a new sheet metal bottom underneath, Mom burned the first batch of biscuits. From then on we continued to enjoy Mom's good cooking.

In early June of 1934 my folks asked if I would like to stay all night with Gene Latham. I usually had to beg for that privilege so now that it was being offered I jumped at the chance. The next morning they told me I had 2 new brothers at my house. I was so excited that they had a hard time getting me to eat breakfast before running up the lane to meet my new twin brothers. Sometime on June 4, 1934 my twin brothers, Harold Wayne and Henry Duane had been born, delivered by a French Canadian doctor, Dr. Rainier, a cousin of the Dionne Quintuplets.

Dorothy Anderson came to stay and help for a while. The Charleston was a popular dance at the time so we moved the furniture to the walls and she showed us the Charleston! Where would she sleep? Upstairs Wanda and Velma had one bed so I insisted she share the other with 8 years old me. That suited everyone but during the night I went sleep walking. Carrying my denim pants down the stairs I spilled slingshot rocks all over, waking up Mom and Dad. Was I surprised when I awakened the next morning in the baby crib and the twins in bed with Mom and Dad!

Then we 3 oldest children caught the measles. They could have been dangerous for the babies but fortunately it missed them. I had just checked out my first big library book, a biography of Kit Carson. For the protection of our eyes, our wise mother kept us in subdued light and would not let me read. As busy as she was in her makeshift circumstances she found time each day to read some of my book to me. What a super Mom we had.

When school was out I turned 9 in August and helped Dad with the work. I operated horse drawn machinery. One hot day we were across the barn lot hoeing weeds in the truck patch when I began feeling faint. Dad, not realizing how sick I was getting, urged me to help finish the job. He was such a loving Dad that I tried to please him. Soon I started blacking out and he lead and half carried me home. That episode of heat sickness could have made me sensitive for life — but it didn't!

We worked hard and harvested the crops. The wheat brought only 12 cents per bushel. That winter a sale of our horses, cows and farm machinery ended Dad's 10 years of Illinois farming. The crops and sale netted Dad $300. That much was seldom seen during the

On the John Daly farm, 3 miles northeast of Armington, on gravel road, on

**TUESDAY. NOVEMBER 20. 1934.**

Commencing at 1:30 p. m., the following property:

**3—HEAD OF HORSES—3**

One bay mare, 14 years old, weight about 1000, a real saddler; one gray mare, 9 years old, weight 1200; one black horse, 9 years old, weight 1300; a good all purpose team.

**3—HEAD OF COWS—3**

One red cow, 10 years old, be fresh January 1st, giving 2 gallons of milk per day now; one red cow, 4 years old, be fresh May 15th, giving 2½ gallons milk per day; one Jersey cow, 5 years old.

One Brooder House 6x9, a good one.

**FARM IMPLEMENTS.**

One Schroeder corn dump, 24-ft. elevator, with wagon jack and horse-power; one box wagon; one rack wagon with basket; one Emerson gang plow, 14-inch; one left hand walking plow, 12-inch; one Surface cultivator, single row; one snoey cultivator, single row; one disc, 8-ft. Setley; one weeder; one hay rake; one 3-section harrow; one endgate seeder; one Setley corn planter and 80 rods of wire; one water tank, medium size; two and one-half sets work harness; six leather collars; other things too numerous to mention.

TERMS—Cash.

**HENRY ROMANS, Owner**

W. G. Beal, Auctioneer.

depression. Some neighbors came by to see what that much money looked like.

Dad hired Everett Wright and his truck to haul our remaining possessions to Kentucky. The family climbed into the Model T Ford car and Dad was headed to his old home in Butler County with 5 kids and $300.00 to start all over.

I had 2 months of the 4th grade behind me and we got settled in time to get the last 2 months in Science Hill School with Dad's cousin, Miss Bessie Romans, teaching. I passed.

1934 wasn't through with us. Later that winter a roaring noise and a jolt awakened me one night. I sat up and saw only black. A storm had knocked our house off its pillars and moved it 3 feet from the chimney. The house was tilted. Mom was holding the twins on her lap and the hot heater was leaning over them.

Dad and I borrowed a house jack and leveled the house. We tore down the chimney and rebuilt it to the house.

Never again did we see a year like 1934!

## Our Old Kentucky Home

### Home Makers and Entrepreneurs

We were busy making the old house into a home. It had been built by  Dad's father in 1900. We added a bedroom. Dad and Mom had a bed in the living room. Across the room was a bed for the twins. The added bedroom with two beds was for me and my sisters, Wanda and Velma.

We carried water up the hill from a spring until we could dig a well.

We built a corncrib of logs where the cracks acted as vents to dry the corn. A stall on one side sheltered the mules and one on the other side was for the milk cow.

I helped clear the 2 acres on the left side of the driveway by taking a corn knife and making beanpoles of the sassafras saplings that covered the field. These I tied in bundles of 25 and carried them 2 miles to Morgantown where I sold them for twenty five cents per bundle.

We mined coal under the hill and with the fireplace converted with a coal burning grate we made more room by removing the potbellied stove from the living room. Twenty five bushels, one ton of coal, taken to an alley in town and shoveled into the back window of a coal house brought a dollar.

## Miss Artie

From late 1934 until the spring of 1939 I attended the one room schoolhouse at Science (Big) Hill on Logansport Road. My teachers included Miss Bessie Romans (my Dad's 1st cousin) James Ayers and Miss Neva Flowers. My 7th grade teacher (1937-8) was Miss Artie Johnson

I recently met Miss Artie as she was leaving after a visit with 100 year old Ione Duke. I handed my camera to a passerby and now have this prized photo!

A popular fund raiser for the one room schools was the frequent Saturday night pie supper. Miss Artie's pie was up for auction. Sam Hankins was the high bidder!

Then in another contest Miss Artie was voted to be 'The Prettiest Woman'. She was too!

Soon after that the crowd took delight in voting Sam Hankins as "The Ugliest Man!" He wasn't; it was all in fun.

Sometime later Miss Artie Johnson became Mrs. Sam Hankins!

Time has given her a fine career and a fine family. She was still very active and a correspondent for The Butler County Banner when I moved to Kentucky in 1997.

To the large army of us who had the privilege of being taught by her, she will always be Miss Artie!

## Lands of Lincoln

On auto license plates, Illinois proclaims itself to be the Land Of Lincoln and it truly is. There in central Illinois is where Lincoln made his home and practiced the politics that lead him to being President. He was a lawyer serving as a circuit rider to surrounding county seats such as Pekin, the county seat of Tazewell County where I was born. The town of Lincoln named for him was a few miles south and some 50 miles south of my hometown of Armington was Springfield, the state capitol.

I moved from Illinois to Kentucky, the state where Abe was born thus reversing his migration from Kentucky to Illinois. Here, I too, studied by firelight and lamplight, walked miles for books to read and swung a mean ax in the woods. Lincoln was known as the (fence) rail splitter. I split tons of firewood. With a broad ax, I hewed 25 cent railroad ties from oak logs. With a mallet and fro I split chestnut logs into slats for fencing and shingles for house and farm building roofs.

I like to tell that I was named after Abraham Lincoln. Me? Named after Abraham Lincoln? Of course I was. I was much too young to be named before him!

About 1940 Dad and I put a fence around our big garden. The fence posts were from long lasting chestnut logs. The railings were weather resistant sassafras saplings. The slats were split from chestnut logs. The only cost was fifty cents for a big sack of nails to nail on the slats. In 1952 I took a self-timed Viewmaster photo of me walking up the driveway past that well preserved fence. I studied that photo to make an oil painting of that scene.

What did Abraham Lincoln find in the woods of this other Land of Lincoln? No doubt the same things I found in the some forty acres of pristine woodland on Dad's sixty acres on Logansport Road.

The depression was still lingering and it seemed criminal to waste food. We tried to not leave a single black walnut to waste on the ground. An occasional White Walnut tree gave us variety.

Hickory nuts were smaller and tedious to pick out but delicious. The scaly bark trees produced larger nuts with thinner shells.

Tiny beech nuts were not good for storage but when you passed a beech tree in the woods you would pause and shuck a few from their prickly outer coat and peel the inner shell away for a few tasty bites.

In late summer ripe persimmons made a tasty treat. Emphasis is on ripe. A green one will make your mouth pucker. That spawned one of my favorite stories: that green persimmon juice can cure baldness. Just when your bald friend's eyes light up you tell him the rest of the story. You rub it on your bald head. It doesn't make hair grow but it puckers the sideburns up to the middle!

Soon after dogwood and redbud blossoms awakened the drab winter woods the sarvis trees leafed out. Ours grew along the top of the Romans Bluff. When their tasty berries ripened it was hazardous to retrieve them as they leaned out over space.

Wild grapevines climbed many trees reaching for the sunlight at the top. Some vines were in strategic places to make swinging ropes for adventurous boys. In the fall the trees were full of clusters of wild grapes. Often classrooms were almost empty of boys as they were out gathering wild grapes. I know, because I was in school. I remembered Dad's razor strop and did not play hooky! There was plenty of time after school and on weekends for me to gather Mom lots of grapes. She canned grape juice for our winter diets.

Both Lands of Lincoln were great for me. I am happy that I didn't miss either one.

## My Kentucky Land

One hundred yard wide Green River bordered the back of our 60 acres on Logansport Road. It included Turkey Rock and the Old Swimming Hole. Green River banks are usually slick mud but this one spot had a sloping shale rock 'beach' making an ideal spot to park one's clothes and wade in for a swim. When Dad was a boy he would hear the steamboat whistle at Aberdeen which gave him time to run to the swimming hole before the sternwheeler got there. One time he was a little late and as he started out a big wave shoved him back on the rocky beach, skinning his rear.

In 1937 when I turned 12 years old he felt it was time to teach me to swim. Soon I was riding the waves behind the sternwheelers. The only ones left were the slow barge pushers. I would catch the wave off the front edge of the barge, go alongside until I got past the paddle wheel, then cut in back as quickly as possible to ride the waves. One day it was a sightseeing group and I saw ladies up on the upper deck. I did *not* do a backstroke as I went skinny dipping past!

Dad and I were at the river one March. I stripped off for a swim. I waded out, breaking the ice in the edge of the water, plunged in and swam out a few yards so I could say I broke ice to swim in Green River. My teeth were chattering as I hurriedly got back into my clothes. I have never been tempted to join the Polar Bear Club and repeat that stunt.

I never developed the patience to wait for fish to bite on my bait. But I didn't mind running the trot line early of a morning and enjoying fresh fried fish for breakfast. There were plenty of mud cats, blue cats and channel cats as well as drum, buffalo and perch.

I once found an arrowhead among the flat rocks so I knew we were not the first to use this swimming hole. How many Native American children played here while the adults did other things like carving the intriguing designs on Turkey rock about 100 yards downstream?

Many think the flat plains of Illinois are boring. Sometimes I was bored but most of the time there were plenty of interesting things to do and observe for a young boy full of curiosity. But Dad's 60 acres in Butler County Kentucky – WOW!

There was the Romans Bluff where there were caves that I could explore or camp all night. There were woods with nut trees which made squirrels plentiful to supplement Mom's fried chicken or pork. In these untamed and neglected woods I found creation as pristine as Kentucky was for Daniel Boone, Abraham Lincoln and Indian lads during centuries past.

We were one half mile from grade school and two miles from an excellent High School and an unexcelled public Library.

**I don't think there was any better place on earth to have spent the years growing from 9 to 18 years of age that could have better contributed to my physical and mental growth and prepared me for what lay ahead, than Butler County, Kentucky.**

## School Days

**1939 – 1940**
With Grade School behind me I was ready to experience town life for the first time as I attending Butler County High School. Morgantown was 2 miles from the farm. The school bus charged fifty cents a month. That was half a day's wages. I walked. It was my decision but I'll bet Dad was pleased. Fifty cents was still hard to come by.

New places and strange faces were a bit stressful that first day. Come lunch time and I took my brown paper bag and headed out across the schoolyard to a bench as far away as possible. I was just getting into it when a pretty redhead, Frances Easley, sat down on the other end of the bench. She liked to have scared me to death. That had to be the shortest bench in town! My peanut butter sandwich got real dry and sticky, or was it my mouth that was dry? I don't know if she got any conversation out of me or not.

I soon got over most of my shyness and grew fond of every classmate in our class. I still tried to keep a low profile. In class I learned to look alert and eager if I didn't know an answer and the teacher would call on someone else. If I knew the answer I would hunker down and look as if I were afraid I would be called on. Ah! Ha! The teacher would sometimes fall for the trick and think here was someone who needed to learn. I would happily speak right up with the right answer.

History was confusing because I didn't have much previous knowledge on which to hang new facts. But as my knowledge grew history became a delight. Arithmetic was easy but boring so I didn't always do all my homework. That sometimes got me an A-. I would butt up against my limitations later.

I didn't go for sports. I was a farm boy and had chores to do.

Sundays were for attending preaching. Our farm was 2 miles from the churches in Morgantown. It was 2 miles the other way to the nearest church in Logansport so we settled for whoever wanted to come to the Science Hill Grade School building and give us a sermon on Sunday. One weekend it was 2 Mormon Elders that had come to town. One of them told us his funny experience. It was a hot dusty day as they arrived at the intersection of R

ochester Road and Logansport Road where our black neighbors were clustered in those days. So one of the boys went up to a house and asked for a drink of water. He was too polite to refuse when a black lady told him to help himself to the fresh drawn bucket of well water with the common drinking dipper. He thought by using his left hand he would drink from the side of the dipper the others didn't use. He was enjoying the refreshing drink when one of the kids said, "Look Mommy. He drinks just like Daddy."

One Sunday as we walked to meeting I heard a thump and looked back. Our pet dog, Old Bum that had moved here with us from Illinois, had been run over by the car that had just passed. He was stretched out apparently dead. Needless to say we didn't make it to preaching that day. Crying, we carried him home where he recovered and lived another few years.

After my freshman year was out in the spring I was feeling that I was no longer just a boy. To Mom's consternation I was insisting that I was going to Illinois and spend the summer working on a big farm and spend time with my cousins. Mom and Dad considered the situation and decided Dad, too, would spend the summer in Illinois.

After I cut a summer supply of firewood for Mom's cooking and hot water needs Dad and I left in the Model A for the 400 mile trip to central Illinois.

## A Defining Summer

**Muscles**.
From the end of my freshman year in the spring of 1940, until the end of my sophomore year in 1941, many things happened to change my life. Five threads would begin weaving through the fabric of my life and will be with me until the end. The first and most dramatic of these was the effect of hard, strenuous work. I left Morgantown, a skinny kid of 120 pounds.

The work I found was with Elbert Richmond. Every spring he sheared sheep for clients that included neighbors, some farmers in eastern Iowa and the Agriculture College in Normal, a suburb of Bloomington. As the Ag students watched the reporters wrote and took pictures and we would be featured in the Daily Pantograph.

With his shears powered by a Briggs and Stratton gasoline engine Elbert could shear a sheep every three minutes. To drag a sheep from the pen, set it up before him, gather up the wool, and tie it into a bundle and rethread the table, then get the next sheep was far more strenuous than anything I had ever done. My stubborn streak would not let me complain about the aches and pains and exhaustion and Mrs. Richmond's good meals and generous lunches got me through the season.

After the shearing season was over we did Elbert's farm work. I enjoyed driving a tractor. The hay making season started and the neighbors gathered to put each farmer's hay in his barn. The first day didn't get started until after lunch. We did a day's work in half a day. I pitched seven loads the same as the seasoned farmers did. I wasn't sure I had any shoulders left that evening.

These activities took place after we milked 7 cows, cooled and bottled the milk and then I took the milk to the customers in town. Then we had breakfast and went to work. I gained 40 pounds of muscle!

My strength and stamina has been a blessing in many ways. But no matter how strong you are, old age will slow you down. It has been my observation that slowing down is inevitable but those who stop don't last long. I sometimes feel that I am like a shark. They never sleep but always swim to keep oxygen flowing through their gills.

Strong doesn't mean longevity. I am thankful that the medics at the Bowling Green Veteran's Clinic found I had a deteriorating heart. The heart specialists at the VA hospital in Nashville have been able to build up my heart and implant a pacemaker and defibrillator for extra safety.

## Aviation

The second thread added in the pattern of my life was not so discernable at first. When I was born there in Tazewell County in 1925 a little 8 year old girl named Libby Jane Forester, in St. James, Missouri took a ride with a barnstorming pilot named Charles A. Lindberg. The night that I was one year and three months old, a plane was droning through the night sky hauling mail from St. Louis to Chicago when the engine quit. The pilot, Charles A. Lindberg, parachuted into a farmer's field just 10 miles from where I was sleeping. His plane crashed into another field. At the age of six I started grade school wearing a Lindberg inspired aviation helmet and goggles like little airplane pilot wannabes all over the country were wearing. Over half a century later, Libby Jane would become my wife. Her sister's son, Charlie Hasler, was one of the Flying Tigers during WWII. So by marriage I became Uncle to one of the Flying Tigers,

The Richmond's had a son who was an aviator. They had financed his flying lessons and after he got his license he was able to enter the army as a commissioned officer and pilot. He was stationed at Randolph Field in San Antonio, Texas. When the U.S. entered WWII such experienced pilots were too valuable to send into combat. They were used to train thousands of new pilots. When Lt. Richmond came home on leave and I took his picture with his father and grandfather it never occurred to me that I could follow his path. But just 3 years after that summer I would be climbing into the cockpit of a Stearman in San Angelo, Texas.

Returning to BCHS in 1942, I found Aeronautics was a major course. This course had been added to High Schools by request of the U.S. government. Aviation was gently touching my future from the year I was born until it finally entered full blown as a major thread in the fabric of my life imbedded in my Tapestry of Memories.

**Operating Vehicles**

The third thread was a love of operating vehicles and machinery. When my cousin Buster, didn't want to drive a truck load of grain to the elevator, I volunteered. Operating different tractors and pulling a variety of machines I found satisfying. I never tired of long hours of plowing large fields. That feeling of enjoyable involvement would stay with me through years of operating airplanes, buses, streetcars, trucks and tractors. In my 40s when I was learning to be a professional over-the-road trucker I asked the instructor if he thought I would be a good one. He said, "Yes, because you love it."

My job on the Richmond farm had given me my growth and a strong muscular body. Their son, a military pilot and officer, gave me a glimpse of an aviation future. I had leaped from the days of the horse (or mule) into the world of tractors and trucks. I never tired of long hours on a tractor that turned a huge field into a seed bed as easily as spading a small garden. Later I would find it just as exciting to take 20 tons of food across the nation. The possibility of a teaching career had faded away.

**Photography**

At the end of the season I used my summer's earnings to buy a set of new tires for the family car. I paid for much needed new clothes for work and school. Then, through the Sears and Roebuck catalog, I bought myself a fourth lifelong thread for my

Developer        Stop bath        Fixer

life's pattern. I ordered a camera and a picture developing set. After using it for a year I began practicing professional photography. I made my living behind the steering wheel but my avocation was photography. It has played a huge role in my life.

Besides taking photographs I spent hundreds of hours standing over the developer trays with either film or prints. Besides my own business I did photography and photo lab (darkroom) work for 3 major studios. Black and white film was coated with a silver salt. The camera would expose different amounts of light according to the different colors of the scene. In the dark I would immerse the film and later the print in a developer bath that turned the image to various shades of darkened silver in a negative form. After the right amount of time the film was dipped in the STOP bath then into the fixer to get rid of the inactivated silver so light wouldn't turn it dark later and ruin the photo. After a thorough washing the film was hung up to dry or prints were pressed tight to a ferrotype plate where they fell off nice and glossy when they were dry.

I had roots in photography. Dad's grandfather, David Coats, was a professional photographer in Butler county in the late 1800s and early 1900s. Dad's 5 year old photo was taken by him

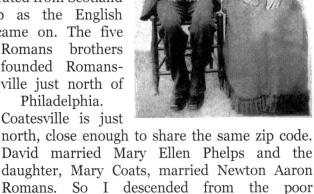

The Coats family is famous for sewing thread manufacturing. The Coats may have migrated from Scotland on the same ship as the English Romans brothers came on. The five

Romans brothers founded Romansville just north of Philadelphia. Coatesville is just north, close enough to share the same zip code. David married Mary Ellen Phelps and the daughter, Mary Coats, married Newton Aaron Romans. So I descended from the poor photographer instead of the thread manufacturing moguls.

Mom added to the mix by using her Brownie

Kodak to fill a shoebox with family pictures. So my heritage in photography is a rich one.

## Grammar

Before 1940 ended I had another hugely important thread to add to my lifelong pattern of life. The sophomore year of high school was the year for English. The first half of the school year was used to learn English grammar and the second half was for English literature.

Through the grapevine the word was: Grammar was the toughest course in all four years of high school. For our teacher we had the firm and intimidating teacher, Miss Vida Lee. That made us doubly scared.

Every night I studied the lessons thoroughly just sure I would never master all those rules and their application. Comes final test time and I took the text book home expecting to cram late into the night. As I looked over a few lessons I said, "I know this material. My worry over the course had made me study hard. Now it is all in my head." I closed the book and the next day took the test and scored 97.

I am convinced that there has never been a better grammar teacher in the school system than Miss Lee. It is a tribute to her that over 70 years later, two of us, June (Baxter) Rice and I, are still writing a weekly story for the Butler County Banner. Mine always includes pictures.

At one of our *Class of '43* reunions Miss Lee introduced to us her husband, Lucian Hunter. She asked him to stand. She introduced him and continued talking. After a little she noticed he was still standing. With hardly a break in her speaking she said, "Sit down, Lucian." We all laughed. That was the authoritative voice of our beloved Miss Lee. At our last reunion she was showing her age. Soon after that I was told she wanted to see me. A few days later before I could go to Leitchfield to see her I learned she had died. I sure hated to fail that last request from her. I sure look forward to seeing her in the resurrection.

Her training gave me the skills to be a good public speaker and writer. It also gave me the tools to develop my skills as a poet. I hope my next book will be a book of poems. In 1934 I became a neighbor to Rollie Beliles for 3 years until his death. He had corresponded in rhyme with a French girl he had met in WWI. He had their poems in a book. Janie and I wrote many poems when we were courting. I would like to see them in a book.

Once I was teaching a group about 8 qualities of speech. I walked to the podium with nothing in my hands. I spoke extemporaneously of the first point. Then I discussed point two. The third point went smoothly. "Now point four is... er...ah ..." with a stricken look on my face I reached for my coat pocket like I hoped for a note that I knew wasn't there.

Suddenly my face brightened and with a gesture declared, "Oh! I lost my poise."

A big sigh of relief swept through the audience!

Maybe it's a good thing for the teaching profession that I didn't become a teacher!

## 1941

Dad and I arrived at his sister's home in Illinois for a second year of work. As we sat down to one of Aunt Stella's fine meals she noticed the difference in me from last year. "You've changed a lot since you came here last year."

Buster added, "That's right. From an ape to a gorilla."

It was great to be with my Illinois cousins again. I thoroughly enjoyed being part of the family groups, the Illinois cousins and the Kentucky cousins.

Dad went to work for Rob Attebery again. Melba was growing up fast as I was. She later married a Mr. Gresham but in 1941 she was writing to a boyfriend in the military service. She would strum on her guitar and sing the popular song, *Don't sit under the Apple Tree/ With anyone else but me.* I used her to practice my new interest in Photography.

I worked with Elbert Richmond again as he sheared sheep. After chores and breakfast we loaded the pickup with the shearing gear and the Briggs and Stratton gasoline engine and drove to the scheduled jobs for the day.

Things were changing fast in farming. That was quite evident when haymaking time came. Instead of pitching loose hay we loaded the rack wagon with bales of hay. In the open field we managed to lift the bales to the guy on the wagon but in the still air by the barn handing the bales to the men in the loft soon had us overheating and exhausted. So the old and new had to be combined. The old power lift was reassembled and the grapple hook was sunk into a bale then all it took to take a bale up and through the door and along the track to the stacking place was just a matter of operating levers.

Another new experience for me was helping Mr. Richmond butcher a young steer. He killed the animal with a .22 caliber rifle, and then used a hoist to lift the carcass by the heels. There we skinned and cleaned the carcass. Fresh beef was a real treat.

We were working by the silo near the barn. Elbert filled me in on a story I heard when I was a kid. Leo Mallory had been killed in a farm accident. It happened right here where we were standing as we butchered the steer. A crew was feeding hay, etc. into a silage cutter when a blade broke off in the machine. It cut off the top of Leo's head and grazed Elbert's skull so hard it harmed his hearing. He had to wear hearing aids or else we had to talk loud to him.

Uncle Arthur Dotson raised a few sheep on his farm. Bobby had a pet among them. I took a picture of Bob feeding his pet. It is one of the best pastoral pictures I ever took. Over 50 years later I used that photo on the front of a handmade book of Bob's life and gave it to his widow, Marianne. Soon the summer was over and I headed for Kentucky for my junior year in Butler County High School.

**1941-42**

Mr Rone picks up passport

Juniors have a special relationship with seniors. We promoted their plays. We hosted the Junior-Senior Banquet. We built and printed the yearbook. As it turned out, it was our yearbook also. Because of wartime conditions we didn't have our own yearbook in 1943.

My photography gave me special opportunities. I photographed plays and events to supplement what the professional photographer's contract covered. After we had the yearbook published we added several photos. I made 25 copies of each print and we pasted them in the yearbook. After 70 years they have survived in good condition.

Bernice Clark (now Curtis), June Baxter (now Rice) and I were busy with poems, posters and ideas for the Junior-Senior banquet and the graduation exercises. We decorated the Gym as a ship for our banquet.

It all worked well because we had a hotshot crew that gave a lot of time, talent and dedicated effort. June Baxter gave untiring talent to the writing, organizing and moving the projects along. Bernice Clark made special contributions in poetry. I contributed poetry and photographs. We decorated the Gym as a ship for our banquet. Every student and faculty member who entered had a personalized passport. We hand-made programs, passports and menu folders.

The group photo for the Senior Class Play has standing: Neel Tanner, Ida Nell Eberman, Urdine Smith, Troy Lee Tuck and Glendon Warren; sitting: Carlton Drake, Claydean Keith, Thera Hampton, Getsel Byers, Betty Brown and Randal Arnold.

A special event put on by the business men of Morgantown was a Temperance Play. The cast included our principal, Mr. Rone back row first on the left. A decade after prohibition ended many were still pushing to ban or limit alcohol. The main remaining organization of the temperance movement is Alcoholics Anonymous with some two million members. They have meetings where they encourage each other to either give up drinking alcohol or be moderate.

What is the difference between an alcoholic and a drunkard? Let a drunkard explain it to you. "Us drunkards don't have to go to all those danged old meetin's."

I was beginning to learn some of my limitations. Arithmetic was easy to the point of being boring. Geometry was fun, more like drawing and art. Algebra was difficult. Trigonometry? Forget it. I am a plodder. I was a straight A student but I had to work harder and longer where others worked faster.

One full-moon night I got sleepy about 11 PM. In the moonlight I went to the river, swam out to the middle in the still, smooth water. High above I could see the tree line on the Romans Bluff and above that glowed the full moon. It was an unforgettable sight. I went back to finish my studies refreshed.

I once read in a James A. Michener book his description of a man he admired. He said the man was slow but accomplished a lot because he was a persistent plodder. I thought, "He is describing me." I only took a casual interest in the point and didn't set it in my mind. Later I decided I wanted to get that statement as a quote. I have never found it. Trying to find an item in the prolific writings of James A. Michener is like trying to find a needle in a very large haystack.

The most historic event of the year was the bombing of Pearl Harbor on December 7. On December 8 we were gathered in the auditorium. On the stage, instead of a play, Mr. Rone tuned in a radio so we could listen, along with eighty one percent of the United States population, as President Roosevelt spoke to congress about the attack on Pearl Harbor. Thirty-three minutes after the speech, congress declared war on Japan. As I walked the 2 miles of gravel road to my home I knew my world had changed but I felt no apprehension. Mom had lived WWI from the age of 10 to 14 and had spoken of how another call-up of men would have taken her father. When I walked in the door Mom was standing over the kitchen stove. I told her that war was declared. Her face quickly turned to me. She had a wide eyed look of fear and horror that I'll never forget. It sobered me.

One day I overheard my dad tell a neighbor, "That Charles can do anything." That confidence in me was nice to hear but also challenging. A big challenge came when he suggested a goal for my looming military service. "Why don't you be an airplane pilot?"

I had never imagined being a flyer but now that became my goal. First, I had to take my senior year of high school and I would have to be 18 years old. That would be in August of 1943.

Our banquet treat to the seniors was a great success. Now it was time for our last school-days' vacation.

## 1942.

To broaden my experience I worked on a different farm after my junior year. Lyle Rhodes had a typical Midwest farm. Both the house and the barn were large. Lyle's father had been deaf from birth so Lyle and Miss Hallie decided they wouldn't have children, instead they adopted Ogarita. I was in Hartford School with her through the fourth grade.

I slept upstairs and to awaken me every morning Lyle would throw the light switch at the foot of the stairs as he did for his deaf father in years past.

We fed cattle and sheep and drove 2 tractors to operate the farm.

Lyle told me about Dad's brother John. Uncle John was only about 20 years old 17 years ago when he and some others worked all day on this very farm. At the end of the day he was sweating profusely and feeling bad. He went back to where he was staying and died soon afterward of pneumonia. I was about a year old at that time. He was the first of Dad's sibling to die.

Lyle and Hallie Rhodes Farm

I was on the Minneapolis-Moline tractor a lot that summer. One day a sudden rain caught me at the far end of a field. I unhitched the plow and in high gear headed for the barn. Racing down the dirt road the big rubber tires were soon picking up mud and throwing it high with a forward sling. Soon I was in a hailstorm of mud! That slowed me down in a hurry.

If we started out with a rainy day I often spent the day in the barn. I would sometime move a roomful of heavy bags to another part of the barn. Once I used a discarded cultivator wheel to build a wheel barrow. There was always something to do on the farm.

One day a cow became agitated and leaped over the manger into the hallway of the barn. After a while she died. We suspected rabies. Lyle cut off her head and took it to Springfield for testing. I was left in charge when the rendering plant sent a truck to retrieve the carcass. A cable was fastened to her rear feet and a wench was engaged to drag her into the truck. But her front legs were lapped around the stair to the loft. I took care of that. I lifted her legs up to clear the steps and turned my face away to avoid the warm gasses that came bubbling from her severed neck. I guess Dad was right when he said, "That Charles can do anything."

There were beautiful things about farming. I helped in the harvest on Uncle Dot's place. The neighbors gathered for the event and the binders cut the wheat and used binder twine to tie bundles and drop then in piles. Others came along on foot to stack the bundles in shocks. Finally everyone gathered for threshing day. The crews would pitch the bundles with pitchforks on to wrack wagons. They would be hauled to the threshing site where they would be tossed in the threshing machine. The wheat or oats would come out of a spout into a wagon or truck to be taken to the elevator by the railroad tracks. The straw was blown out another spout onto the straw stack.

The most beautiful part of the day was the threshing dinner. While the men were working, the wives were preparing a rich and bountiful dinner and lots of iced tea. We washed up in the washbowls, combed our hair by the mirror hanging on the tree, then workers and children sat at a long table in the shade and ate a meal fit for kings and enjoyed as only hard workers can enjoy a meal.

Workers were leaving for the war so to get the work done farmers were buying new machines to do the harvest by themselves. Tractor drawn, the machines could cut and separate the grain and leave the straw in the field. It combined the cutting, hauling and threshing the grain into one operation. Not surprisingly, this machine is called a *Combine*.

All the farm boys that went to war could not find work where they left it. One hundred acre farms were absorbed by thousand acre farms. One man sitting high up in an air conditioned cab with a radio could do with that machine what a whole crew did before. A way of life disappeared. Too bad. It was a rich and satisfying life. I am glad I had a taste of it.

### 1942 – 1943

It was time to leave my summer job in Illinois and go back to BCHS for my senior year. Uncle Dot (Arthur Dotson) said that after another month of finishing up the harvest he was going to come down to Kentucky for a visit. I decided to miss the first month of school and come with his family.

The war permeated our lives. Some boys turned 17 and quit school for the military service. A big surprise was a course in Aeronautics as requested by the government. Since my goal was the Air Corps I would stay in school and wait until I was 18 before I joined. The new text books, one for class and a different one in the library for research, arrived a month late just as I arrived.

Dad was happy to have a visit from his sister Stella and her family. We took them to a movie at the theatre on Main Street. It was about the battle of the Alamo in San Antonio. It never entered my imagination that I would be there in person in a little over a year.

Uncle Dot had hardly ever seen a movie in his life. He came out of this one saying, "If they had killed that woman I would never have seen another movie." I don't think he did anyway. Less than 4 years later, our beloved uncle, Arthur Dotson, died from the lung damage he had received when the Germans gassed him in WWI.

My sisters, 16 year old Wanda and 13 year old Velma, were dating service men. Velma had overtaken Wanda in growth and they could wear each other's clothes. Imagine the shock as one of the G.I.s at the end of the date learned that his partner was only 13 years old!

One soldier they met was Eddie Loible, son of a sugar beet farmer in Wyoming. We invited him to spend a weekend with us. On Monday morning Mom served her usual sumptuous breakfast, Eddie counted the eggs on the platter and asked, "Is that enough for the boy, too?" As usual I was lingering in bed.

Mom explained, "Charles likes his eggs a certain way so he cooks his own."

"When he gets in the army he'll have to eat what he gets." Soon I was breaking two eggs into the skillet, smearing the whites and yolks together then letting them cook into a solid scramble. When Eddie saw my plate he exclaimed, "Good god, that old boy is going to make out all right. That's just the way the army cooks them!" He observed that anyone seeing the humble homes on Logansport Road would think we were the poorest people on earth. "But get behind these doors and you are living and dining like kings."

Another remembrance of that year was a scene on Main Street when a fisherman held up, for a group of us to see, his 67 pound catfish he had caught in Green River. Dad said when he was young 100 pounders were common but in 1943 this 67 pounder was a sensation!

The war was a constant presence in our lives. This was especially noticeable in school. One day the whole school was gathered in the auditorium. Among other things we had a sing along. Someone requested that we sing a popular war song, "Praise the Lord and Pass the Ammunition."

On the stage, our principal, Mr. Rone, became very serious. As we quietly listened he said, "Respectfully, I prefer that you not sing that song here. It is about the gunner getting killed and the Chaplain taking over the gun to shoot the enemy. That is against the Christian principles of why he is with a military group. He is there to attend their spiritual interest. This song is about a chaplain who forgot his place and joined the military action."

We respected his request and moved on to other songs.

The big shock of the year came during the December holidays. A young man in a pickup speeded around a curve and drifted into a head on collision with the pickup driven by Mr. Rone's brother, Shirley. Mr. Rone was in the passenger seat. They were trapped in their seats and burned to death. Shirley was married to my cousin, Dorothy Anderson. This was a family tragedy, a school tragedy, a whole county tragedy. Mr. Foyest West was our principal the rest of the school year.

I loved to read and study. The world was full of things I wanted to learn about. The last thing I wanted was to get up in front of an audience and give a speech. Perhaps missing the first month of school would lower my grade average. I was very pleased to see June Baxter win the honor of being the class Valedictorian. Some 50 years later she confided in me that I had had her worried. I laughed and said, "I was worried about the same thing!"

We would soon graduate and leave a wonderful world of experience and memories behind us.

## News (Barber Shop)

Classmate, Royce Pendley was the son of Dotson Pendley who had a barbershop on Main Street. Dotson's gift to all the graduating boys was a free haircut.

Once while waiting my turn for a haircut the radio was reporting the riots down south. The men in the shop reflected the prejudice of that time by laughing at and referring to the black people trying to get justice and fairness, as a bunch of monkeys. I did not like to hear that but another prejudice of that time was, "Young people were to be seen and not heard." So I kept quiet.

Beecher Carson shined shoes at a barber shop on Dogwalk. I heard him say, "Anytime a black man thinks a white man thinks anything of him, he is deceiving himself." I didn't like to hear that either.

Beachie and his brother Jim, big men like the Mills brothers, bought 4 gallon of poke greens from me every spring. After that one sale, Beechie or Jim would say, "No more. I'se done poke pizened already." I was fond of those guys. They were not just customers, they were friends. As long as he lived I would visit Beechie every time I came home for a visit.

Grady Norris had a barber shop on the right side of Dogwalk just as you turned off of Main. While here on a visit he gave my grandson, Nathan Roder, his first haircut. When Grady died his widow ask if she could have copies of the pictures I had taken. She had no other pictures of him. When I was building my lawn mowing business in 2001 Troy Lee (Sally) Tuck asked me to come by and quote him a price for mowing his lawn. He asked, "Does that include weed eating?'

My answer was, "The haircut is not done until the sideburns are trimmed."

"Oh! We are going to get a Grady Norris haircut!" He remembered Grady.

In Armington, Illinois in the 1930s there was one barber shop with two barber chairs and a pool hall in the back. The two barbers were Arthur Ludden and Bob Mobley. Bob gave me my first haircut, probably when I was 5 in 1930.

In the 1970s and 1980s I was hauling frozen Flavor Pac food out of the northwest for North Pacific Canners and Packers. Ragner (Hokie) Hokanson owned the trucks and handled the shipping department. His son Larry was one of the drivers. One trip, Larry and I found ourselves loaded and heading west through Illinois. I invited Larry to detour with me to the farm north of Armington where my cousin, Buster Dotson was managing the big farm. We had plenty of time and Larry pitched in and helped with some of the work. He was delighted to taste life on a Midwest farm. We needed haircuts so after a while we drove to Armington.

Arthur Ludden was long gone but there was the aged Bob Mobley still cutting hair. So that day, over 50 years since my first haircut in 1930 I got a haircut by the same barber. Some threads that weave through the fabric of our lives go on for a long time.

My present favorite barber is 99 years old. My wife, Janie, likes to cut my hair. She is particular about the way I look. My next favorite barber is Janie's daughter, Melinda Wilkinson, who has a barber/beauty business in Phoenix, Arizona. When she visits I get a real professional haircut. Too bad Phoenix isn't closer to Morgantown.

## 18

I'm a high school graduate at last but I won't be 18 years old until August 3. I decided I would work a short summer in Illinois. I would ride my bicycle for the 400 mile trip. I trained for the long ride. I pulled the long challenge of Big Hill until I could go uphill sitting down with another boy on board for extra weight.

Early one morning I started off in the dark. Crossing Green River on the Logansport Ferry a truck driver hauling milk to Owensboro offered me a ride. That gave me a good energy saving start. At Decatur, Illinois just 50 miles short of Armington and the home of that tasty Karo corn syrup I got concerned about some dark clouds coming in from the west. I had just passed a side road going about a mile to an industrial center. There by a railroad yard was a hotel. I turned back and got in the shelter of the hotel just as the storm struck.

When I asked for a room the clerk ignored me. I looked too young to have a legitimate need for a room. I stood by and chatted about my Armington roots but this late afternoon storm made it unsafe to go there tonight. He finally relented and for fifty cents assigned me a room on the sixth floor. I asked for a safe place for my bicycle. He changed me to the second floor and said I could keep my bicycle in my room.

For light there was a bare bulb hanging from the ceiling. There was no lock on the door so I wedged the back of the big stuffed chair under the doorknob. The second story window was about even with the tops of the train engines as they shifted cars around all night in the yard that began almost under the bedroom window. But tired me, I slept soundly unperturbed.

The next morning I sat at the bar and ordered ham and eggs. For fifty cents the large platter was filled with ham, eggs, hash browns, biscuits and gravy. Even this growing teenager couldn't eat all of it.

The summer work made the time go fast. I spent weekends with my Dotson family cousins. Buster would drive the family Plymouth and Buster, Bobby and I would go to a movie in Minier. Then we would go to the Minier Ice Cream Parlor. I would get a quart of chocolate milk and a chocolate cake roll with ice cream in the middle. That was our weekend celebration!

While Buster drove home Bobby and I were reading comic books. I finished mine and was looking for mischief. As we approached the road to turn east I said to Buster, "Go straight ahead and let's wake them up in Armington." He scoffed at the idea and turned east toward the driveway to the old Daly farm and the Dotson farm just beyond.

I am in the back seat alone and Bobby is up front still reading his comic book with the dome light on. I got down on the floor and reached up to the door handle. The back door of those old Plymouths opened out and dangerously backward. I opened it a little and slammed it back shut. Buster looked back and his passenger was gone. The back seat was empty. He slammed on the brakes and took a better look. He reached back, and like a mother cat picking up a kitten, picked me up and sat me on the seat! He never said a word.

This warm night we went to bed on quilts in the grassy front yard. Buster was thinking of the Bing Crosby Road picture we had seen,

"What a wife that Dorothy Lamour would make." About 3 times he said it and each time Bobby or I would say we wouldn't want a wife that showed off in the movies. About the third time we said it he thundered, "OH! SHUT UP." We prudently did and were soon asleep.

The summer of work and fun passed fast and I headed for Kentucky and a rendezvous with the end of my childhood.

## My Day at Western

The comic said he went all the way through college in one day. He walked in the front door and they kicked him out the back door.

My total experience at Western, then called Western State Teacher's College, was about as brief as the comic's but more productive. I was sent there to take an aptitude test for enlisting in the Army Air Corps. You had to score 180 to be considered. Three other contestants scored 180, 181 and 184. Then the tester counted mine and shook his head. "I am going to count this again." I thought he was trying to find me another point. After the recount he said, "That's right. You scored 257 out of 270." I would soon be trading my graduation suit for a cadet uniform.

Later I scored high on the shooting range. I left boot camp in Missouri wearing the medal of Expert in 3 weapons. That's not surprising considering all the squirrel hunting I did with the .22 caliber single shot Stevens Favorite. That was the only medal I acquired during my 2 years in the military.

BOOK 2

Silver Wings

## The Long Road to Jefferson Barracks

August 1943. Eighteen years old at last. Now I register for the draft (Selective Service) and apply for service in the Army Air Corps. That was my first draft card. When I left the service 2 years later and moved to Oregon, I had to register again and let them know where I lived in case they needed me again.

First stop: Bowling Green. At Western State Teacher's Collage I take the Aptitude test and pass with a high score.

Second stop: Louisville. I am given a physical. They have a problem with the lab work and Dr. Miller did tests for them and I passed. Now, there was more waiting at home. Third stop, Evansville, Indiana. I receive notice to report for induction. I say goodbye to the family and catch the bus. A group is sworn in and told to go home until called. They were not ready to feed me yet. I wasn't prepared for that and had barely enough money for a ticket home. The Greyhound took me to

Owensboro. It was too late for the Fuqua bus to Morgantown. I had to wait until the next morning. I spent time in a bowling alley until they closed at midnight. The bus depot was closed. I saw a moving van parked on the street with the back doors ajar. No one was around. I crawled up in the trailer where I found a stack of quilt like pads for wrapping furniture. I lay on the stack and pulled one over me and set my mind to wake up at 5am. I hoped I wouldn't find the back doors locked and the truck headed for parts unknown. The next morning I had breakfast and boarded the bus for home where I walked in on a very surprised family!

In a few weeks the notice came. I was to go to Jefferson Barracks, Missouri after I checked in at Florence, Kentucky.

Fourth stop, Florence is across the Ohio River from Cincinnati. So I went east so they could put me on a bus to go west!

Jefferson Barracks that winter was a miserable place. We were housed in huts with double deck bunks in each corner. Each day was grueling in either freezing cold or rain and mud. We did exercises and 20 mile cross country runs. My hard farm work had prepared me well but it was still rough. All seven of my roommates ended up on sick call at one time or another.

The food was good and I never missed a meal.

During WWII it was common to see civilians offer to do something nice for the service men stationed near their homes. So one Saturday when most guys had gone to town I was hanging around the recreation room when the word came from the office that 2 motherly type ladies were looking for 2 volunteers. I was one of the fortunate ones available. They wanted to share tickets for the Ice Follies in downtown St. Louis. I saw that show for the first time by the generosity of these two ladies. That was a memorable event during my 2 months at Jefferson Barracks. On the firing range I scored expert so I could wear the wreath with tags for qualifying weapons,

## The Hinkle Fieldhouse

After I finished boot training in Jefferson Barracks, Missouri in the winter of 1943 I was taken to Butler University in Indianapolis, Indiana. There the Hinkle Field House became my home for the next five months.

Butler University had become an army post. The boundary included several blocks of residential homes. One cadet's home was within the boundaries so anytime he was off duty he could visit home.

**The Gymnasium**

When we arrived we were restricted to the base for 2 weeks. I spent one afternoon swimming in the Olympic sized pool in the field house. I swam 100 laps and was too bored to do more. Later in a competition my group begged me to represent them. I explained that I was a plodder and could endure but couldn't outswim anyone. They insisted so I swam in the contest and, predictably, came in last but I was cheered for going the distance.

Hinkle Field House Butler U. Indianapolis, Indiana

We were awakened every morning with reveille over the PA system followed by a popular music recording that brought on lots of whistles and shouts. I asked, "Is that some college song?" Those who heard me laughed at my ignorance. "I didn't have a radio on my tractor," I said.

My comedian side showed up one day. On my 3 high, top bunk, I stood on my head. My feet sticking six feet up in that sea of bunks was a stand out attention getter. Not a good example for a bunch of rookies there learning to be dignified officers! It caught the attention of the cadet in charge. "Stop that. Use your head." He admonished.

"That's what he was doing," someone quipped.

As soon as I had open post I looked up my relatives.

The Meridian bus route, cutting a diagonal to the base in eastern Indianapolis, became my commuter ride.

## I Meet Norma Montague

I never met my great Uncle Isaac Lucky Andrews. He was Postmaster at McAndrews, Kentucky and known as the largest (400 pounds) Postmaster in the U. S. His grave marker indicates that he was a veteran of the Spanish American War as was his brother Ollie who lived in Morgantown. His sister, Maude, married John Robert Vincent in Muhlenberg County and was my Mom's mother. Mom kept up with her relatives so when the Army Air Corps sent me to Butler University in Indianapolis for 5 months in 1944 she told me that Uncle Lucky's 2 daughters lived in Indianapolis and I should look them up.

Hazel was married to Stanton Montague who was chief deputy sheriff of Marion County. Their 18 year old daughter Norma showed me the town. Her Dad let me ride with a deputy on police business.

The Montague's daughter, Norma would be Mom's second cousin and my third cousin. She was a beautiful 18 year old who was a look alike of Alice Faye, the beautiful movie star. It never once occurred to me that a third cousin could also be a girlfriend. During my 5 months there at Butler U. I saw her as another of my many cousins. When Cadet Rockwell went with us on picnics, movies or other outings I remember twinges of jealousy if she gave him too much attention. If I saw Norman Rockwell featured on the Saturday Evening Post I would see 'Norma Rockwell' and I didn't like it. So I had some but not too serious a possessiveness toward my newly discovered cousin/friend. My heart may have been talking to me but I wasn't listening. Years later Norma told me that those 5 months in the spring of 1944 had restricted her social life as she had the task of entertaining me, her country cousin.

## The Meridian Bus

My concentrated interest at Butler was to learn physics, public speaking and, in the fifth month, my first experience of flying. Piper Cubs were used to introduce us to flying. The college experience, besides filling in our education requirements, was to polish us as eventual officers. It was supposed to get some of the country out of us, a hopeless task. I have remained a country boy knowing I can handle the city life but few city boys could handle farm life as I could. My five months with my city relatives probably prepared me for city life as much or more than the college experience.

My social interest could easily have expanded beyond the family circle.

One evening I was riding the Meridian bus back to my GI home. I was standing near the back facing the left side of the bus. On the back seat was a young lady (18 – early 20s) reading a book about birds. In front of me was a middle aged woman. After a brief exchange between the two I surmised that this was a mother and daughter. I addressed the mother. "I see that your daughter is interested in John J. Audubon and his bird paintings."

"Yes. She is a member of the Audubon Society." Having read hundreds of books during High School I could converse about many subjects and this is one of them. After a few minutes, this mother who had probably been very protective of her daughter with all these service men in town now turned to her. She got her attention from the book to which she had maintained a studied attention during my conversation with her mother.

"I want you to meet this young man, Charles Romans."

I acknowledged the introduction. Now what would I do? Would I ride on to the end of the line and get off at my stop on the way back giving me time to get address and phone number? What would I do? I ran! After the brief introduction the next stop was Butler U.

I rang the buzzer and stepped off into the night and headed for the bunk house.

War time brought many brief encounters with strangers. I wonder if through the years that young woman and her mother remembered that pleasant encounter as I have.

Have they, too wondered, "What if?"

Racial tensions were up north as well as down south. Hazel Montague was in law enforcement also. She was a truant officer. One day Norma's younger brother and I were riding with her in an unmarked county car when, at a red light, a car bumped us from the rear. It was driven by a white man with a black passenger. He backed up and hit us again. When the light changed Hazel put the car in reverse and gunned it. She gave them a bump I'll bet they remembered. Her son and I laughed in approval and later told Stanton about the incident. He said, "I don't blame her but she shouldn't have done that."

One dark winter evening I was standing near the front of the Meridian Bus going back to the base. Most of those standing were off already so as a frail black grandmother was struggling to get off with her package I stepped over, took the package and handed it to her after she was safely off. As the only one standing I resumed holding the strap as the bus proceeded. I never noticed how quiet the bus had become until a lady behind me said, "Young man, that was a good thing you did. It's a good thing all of us aren't panty waists." I didn't know anything to say. I was surprised that I had shocked a busload of northerners by helping a LOL that happened to be black!

Our last month at Butler U. would introduce us to flying. We went to a local airfield and I was introduced to an instructor. We went out to the flight line and I walked up to the first airplane I had ever seen on the ground. I fastened the seatbelt in the back seat of this Piper Cub. Soon we were racing down a roadway that didn't go very far. Before getting to the end of it we leaped into the air and didn't need the road anymore. Soon after getting to altitude the pilot asked if I would like to do a spin. I wasn't sure about that but I was there to become a pilot and didn't think it wise to say 'no'. Soon we were spiraling toward the ground as though to bore a hole in the earth. I was relieved when we came out of the spin and started climbing again. Soon he asked, "Would you like to do another one?" Again I was afraid to say 'no'. Soon our first hour of flying ended and we would do a total of 10 hours before heading for Texas.

**San Antonio, Texas**

All too soon my college days were over. We boarded a troop train for Texas. I was sleeping in an upper berth and felt the train stop. I pulled back the window curtain and saw a cowgirl watering her horse in the town square. We were in Texarkana, Texas. I really felt out west!

We proceeded to San Antonio where we would spend the next 10 weeks in the San Antonio Army Air Corp Preflight School. Elbert Richmond's son, the veteran pilot from Illinois, was stationed in San Antonio. I never saw him there. He was stationed on Randolph Field.

We had a name – Class 45C. This was the first real taste of army life. In Missouri we were housed in huts. In Indiana we were in a college Gym. Now we were in large barracks with a foot locker at the foot of each bunk. We washed up and shaved in a large room with mirrors and sinks along a wall. A long row of toilets sat along the back wall - in the open. When not in class we went on work details to trim the lawn. I tan well and stand the hot sun but I dutifully took a salt pill and immediately got sick. I got along fine without extra salt.

The classes were easy. I usually had a comic book in my lap to read while the rest learned what I had learned in my high school Aeronautics class.

In the preflight class was an older man, Cadet Primrose. He, like me, was a quiet kind of fellow. He had been in the army for a few years and had transferred here for flight training. He recognized me as a tenderfoot from the country and took it upon himself to go with me every time I went to town. He said he wanted to see that I didn't get in any trouble.

My first goal was to explore the Alamo. The other big attraction in San Antonio for service men was the big Breckenridge Park. One weekend day we saw a crowd around the rim of the snake pit. We joined the spectators and watched 2 men down in the pit walking around among the snakes. They were wearing high topped boots. They chose 2 large rattle snakes. After showing those off they proceeded to butcher them and fry them in a skillet over an open campfire. Some say fried rattler is a lot like fried chicken. I was going to try a piece but it was all gone before the platter got passed to me.

One day we met 2 girls. They were sisters out for a walk. We talked a while then did *The San Antonio Stroll* together the rest of the afternoon. We saw a photo booth where we could get pictures taken. With Primrose's approval I had my picture taken with one of the girls. Her name was Estella Rosalie Gonzalez. I sent the photo home to Mom and she saved it in the family picture file – the shoebox.

San Antonio became one of my favorite cities along with San Francisco and New York.

## San Angelo

After 2 months in Missouri, 5 months in Indiana and 10 weeks in San Antonio for Preflight School it is finally time to fly. Class 45-c was excited as we were transported west to San Angelo. Goodfellow Field would be our home for both Primary and Basic training. First it would be Stearman bi-planes. They were tail draggers meaning they had tail wheels and could ground loop on landing if you didn't keep firm control.

Each instructor was assigned 4 students. I was assigned to Lieutenant Stewart. Lt. Stewart was a skinny, mild mannered person who resembled Hank Williams. He was known to end the class with only one student after 'washing out' the other 3. Right away one cadet was eliminated because he got air sick every time he went up.

It was time for the first flight. I strapped on my parachute, put a note pad and pencil in the pocket on my flight suit. The pocket was convenient, just below my knee. I climbed into the rear cockpit. Stewart took off, climbed to altitude and headed for the practice area.

Suddenly the plane was upside down. Instinctively my elbows went out under the rim of the cockpit. My notebook came floating past my face. I grabbed at it with both hands. It got away and my elbows went back under the rim of the cockpit. I felt as if I was about to fall up to that earth over my head. But my seat belt held and I became a forever believer in seat belts.

Stewart could talk to me through a tube to my earphones but there was no return to him. He would show me a maneuver then tell me to do it. If I didn't perform to his satisfaction, he would yell in my ear and whip the control stick back and forth so my control stick would hit my knees. But with my long legs I could spread my legs out of reach of the control. When he couldn't feel a bump he yelled, "Where's your dammed knees?" So I slapped the stick back and forth with my hands so I wouldn't get bruised knees. His training theory was: If he could rattle his student so could an enemy pilot.

Where was that mild spoken trainer I had been assigned to? Up here I was flying with a demon. The only levity I saw from him was the day he had a dogfight with a hawk. It was a wild ride. I saw the Hawk peel off in a direction he didn't see and the chase was over. That wild man always bailed out before we landed because the pilot that climbed out was the soft spoken instructor I first started with!

## Solo

The day of my first solo his only comment was, "Do a spin."

It was a sunny Texas day with towering cumulus clouds filling the sky. I climbed up among them trying to find an open space long enough to stall into a spin. I thought I had found one. I flew close to a big white column and turned toward one some distant away. I pulled the nose up into a stall. As the heavy engine pulled the nose down I applied right rudder and held the stick back. My power off nose dive became a classic spin. What was not according to plan was — I went into a cloud that had been below me. I was in a dense white fog. I kicked the rudder strait, opened the throttle and when I had flying speed I leveled out; fortunately, I came out under the cloud.

Now, where was I? It was the strangest land I had ever seen. Nothing looked familiar. Now I knew how Dorothy felt when she went for a spin in Kansas and landed in a strange place! Like other teens I had to find myself. I hit on a plan. Going by the compass I steadied the plane on straight north. Now San Angelo should be in a certain direction. I looked where it should be and to my surprise it was there. It was a solo I would have no trouble remembering.

Now I could take the plane out by myself and practice, practice, practice. It was a beautiful day under the Texas sun. That day the sun would save two lives. I arrived in the practice area and found a long field to practice turns. I dropped down to an estimated 500 feet, then paralleled the fence row at 500 feet out, if my eye judged it right. At the end of the field I turned left. Each time around the field gave me practice on 4 left turns. The trick was to make the turn without losing altitude. Banking the plane on its left side made the plane slide down to the left unless right rudder was applied. The extra drag had to be compensated by more throttle or angle of attack. I wanted to be smooth when Lt. Stewart checked me out.

I did my routine scan of the area and saw no other planes. I settled down to await the end of the field. The summer sun was north of me as I traversed the north side of the field. I amused myself by watching my shadow that travelled almost on the fence below me. Something caught my eye. Up ahead was a shadow coming toward my shadow. I looked up and down the sun ray and saw nothing higher or lower than me. I pushed the nose down to see what might be in the blind spot straight ahead of the big radial engine. There was another Stearman closing dangerously fast for a head-on collision. I reacted by pulling up. My wheels must have been within inches of his prop. I headed straight for Goodfellow Field. I did not enter a flight pattern. I did my first straight in landing, checked in my parachute and went to the bunkhouse and stretched out to think about it. I never spoke to anyone about the experience and flew the next day as usual. Class 45-C was the first class to finish the training without a fatality. I think this was the day I helped make the new record.

Of Lt. Stewart's four students I was the one to survive and move on to Basic Training which was on the same field, only different planes.

## Baby Shoes to Silver Wings
After completing primary training in the bi-plane, the open cockpit Stearman, we continued into the basic training phase in the sleek low-wing plane, the AT-6. Class 45C was the first class to use the advance trainer for our basic training. It was a delightful plane to fly. We did a lot of solo cross country trips for practice in navigation and flying. I would be cruising along listening to the radio to pass the time. I would sometimes, out of sheer exuberance, shove down the right rudder while pulling the control stick full back. The plane would roll in what we called a snap roll. A quick return of the controls to normal at the right moment left you flying straight and level as before. The plane and I were dancing to the music.

One day while doing touch and go landings on a dirt field we were coming in for cross-wind landings. I came crabbing in with the nose slightly upwind then used the rudder to kick the plane straight with the landing strip at the moment of touchdown. The plane wobbled up on one wheel and I was close to going into a ground loop.

My right foot was trying to push the rudder through the floor as, over my left shoulder, I watched as the wingtip whipped dust off the weeds just scant inches off the ground. As I slowed, the plane settled down and I came to a safe stop.

I felt heat on my face. Flames were streaming past my canopy. The engine was on fire. I held the brakes hard and opened the throttle and blew out the blaze.

The officers who were observing and grading our performance came over and inspected the wing tip and saw no evidence of contact with the ground so waved for me to continue.

We were on Goodfellow Field in San Angelo, Texas during 1944 for both primary and basic training. San Angelo was beginning to feel like home. During open post time I would go downtown and browse the magazine racks. I was interested in photography and songs. One Popular Photography magazine featured a picture of a fox taken by Mrs. Harold Medbury, a neighbor in Illinois. That touch of home was exciting.

I bought the *Latest Hit Songs* magazine to see some lyrics of what I heard on the radio. On page 6 a song caught my attention. Mom would like this song, *From Baby Shoes to Silver Wings.* In a few months I would be getting my silver wings so these lyrics fit our experience. I clipped it out and Mom saved it and gave it back to me years later.

On October 24, 2013 I went to my Morgantown mailbox and pulled out a copy of this same music magazine! How did that happen?

I wondered if that magazine could be found. On eBay, the Discount Merchandise Distributers of Laurel, Maryland had bought a huge lot of comic books and old magazines at an estate auction. Of *Latest Hit Songs* they had a set of 4 magazines listed on EBay, 3 of them from 1944. That gave me a 25 per cent chance that one of them would have my song. So I took the plunge and ordered them. The October, 1944 issue was the right one!

For years it was a custom to take the baby's first shoes and have them preserved by having them bronzed. My folks didn't have my baby shoes bronzed so I don't have them but I do have my silver wings.

A joke of that period tells of a country bumpkin training hard and winning a gold medal. He was so proud of it he had it *bronzed*! Think about it!

## Speech

I attended the first months of the fourth grade in Illinois then completed it in Butler County, Kentucky. My *northern brogue* was quite contrasted to the southern dialect of the south. My 'noo' had become 'new'. The laughter was friendly but it bothered me. As fast as I could I dropped the northern accent but was reluctant to adopt the southern. I developed what I call 'text book English'.

During High School I spent summers in Illinois and the school year in Kentucky. I developed an interest in language. One year as I was about to leave for Kentucky I made my Uncle Dot (Arthur Dotson) laugh when I told him I was going to leave *You-uns* and go see *You All*. I don't know if that was northern talk or something Uncle Dot brought with him from Tennessee. The use of some words was strictly farm related. If the boss told you to do a good job of stripping the cows he meant to get all the milk. Otherwise her system may think it is time to wean the calf and start drying up. I told Uncle Dot it sounded like he wanted us to take off all her clothes.

In 1944 one of the instructors at Goodfellow Field entertained the cadets by telling where they were from by their speech. I wasn't present when someone asked him, "Where is Romans from?"

"He has me puzzled. Some in the Detroit area speak as he does. There are places in Texas where the talk is similar to his but I can't pin him down for sure."

Having a multi-state background made it easy for me to make friends. If a cadet was from Iowa, Illinois or Indiana I would say I was from Illinois and talk of Midwest life with him. A contentious fellow heard me one day and said, "Why don't you tell him you are from Kentucky? Are you ashamed of it?"

"No." I replied. "I really am from Illinois. I just say I'm from Kentucky when I want to brag."

When I left San Angelo I had logged 103 hours in the Stearman and 80 hours in the AT-6. Since we had used the Advanced trainer for Basic what would we use for Advanced training? Excitement was running high when we learned we would be training in B-25s. Soon we were sent to the Texas Panhandle city of Pampa and the Pampa Army Air Corp Base.

## Pampa, Texas

Basic training in the AT-6 was over. Class 45-C was excited when we learned we would be the first class to take Advanced training in the fabled B-25. We moved to the Airfield at Pampa, Texas. Jimmy Doolittle had led a raid of 16 B-25s on Japan in April 1942. One exercise we performed was a short field takeoff. We would hold the brakes and slowly rev the engines to high RPM. When we released the brakes the plane would leap forward and we would try to become airborne before the end of an imaginary aircraft carrier. Now we knew somewhat of the experience of the 16 pilots who took off from the aircraft carrier Hornet to bomb Tokyo.

I may have seen some of those planes as they trained. In 1942 on our Butler County farm I looked up to see a flight of large planes thunder overhead just above the treetops. The training base for Doolittle's raiders was in Northwest Florida. My home was well within range of a practice flight.

Doolittle had seen the need for instrument flying and had developed the ability and means. At Pampa we became instrument rated pilots as well as multi-engine pilots.

We ranged over a large area of Texas, New Mexico and Oklahoma. Each crew consisted of an instructor and 2 students or just 2 students. When the instructor was training one student the other would sit on a bench behind the pilot's seat. I was sitting on the bench one day; I was reading as usual. A gallon of extra hydraulic oil was sitting in an enclosure beside me. The student was learning instrument flying so had a dark curtain over his windows. The instructor put the plane in a steep climb and turned it over to the cadet. He saw by the artificial horizon instrument that the nose was high. Vigorously he pushed the nose down. The oil can came floating out of its nest and was floating around in front of me. I was holding to my seat to keep from floating to the ceiling. It was my first experience with free floating weightlessness. It was an unforgettable experience.

I met neighbors. Two widows stand out. Mrs. Moore said that when she married Burns Moore he was working in the oil fields of Borger a few miles north of Pampa. The town had no jail so they chained their prisoners to a tree!

Mrs. Magee had a very funny story. She got up in the night to use the bathroom. She left the lights off so as to not disturb Henry. She sat down — in somebody's lap. She jumped up and ran out of the house. When she came back in Henry confronted her about why she had run out. "I thought there was a man in the house."

"I am a man," he said.

I met Roy and Effie White. They were a nice moral middle class family, the kind I liked for friends.

On July 3, 1917 the American Expeditionary Force lead by General John J. Pershing landed in France. The Germans were invading France and France needed help from the USA.

General Pershing was aware of history and knew that Lafayette volunteered from France to serve as a General under General George Washington. So France helped America win freedom from the British and now it was time for the Americans to help France get freedom from the Germans. So General Pershing's aid dramatically announced, "Lafayette, we are here!"

In my stereoscope collection I have a 3-D photo of General Pershing in France. I met the General through books and pictures. But Roy White saw the General in person there in France in WWI and served under his command.

Returning to civilian life in Texas, Roy was busy for some time making boots and saddles for the Texas cowboys. While living in a boarding house run by 2 sisters, Effie and Ellen he found his lifelong partner. Effie Winifred Kendall became his wife. Her sister Mary Ellen married and later as the widow of Mr. Turcott became the beloved 'Auntie' of his two children.

Eventually he leased out his shoe making equipment and opened a service station in LeFors, Texas where Garland and Nell Roy were born. During the radical nationalism of WWII this old veteran was boycotted out of business because of his religion by the people who owed him many hundreds of dollars for the gas bought on credit.

He moved his family to Pampa and worked at the local Carbon Black plant for the remainder of the war.

I was looking for a place to go to Sunday services and when I found one I met Mr. Roy White. In my off time from the Pampa Army Airfield I was welcomed to his home. It was a few weeks before I learned he had a beautiful daughter when she came home for a weekend from Oklahoma City where she was taking a business course at Draughn's Business College.

In my senior year 1942-1943 at BCHS Aeronautics was a course included at the request of the government. Miss Hood's math, Miss Lee's grammar and Mr. Spickard's Science came together in that course to help me learn about flying airplanes and the related fields of weather and Navigation. Before radio assisted navigation and computers, navigation was by compass, gyros, pencil, paper, rulers and Jeppesen E6-B Flight calculators using air speed, ground speed, wind velocity and direction to plan your flight. That was called Dead

Reckoning.

In 1945 I put my knowledge to the test. Army Air Corp Class 45-C would soon get our wings but we had a special test to perform. With 2 student pilots in each B-25 we were to fly 300 miles from our base in Pampa, Texas to Oklahoma City and back. Instructors were flying the same route observing our performance. We flew low level outbound and came back at 20,000 feet using oxygen. I took responsibility for the outbound trip.

It was soon apparent that an unknown wind was taking us to the left of my plotted course. I maintained the heading and airspeed until half way there. Then noting our location I recalculated my heading and airspeed. The Oklahoma airport had the old A and N (Daw Dit and Dit Daw) radio signal with a cone of silence straight above the station. I crossed that cone of silence just as the second hand was crossing 12 on the clock exactly on our ETA(estimated time of arrival) that had been assigned to us.

I turned the plane over to the other pilot and had time to think of that beautiful 18 year old Nell Roy White from Pampa who was now working in Oklahoma City and living in a boarding house. In less than 3 months she would be my wife.

Back in Pampa the instructors were discussing with different crews their performance. Our instructor glanced over at us and said, "You were right on." That was nice to hear.

I got my Wings in May 1945 and was assigned to fly and train Navigation Cadets in San Marcos, Texas. I left Pampa in an officer's uniform with gold bars on my shoulder and a USAAF class ring with a black onyx set. I was still a teenager!

The war was over in Europe when I got my commission in May. But a 'D-Day' kind of invasion in Japan was anticipated. Good pilots would be needed. But then the Atomic bomb was dropped and the war ended.

A lot of causalities would have been sustained if the invasion had taken place. I was pleased that I could handle a plane in such a steady manner. But recently I happened to think — I would have been a good steady target for enemy gunners. The atom bomb probably saved my life!

Whew!

Pampa, Texas became an indelible thread in the fabric of my experiences and a prominent pattern in the tapestry of my life.

## To San Marcos the Long Way

I had 2 weeks leave. I spent the first 2 days in Oklahoma City. She was working in an office and boarding in one of the large Midwest homes that had an unused room I could use. The landlady was German and she told Nellroy she should marry me because she was sure I was a good German man! I proposed to Nell Roy but she didn't feel she was ready to marry. She did accept my wings and though she was wearing a see-through blouse she modestly turned her back as she pinned on the wings. My next stop was Indianapolis. My sister Wanda was working in Indianapolis. We got together and had our picture taken at the Kindred Studios. My cousin Norma was engaged to an Air Corp Captain. She took a vacation from her bank job to visit Kentucky with me. My folks were very pleased to have a visit from Uncle Lucky's granddaughter.

After a brief stopover in Illinois where I visited my cousins and Dr. Ross, the old family doctor, we proceeded to my home in Kentucky to spend the rest of my leave with my family.

All too soon it was time to catch a bus for San Marcos. I arrived and was assigned to the end of the field that used twin Beech twin engine planes with 3 seats and desks for the navigation students. I was a little disappointed not to get a DC-3 assignment at the other end of the field where students were taken for longer flights, even over water, and trained in celestial navigation using sextants. But the twin Beech was a neat plane to fly.

After getting settled and getting used to being an officer I got a letter from Nell Roy. She was accepting my proposal. We decided on July 7 for the big day. The big day wasn't so big except to us. It was to be a wartime wedding by a justice of the peace in Austin, the capitol of Texas. Like my father I was getting married at the age of 19, just 3 weeks short of 20. I went to the courthouse to get the license. The clerk asked the age of the bride. "Eighteen," I replied. He entered her age.

"What is your age?" he casually asked. I told him I was 19. "Uh oh," and he slammed the book shut.

"I've got it," I said and laid down the permit with Mom's signature, required because I was not yet 21 years old!

I reserved a hotel room and found a Justice of the Peace who agreed to stay in his office until her train arrived. After a brief ceremony I almost left without giving the JP anything for his service. At the door I turned back and gave him ten dollars.

Nell Roy had dinner on the train so she went to the room to freshen up. I had not been able to eat all day. I decided I should have something for nourishment so I went to the bar and ordered a glass of milk. After drinking that, I was afraid my breath would not be fresh, so I had a Coke. The guy on the bar stool beside me, said, "Now I have seen everything. A man has a glass of milk and a Coke for a chaser!"

## At Home in San Marcos

My first home with my new bride, Nell Roy, was in San Marcos, Texas. Harvey Samson, from Boone, Iowa had been assigned to San Marcos also. He had acquired a scooter and after breakfast he would pick me up and we would ride to work on his scooter.

Charles E. Romans
Morgantown, Kentucky

Harvey L. Samson
1704 Boone Street
Boone, Iowa

Nell laid out my clothes for the day. They were the wrong ones. Uncle Sam dictated what uniform I should wear according to my duties for that day. Nell was offended and never again had anything to do with what I would wear.

It was an Idyllic time. Nell's friend, Edna, from Pampa made her home in San Antonio with her husband, Jack and their daughter, Peggy Sue. We would often spend the weekend with them.

One weekend a big football game was played in Austin, just north of San Marcos. I, and some other pilots, needed flight time for a maximum paycheck. On Sunday five of us climbed in a Twin Beech and flew to Austin. Three of us sat at the 3 desks used by the navigation students. We watched the game from about 4000 feet and listened on the radio. Circling below us were Piper Cubs and other small planes. Above us were B-25s and DC-3s. After the game we headed for home.

I was in the first seat behind the copilot. I watched as the pilot lowered the landing gear and flaps and lined up with the runway. After the wheels are solidly on the runway raising the flaps takes away more LIFT and settles the plane tighter to the runway for braking. I watched as the pilot touched down and, keeping his eye on the runway reached down to raise the flaps. *The handle he raised was for raising the landing gear!*

The right seat pilot saw what was happening. His right hand flew across and he slapped the landing gear lever back to the down position in time to prevent a belly landing. Whew!

Nell's family came from Pampa to visit us. I liked Roy. He was a WWI veteran and after the war had, besides shoe repair, made saddles and boots for Texas cowboys. He had the leather shop with his brother.

Roy and Effie White brought her sister, Ellen with them. Since Edna had been their neighbor in Pampa they were glad to see her again as well as her daughter, Peggy Sue.

I enjoyed the company and did not foresee what it would be like to live a few blocks apart in Portland, Oregon. Eventually, I could relate to the song recorded by Slim Whitman, also by Kenny Roberts. The popular song was *I never see Maggee alone.*
*She brings her father, her mother, her sister and her brother,*
*Oh! I never see Maggie alone.*

While I was flying navigation cadets on their training flights, Nell searched for an apartment. She finally found one recently vacated and we moved in. Now we could have some home cooked meals. The first one was a big pot of pinto beans and a pone of cornbread. We sat down to dinner. I crumbled cornbread in the middle of the plate and proceeded to stack on the beans in anticipation of a real feast. Suddenly I noticed that Nell wasn't eating. Her hands were folded in her lap as she stared in wide eyed wonder. "I never saw anything like that before," she said.

One day the flight plan was to fly to the Mexico border then turn east for a 20 minute leg of the flight and from that point straight back to the home field. When we got to the border I got no instructions from the 3 students at the 3 work stations in the plane. Finally 20 miles into Mexico the order came to head east. For 20 minutes we paralleled the border before getting the order from the budding navigators to turn for home. This performance could have been fatal in a war zone but they were here to learn what I learned in the aeronautics class in Butler County High School. Some of these I helped train may have served in Korea and Vietnam.

At Pampa when I became aware that I was making a good record in navigation I was somewhat concerned that I would be commissioned as a navigator. Two events stand out.

Besides the study of flight and navigation in our High School course in Aeronautics I think our course in Geometry under Ms Lucille Hood honed my skills in drawing vectors, lines and circles. This added flair to navigation assignments.

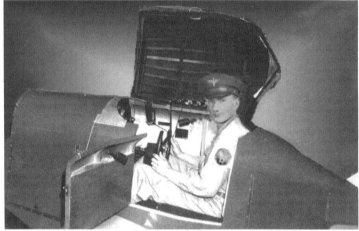

We spent many hours in a Link Trainer in simulated flight and navigation. One assignment called for flying a certain pattern. After getting seated in the Link Trainer you closed the door and hood. Now you were in a plane at night or in a cloud and had to fly by instruments. The assignment: Fly 2 minute legs, do a 270 degree turn which basically left you turned left. Doing this 4 times would leave you back where you started. A robot pen on the instructor's desk recorded your route along with any mistakes. I would blindly fly this maneuver and the pen would match the starting line.

Operating farm machinery had made me skillful in operating planes and my schooling had made me skillful at navigating. So which would I be?

I guess I shouldn't have been surprised when I was assigned to the school for navigators at the San Marcos Airfield where I would be the students' pilot and in-the-air trainer. The Twin Beech was a delight to fly and one of the most popular business planes ever built. I was a little disappointed not to be assigned to the other end of the field where they used DC-3 aircraft and long flights with celestial navigation.

One weekend Nell and I bought steaks and put them in the ice box and went to a movie. An usher came through and announced that all pilots were ordered to report to the base. A storm was coming in from the gulf and the planes were to be moved out of harm's way. When I arrived all the planes had pilots so I signed on as co-pilot on a plane being sent to Indianapolis. This provided me with my only experience with a rated navigator as you will see.

After 2 days we were called to come back to San Marcos. Over Arkansas we were losing oil pressure in both engines. We spotted a field with lots of planes so we put our plane on the ground at Walnut Ridge, Arkansas. It was a bad choice. It was a closed field and they had no oil for us. Fifty German prisoners of war were dismantling old planes. The major in charge ordered oil for us but we had to wait for it two long days. Thanks to an excellent German cook we really ate well. I really enjoyed the excellent Salisbury steak. The major said bread had been a big problem. He would order for 50 and get enough for a few but since he had told them to send bread for 500 he had a warehouse full of excess bread!

The movie house was playing *Boston Blackie Booked on Suspicion* and *The Picture of Dorian Gray*. I saw the double feature twice the first day and when we didn't get away I did the same thing the next day. The highlight was in the *Picture of Dorian Gray* when Angela Lansbury sang *Goodbye Little Yellow Bird*. I became a lifelong fan of Mrs. Lansbury.

When we were cleared to go home the arrival time was critical. Clouds were due to cover the field late that night. We had a hitchhiker. An officer had asked to go to Texas with us. He was a rated navigator so we let him handle our navigation. Late that night we were due at San Marcos but no airfield showed in the dark. I flew from the right seat while the pilot and navigator pored over a map. I saw a green flashing light which indicated an airfield. I buzzed the field and got the name off the hanger. The other two found the location on the map. We took up the proper heading and in 30 minutes landed in San Marcos just as the clouds arrived. The steaks in the ice box were rotten.

The navigators I helped train may have served in Korea, Viet Nam and other places. If so, I hope they were experts.

Rockwell and Soen were two 45-c classmates also stationed here at San Marcos. We often got together at the Officer's club on weekends. I know that it is said that alcohol in moderation is healthy but I have never liked the taste. The Bible condemns drunkenness and recommends moderation. So on a hot day a cold beer was refreshing but after half of a bottle I could stand no more.

One weekend Albert Soen's wife had arrived from Moline, Illinois for a visit. As we were enjoying the cool of the evening at an outside table at the officer's club I mentioned that I had never drunk a whole bottle of beer at one time. Mrs. Soen said, "If you drink that whole beer I'll give you a kiss."

No one noticed as I slowly emptied the bottle. When I called their attention to it Mrs. Soen started around the table and I started running across the lawn with Rockwell and Soen in hot pursuit. They held me while Mrs. Soen planted a kiss on my cheek to everyone's amusement including my new bride, Nell. We had visitors from Pampa. Nell's parents came for a visit. Wearing my gabardine summer uniform I posed for a picture between Nell and her mother, Effie. Our first months of marriage spent in San Marcos, Texas were an Eden like honeymoon and passed all too soon. The war was over and pilots were in excess. Discharge was available for the asking. I asked. I sent Nell home with her folks and expected to soon follow. I sent most of our money with her. I asked for discharge at Amarillo not far from her Pampa home.

I checked into a free barracks and waited for my discharge and travel papers. I got them right away. I would be leaving in two weeks.

# BOOK 3

# Settling In Oregon

**Two weeks!** I had kept only five dollars for food. I went to the PX and bought a 2 pound box of crackers and a 5 pound block of cheese. For two weeks I had cheese and crackers 3 times a day. That left me 15 cents every other day for a movie.

I was a big fan of Jack London and stories of the Northwest so I liked the idea of moving there. When I learned that the Whites were planning to move to Oregon I told them I would bring their daughter out there as well. Now with my discharge in hand we could all go together. Sometime later Auntie and Nell's brother, Garland would join us in Oregon.

That October the 4 of us loaded into Roy's 1938 DeSoto and 26 foot travel trailer and headed west. We didn't get far and for a while it seemed we would not make it to Oregon.

The postwar country was still a land of shortages and ration cards. Unavailable tires were needed for the trailer. Farm implement tires were not rationed so Roy bought 2 plus a spare and fitted them on the trailer. The first one didn't even get us out of Texas. The second blew out in Tucumcari, New Mexico. The Oregon Dream seemed impossible. We had a family discussion. Tucumcari was too small but Albuquerque was an up and coming town. We could live with that. We hired a truck to take the trailer over. Going west, there is a long downgrade lined with businesses as you approach Albuquerque. One business had a large sign, "New tires. No ration card needed." Yeah, yeah. We just kept going. But we debated. Why did he have the sign up if it wasn't true? Curiosity got the best of us so after a few miles we turned around to investigate.

The dealer had surplus airplane tires! He fitted 2 on our trailer by using a cutting torch to cut *out* the center of the airplane wheels and welding *in* the center of the car wheels and soon a surplus army pilot was rolling toward Oregon on 2 surplus airplane tires.

As we headed up the Pacific coast Route 1 Mrs. White found the precarious high points overlooking the ocean terrifying. She was having a panic attack. We stopped, unhooked the trailer and leveraged it around to face downhill and hooked it up again. We went down to a road leading east to the inland route and made it to Portland. We

parked in a small trailer park at 10901 N. E. Sandy Blvd., our first Oregon address. The Meiers who owned the trailer park sold Nell and me a homemade 16 foot trailer for $125.00. We owned our first home. As a first step in learning our new city they told us that Fred Meyer was the main store for shopping. At first we thought they were directing us to a relative but they pointed out that the name was spelled differently.

Next we moved to a larger trailer park on S. E. 82nd Avenue. Behind the trailer park on 84th Ave at Lincoln Street Nell and I bought the west half of lots 21 and 22 of Larson Place. It would be our

home for the next 35 years. Since Lincoln Street is the 2100 block SE we numbered our home 2102 but since the Paul Meyer home across 84th had been mis-numbered 2201 we changed ours to 8404 S. E. Lincoln Street.

After having a cesspool dug I built a 1 room square house with a bathroom and closet. It would later become a bedroom in our big home I would build around it. Equipped with a birds eye maple

veneered bedroom set and our kitchen and dining room still in the trailer we had a comfortable starter home. Roy built a shoe shop and home on a trailer frame at 85th and Division. Later he moved it down the block, added on the back and bricked the front and had a home and a shoe shop. Our future children would be 4 blocks from their Pappy Roy and Grammy. The back of Binnsmead Grade School was only one block away and the berry field in front of our home later became Binnsmead Park and part of the school playground. Our daughter, Charla Kay, was born in 1949 and Roy and Effie were a big part of her life. Grandparents are the best babysitters in the world. Roy and Effie were the best.

I liked Roy White and out of respect I always called him Mr. White. WWI veterans and those who served Texas cowboys in the frontier style before and after that war are gone and those of us who knew them have lost a direct link to a bygone era.

## Country Boy Needs a Job

Several times between Pampa, Texas and Portland, Oregon Nell reminded me that I didn't have a job. Was I missing something? Do women think with a different logic than men? Well, yes, but I could not fathom why I should be worried about a job until I arrived where the jobs were.

I was first attracted to the streetcars. That would be a good job for a former Midwest tractor driver. But I was turned down. In effect I was told to grow up and try again. You had to be 21 years old. I read of an opening at a roofing company warehouse. I had plenty of muscle and was not afraid of hard work. I was turned down. Reason: Over qualified. That was the first I knew that getting to be a pilot and officer as a teen ager made me too smart to do manual labor! United Airlines needed a baggage handler and that was my first postwar job. One afternoon I loaded the baggage and saw the passengers board the plane and take off. The next morning I felt a personal touch in a major tragedy as I read that they had smashed into a mountain in Idaho.

United Airlines is the only company I worked for that, despite mergers and acquisitions, has kept its name for decades later.

## Earthquakes

One day the hanger doors began shifting back and forth. I was experiencing my first earthquake. I worked at UAL only a few weeks but a new thread had been added to the fabric of my life.

It was 4 years later that another earthquake got my attention. My daughter, Charla Kay had been born in February. That summer Nell went back to work and I was babysitting. We were both napping when the house began to shake. Realizing it was an earthquake I picked up Charla Kay and hurried out into the yard.

Peter and Emily Walthard were good friends and neighbors. One day Emily went shopping 9 miles east in Gresham when an earthquake began giving the area a good shake. Emily looked at her companion and said, "I'll bet Pete is home thinking he is having another dizzy spell." When she got home she looked at Peter and said, "You had another dizzy spell didn't you?"

"Yes, the worst I've ever had. But how did you know?"

In the early 1970s I was trucking twice a week to Los Angeles. I was home when a tremendous earthquake hit LA. Freeways fell, disrupting traffic. When I drove there a few days later I had to make detours to get to my delivery points. Another week and I had a few days off and we took my boys, Henry 7 years old and Vincent 5 years old, and went to Disneyland. We got a room in the historic Alexandria Hotel in downtown LA with pictures of W. C. Fields and other notables on the hallway walls. It had been an elegant place in its heyday. Our room was a large 2ⁿᵈ floor room with beds along one wall. My wife and I chose the first bed and the boys took the second one about 10 feet over. We went to bed with the recent earthquake on our mind. The next morning I was awakened by the bed shaking. I glanced over at the boys. They both seemed to be unaware of the shaking. The bed started shaking again. I awakened my wife and said. "We are having another earthquake!" Someone started laughing. The mound where Henry slept was only pillows stuffed under the covers. Henry was under our bed giving us a scare. I found that I was not the only prankster in the family.

## Nell Roy's First Oregon Job

Nell's first job was with the Loose-Wiles Biscuit Company, that later took the name of one of their subsidiaries, Sunshine Biscuits. She

excelled as a bookkeeper in the office. That was a real asset in those days of hand bookkeeping. She recommended me for an opening in the factory. Soon I was stacking crackers as they came out of the hot oven. This upper floor was a scene out of a Charles Dickens novel of old London, England. All were interested as the hawk nosed manager, Leonard Grindal, romanced Elsie, a short dumpy factory worker. It was a lively and friendly place to work. Mr. Joseph Loose from back east came through the factory one day and watched us work.

Nell and I took the electric Hawthorne bus to Grand Avenue then the Bridge Transfer street car took us to the eastside factory just a

short way past Burnside where northeast Portland begins. That spring a wheat shortage threatened a slowdown in the bakery so I moved to a job with the Damascus Milk Company on S. E. Belmont Street. Not a lot later Nell Roy got a chance to move to a better job at the Paget Mortgage Company on the west side. She enjoyed being downtown. During her noon hour she would eat her sandwich then walk off the calories while window shopping. She often found and bought stylish clothes. She was a real dresser. She never did become overweight.

Lowell Paget was an interesting person. He was the third generation to own the mortgage company. He smoked but out of deference to his father's memory he always stepped out of the office and smoked on the street. One son joined him in the business. The other son was a doctor at the Mayo Clinic. He once said to the office help that the farmers of the nation were the only ones that added anything to our growth. Everyone else lived off of them and each other.

Mr. Paget was a prominent Oregonian often called 'Mr. Republican' as he was one who went to Washington to cast electoral votes in national elections. He always drove a nice modern auto but observed that really rich politicians drove a luxury car for the family but an older jalopy for politicking.

A joke about a mortgage: This one has whiskers. The old farmer had saved for years and finally had enough money to buy a farm. The banker helped him with the real-estate transaction and accepted his pay in full. Then he handed him his deed. The farmer refused to accept it. He said, "I want a mortgage." The banker said, "You own the farm. Why don't you want the deed?" The farmer replied, "When I was young my Dad had a farm. He had a deed and the bank had a mortgage and the bank got the farm. This time I want the mortgage."

## Milk Man

I told the manager at The Damascus Milk Company that as a 15 and 16 year old I had milked the cows, cooled and bottled the milk and delivered the milk to the doorsteps in Armington, Illinois. "You've done it all," he said as he hired me to run a route in the neighborhood of Eastmoreland. I drove a Divco special stand-up-and-drive milk truck. The homes of the well-to-do of Eastmoreland have long driveways and the delivery box is at the back door. If a note in the empty bottle said to leave an extra pint of cream it meant 2 runs up the long driveway. I added 26 new customers my first month on the route.

On the upper part of my route one of my customers was a fellow employee. His dog, a medium shaggy haired grey, watched me from his bed box as I crossed the porch to the milk box. He didn't appear to be friendly. I kept an eye on him. One day, to test him I pretended to not be watchful. Sure enough, out of the corner of my eye I saw him leave his box and come sneaking toward my heels. At the right moment I turned and landed a kick under his chin. He never made a sound, just returned to his bed. Never again did I see him leave his box.

Another day a large shaggy dog found a warm spot in the middle of the street. I stayed in the middle and slowly approached. He raised his head to see if I would move over to pass him. Finally he grudgingly stood up and moved barely enough for me to pass by a couple of inches. As the open door passed him I heard a deep throated grumble – ooo ooo ooo. I knew exactly what he called me! We farm boys know their language.

I was undecided about my job. I would soon be 21 and could now operate streetcars. But the milk company was a progressive company and I was proving to be a valuable employee. My good friend and neighbor, Peter Walthard, made his career here in the ice cream department. It became known that we would be owned by Carnation Milk Company. Maybe there was a good future with this company. When the driver with the route east of mine complained about his workload they put several of his customers on my route. With my own new customers added I was soon working 9 hours for 8 hours pay. A job where the customers ran to catch me instead of me running up their long driveways was looking better all the time. A month after my 21st birthday I went to see Mr. Woodcock at the Portland Traction Company.

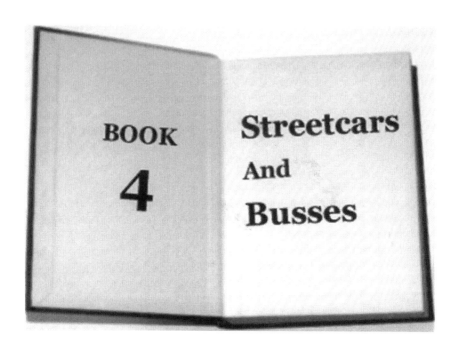

BOOK 4

Streetcars
And
Busses

## Horse Cars and a Lost Doll

At last I was 21 yrs. old and could apply for the street car job. But first I had to present a letter of introduction from someone who knew me. What better reference could I get than from my neighbor, Mr. McCallum? He was retired from the Portland Traction Company. When he started, the streetcars were pulled by horses! He told of primitive autos getting stuck in the muddy streets too close to the rails for the streetcar to pass until they helped them get unstuck. Were those the Good Old Days?

His wife was a nurse and proud to be from England and held tightly to her British accent. I asked her once if they had a 4th of July in England. She said "Blimey NO!" so I asked her what they called that date between the 3rd of July and the 5th of July. She looked at me for a moment then declared, "I'm never going to speak to you again." She did though. She was a fine lady and a Christian sister. She died at the ripe old age of 103.

Thane Weisberg and I applied for the bus company job at the same time. Mr. Woodcock hired us both but since I asked for 2 weeks to quit my milk route and train another milkman Thane was put first on the

Portland Traction Co.
Streetcar Operator 1946-1967

list so for the next 21 years Weisberg and Romans were consecutive names on the seniority list. When I was an aviation Cadet we were listed in alphabetical order. Cadet Pontius' name followed by my name Romans fascinated our officer in charge as he pointed out to the whole troop one day that Pontius Pilate was the Roman governor that prosecuted Jesus.

At the bus company if you got a "See me" in your driver's mail slot you had to go see Mr. Woodcock in his office. Until you saw him you would be wondering where you got caught goofing up. You likely took an expired transfer from a passenger that was an incognito inspector checking up on you!

You carried a changer on a harness on your chest so you could sell tokens 3 for a quarter. At the end of the day you turned in the unused rolls of tokens and the money for the ones you sold.

The clerk, Archie Bugh, could count a pile of change faster than anyone I ever saw. One day I went over to his home to discuss photos and I met his charming wife. Her home was filled with dolls and ornaments. I was fascinated. She told me about one doll that wasn't there. As a little girl in England she had the same birthday as Queen Victoria. She was one of the little ones sharing the Queen's birthday that was invited to meet with the Queen. She was 5 years old and the Queen lifted her up to sit on her lap. In addition to all that, she was given a doll. WOW!

Sometime later her family migrated to America. Standing at the rail of the ship's deck she accidently dropped her special doll overboard. For an interminably long time she could see the doll bobbing up and down on the waves behind the ship. Needless to say, she was one heartbroken little girl. As she told me the story I could tell that even after a half century she still felt the loss.

My dad was 1 year and 8 months old when Queen Victoria died in 1901. I was awed to meet someone who had met, yes, more than that had sat on the lap of the great Queen.

1946 was bringing me new jobs, new bosses, new friends. Was I touching history or was history touching me? The history I learned in BCHS seemed less ancient all the time!

## Kentucky Meets Virginia in Oregon

The Portland Traction Company never hired women until WWII made it necessary. After the war they stopped hiring them but the ones already hired could stay. Their numbers were gradually reduced by attrition. At a time when bus drivers were thought of as men it was startling momentarily to hear that a bus driver had quit to have a baby!

Women were not the only ones discriminated against. Black Americans were not hired at that time. By the check-in window a sheet of paper had missed the waste basket. I picked it up to keep the room tidy but glanced at it. It was a letter to the division manager congratulating him on keeping blacks out of the work force!

I met Russell Hughart. He had been a driver before the war and during the war he was called into the office and told he was fired. They didn't want one of Jehovah's Witnesses working there. He joined some others and formed the Radio Cab Company and became competitors of the bus company. Their radio dispatched cabs were progressive for the time. One lady called for a cab and was prepared for the cab to drive from the cab company yard. Russell was two blocks away and was soon in front of her door. She refused to ride with someone that drove so fast until he explained about the radio.

I was still learning routes. I went out into the bus yard to find bus such and such and learn another route. My trainer was one of the women drivers, Opal Lanier from Virginia. She was really surprised when she learned my name and she exclaimed. "Before I married I was Opal Romans." We wrote to our respective mothers but no kinship was discovered but we likely descended from the 5 Romans brothers who came from England on William Pitt's ship and founded Romansville near Philadelphia.

## Hot Beef Sandwich

One morning I was completing my morning shift on the Mt. Tabor street car. A young driver, Vern Albertson, took over at 28th Street and continued on toward downtown Portland. He had had no breakfast and no prospect for any lunch for the next 8 hours. Since I had a 4 hour break on my split shift I told him I would bring him a sandwich after a while.

I walked the 10 short blocks to the Car Barn Diner and had my morning coffee and snack. I then studied the menu. Ah! Hot Beef Sandwich. I'll bet that would suit my friend. I ordered it.

I was dismayed when the waitress set before me a big platter with an open faced roast beef sandwich, a generous portion of mashed potatoes, all smothered in gravy. What kind of brown bagger would that make? I covered it somehow and carried it to the Mt. Tabor line and caught an outbound car and met Albertson as he was going west on his next trip.

He was soon sitting on one of the wicker seats enjoying his still warm lunch while I took the car as far as 28th Street. I returned the dinnerware and at the first opportunity I tried one of these delicious hot meals that sold for the price of a sandwich. I was hooked!

It became one of my favorite meals. Later while trucking I had hot beef sandwiches in every Northern and Western state I trucked in. But there was going to be a lean time.

Some have said that Kentucky is a foreign country in the middle of the United States. While in a Spanish home on business the husband told me they were refugees from Cuba. I told him I was a refugee also. He wanted to know from where so I told him, "Kentucky." He protested that that was in this country. I told him I left Kentucky for the war in 1943, got captured by a young lady in Texas, was taken to Oregon several years ago and hadn't got back to Kentucky yet!

I didn't get much sympathy from him!

Finally in 1997 I moved back to Butler County, Kentucky.

Soon I looked for a hot beef sandwich. There was none on the menu anywhere around here. I looked far and near for months and years. I was in a desert as far as hot beef sandwiches. One day I expressed my frustration to a waitress at the Kountry Kitchen. Why don't you have a hot beef sandwich on the menu?

She pointed to a line on the menu. Manhattan. *Manhattan?* In Morgantown a Hot Beef Sandwich is a Manhattan! I had found my hot beef sandwich. The famine was over!

When you move to a foreign country even with a familiar language it may take a while to learn all that is new or different.

Manhattan, Manhattan, Manhattan, Manhattan, Manhattan ...

## Sleep

When I was about 12 years old I wanted to stay awake all night. Dad and Mom set the rules. Put out the lamp and be quiet so the others could sleep. I sat in front of the warm fireplace and lasted about a half hour and went to bed.

In the Air Corps I enjoyed night flying but was never out all night. On my first night shift on the city buses I was soon fighting sleep. I had heard of NoDoz pills so I stopped at a neighborhood store about 10 pm and bought a bottle and took 2 pills. Wow! Did I have trouble staying awake?! A NoDoz pill contains as much caffeine as two cups of coffee. I've known since then that caffeine puts me to sleep!

Pediatricians are the doctors of choice for children until adolescence. They know that downers stimulate children and a stimulate, such as the caffeine in coffee, sedates them until their metabolism reverses during adolescence. That's proof that I am still in my first childhood!

I finally worked enough odd shifts to break my body from a routine sleep time. I still like to sleep when I am sleepy and read and do other useful things when I am wakeful no matter what the time, day or night. When I am wound up for a long haul a 15 minute nap will usually break up a spell of drowsiness. That pattern paid off when one of Portland, Oregon's rare ice and snow storms came one night when I was on an owl shift.

I was out on the Powell-Broadway route without chains when the storm hit. My 6am relief driver didn't show up. I kept driving. My midwest icy road experience helped. I would not stop on a slope or at the curb. Passengers would have to board at the top of the grade and in the middle of the intersection where it was level. Until the overworked mechanics got chains on the other buses I made a round trip and passed every other bus on the route, stuck, unmovable against the curb. I gave service all day and then another night shift. The next morning during the rush period I had another full load, crossed the Ross Island Bridge and before I got to 6th street where I could turn off this hill a lady ran across in front of me desperate to catch a ride to work. I was forced to stop where I could not start moving. She had to walk the half mile or so to town along with the whole bus load of passengers. I carefully rolled and slid backwards and got against the curb. I reported my location to the dispatcher, propped my feet up and went to sleep. I had been driving over 30 hours! That was not illegal.

**Pat Daniels**

You hear of those riders who spend a lot of time riding the public transportation vehicles. Pat was well known to the bus drivers in Portland. He was a little guy about 5 feet. He joked that his phone number was 002 Short! He had a job delivering blue prints around town for a company in NW downtown Portland. His vehicle was a bicycle. After work he would ride the buses or talk with one of the inspectors on a corner or in the inspector's car. He knew a lot of what was going on in the company. You could learn a lot from Pat. He was the Bus Company gossip.

Pat lived with his folks and brother in SE Portland a block off the 52nd Avenue bus route. I became a friend of the family. When his dad was old and dying I would sometimes stop by and shave him to make him feel better. Pat had a reserved dry humor way about him and could sometimes be a little moody. One 5 PM he was in a bad mood and caught his bus straight home. I happened to be the driver.

Downtown Portland is on the Willamette River that soon empties into the Columbia River just north of town and thence to the Pacific Ocean 80 miles away at Astoria. So we start our trip from downtown at only 50 feet above sea level and all routes have to go uphill. My bus that evening was an old 900 series gas bus that could barely move upgrade with the heavy rush period load. Pat was sitting by the door on the bench seat that faces the aisle just across from my driver's seat. He is getting impatient. "Can't you go faster than this?"

"Yes," I replied.

Then why don't you do it?" he growled.

"I have to stay with the bus." That didn't help his mood any! I stole that line from Rod Brasfield when he visited Portland with the Grand Ole Opry show.

One year I had a vacation when my wife didn't. So it was agreed I would visit Butler County for a family visit without her. With his mother's blessing on the offer I invited Pat to make the trip with me. As I posed him for a picture on the edge of a canyon in Idaho it was certainly different scenery for him. The farther away we got and the stranger the scenery the more scared and homesick he became for his mother. He was reduced to tears.

"Pat, I can't put you out here in the middle of nowhere. Hang in there until we get to Denver and I'll put you on a Greyhound bus for home." He was right at home when he got on the bus and he liked the driver. When I got home he told me how the driver promised to show the passengers a pair tree on the courthouse yard in Salt Lake City that never had pears in the tree but always had pairs on the ground. Sure enough when they got there he saw no fruit on the tree but there were lounging couples (pairs) courting in the shade under the tree.

Pat made the work day pass faster. With my jokes and tricks added to the mixture we made a good Pat and Mike comedy team.

One day he came to ride my bus and was obviously in deep distress. When we were alone at the end of the line I asked, "What's wrong, Pat?"

Miserably he said, "I can't tell you. It's about my brother. It's too terrible. It was in the paper."

On my split shift I went to the Oregonian office and asked what news was in the paper about his brother. He had been arrested for soliciting as a gay person. Pat had felt shamed speechless. My! How times have changed!

Before I left Portland for Morgantown in 1997 I visited Pat in his rest home in NE Portland. He had had a stroke. He is probably gone now. He enjoyed his simple life and made others laugh.

I remember Pat. I won't forget him.

## Council Crest

At the Portland Traction Division where I worked I was operating vehicles on all the bus and streetcar lines except one – Council Crest.

Council Crest is a hill in the southwest part of Portland that looms 1000 feet above the downtown part of the city. Leaving downtown you climb gradually to SW 23rd Ave and Burnside, the dividing street between NW and SW. There the 23rd Ave streetcar turned north on 23rd past fine old homes turned boarding houses, upbeat specialty restaurants and, eventually, industrial sections ending at Montgomery Wards. Across the street at 23rd and Burnside in a Y was Henry Theille's restaurant. Henry's widow had continued with a new husband and when he turned 100 years old, I and many others celebrated with him by dining there one last time. Soon after that the restaurant closed. I still miss the wonderful German Frikadellen served there. But down 23rd avenue Rose's still serves her great sandwiches. When you visit this area you are really *Up Town.*

The Council Crest street car has turned left at this point heading into dangerous steep grades and curves. The street becomes Vista Avenue at this point. The car leaves Vista at Patton Road and skirts the hill on a private right of way. Below on the right you can see the grey rooftop of Stroehecker's grocery store on the street below where you can buy the staples plus exotic fine foods. This is the only commercial enterprise allowed in this exclusive residential neighborhood. At the top, the rails circle the peak, looking down on the Tualatin Valley far below and the route terminates on the east side. The operator waits to begin his downhill trip here with the woods and City Park and lookout covering the very peak on his left and the turnaround of the residential street on his right. One little boy asked his mother as he climbed the steps, "Is this where they let the drease drip?" Yes the machine did drop grease and stain the pavement here.

An exclusive few drivers covered these Council Crest runs. I wanted to be one of those operators. How?

First you had to gain experience on other routes and have a good record for one year. I met that requirement in 1947 at the age of 22. I applied for a chance to train for CC and was accepted. Now, on my own time, I had to ride and practice with one of the old timers for 20 hours on daytime runs and then for 20 hours on nighttime runs. Now before taking a run the company had to show they had thoroughly trained the operator and have the paper signed by the Mayor. They wanted their affluent citizens to be in good hands. They included Mr. Meier of Meir & Frank (later sold to May company) and partway up vista I passed the old dark grey Victorian home of Dr. Janet Thayer. In 1949 she delivered my daughter at the Emanuel Hospital. The mayor at that time was Dorothy McCulloch Lee, the first woman to be Mayor of Portland. I had seen her the previous year as she would be at the car barn at 4am electioneering in the driver's room as they came to work. Over half a century later I would be in Morgantown in time to see the first woman mayor elected there.

My training was complete. From then 'till the end of the street car era Council Crest was my favorite run.

My youth was only mentioned once. One Sunday morning I had only 2 old dressed up gentlemen on board as I headed down the hill. Unbeknownst to me the car before me had slid on the fall leaves and *that* greased the rails. For my car it was like black ice. As soon as I applied brakes the car took off. Careening around curves I was going faster and faster. Stomping on the sander, yanking on the hand brake and applying the full electric brake with little results I was expecting the electric derail up ahead to throw us off the rail and into the curb to be rescued later. But my efforts paid off. We made what appeared to be a normal stop just short of the derail. As I waited for it pop shut for me to proceed one of the old guys said, "Taking those curves kinda fast aren't you, Sonny?

## Dinty's

A public transportation driver sees a lot of big city drama through his front window and even helps make some of the drama. As passengers exchange stories you hear interesting things that add a tidbit to your view of the city and humanity. Some passengers like to sit close by the driver and chat with him. Contrary to what some say about a driver's attention being fully on his driving a driver can be aware of lots of things around him. An alert driver is a safe driver.

The streetcars and later buses left Fifth Avenue downtown and went up Washington Street past the Aragon Studio at Tenth and soon after blended into West Burnside. At nineteenth you passed the Multnomah Stadium on the left and about 21$^{st}$, there was Dinty's restaurant on the left. Yes it was *Dinty's* like in the comic strip *Bringing Up Father* where Jiggs was always going to Dinty Moore's to eat corned beef and cabbage much to the disgust of his high society wife, Maggie. Dinty's was there a long time before Denny's filled the country.

Frequently, an old fellow, neatly dressed in a suit and hat, came in for breakfast. He always sat at his favorite table and the waitress greeted him with a cheery, "Good Morning." and served him his regular order with a friendly smile.

He enjoyed his leisure meal. He then left his usual dollar tip and left to be back to breakfast here again in a day or two or three.

One morning the waitress came over to clear the table and pocket the tip as usual. She was busy for a while and he was long gone when she took the tips out of her apron pocket to fold them away. Oh! No! It wasn't a one dollar bill the old man had left. It was a *ten*! "He can't afford that," she thought. So she kept the ten in her purse until he came in again a few days later.

She went over to his table and said, "I think you made a mistake the last time you were here."

"How's that?" he asked.

She laid the ten dollar bill on the table and said, "You left this."

He sat for a moment looking at the bill and said, "Yes. I did make a mistake."

He slowly got out his wallet and tucked the bill away.

Then he placed another bill on the table. "I meant to give you this."

To her surprise and delight he was giving her *One Hundred Dollars*.

This cheerful waitress had been a bright spot as his life wound down with old age and he wanted to reward her and even made it larger for her refreshing honesty and concern.

## Our First Auto

After WWII cars were scarce. We found a 1936 Ford V8 for sale for $500. After I got the job driving split shifts on the buses I bought a red Cushman scooter that got me to work twice a day for two weeks on 25 cents worth of gas. When we arrived in Portland we parked in a small trailer park at 10901 N. E. Sandy Blvd. In the park was a homemade 13 foot trailer for sale for $125.00. We bought a lot for $500.00. Now we had a home of our own. When I got enough of our new house built to move in we sold the trailer for $140.00.

The 1936 V8 was a step up from Dad's 1929 Model A. When Ellen Turcotte, Nell's aunt, left Pampa, Texas and joined us she mentioned selling her Model A for $100. I hadn't known she had one stored in her garage. If I had known...

When Nell's brother Garland joined us he was driving his Dad's car down by the Steel Bridge waiting for a green light. The car beside him was a model A. Garland could not stand for another car to outrun him so he was poised for a jack rabbit start. But before he could hardly press the accelerator the Model A leapt forward leaving him behind as it raced over the bridge. He saw the driver park over town and asked him what he had under the hood. He had installed an airplane engine!

Souped up Model A Fords, V8 Fords, Street cars, Electric buses – it was the late 1940's alright. Big changes were not far off.

On the scooter I took off for work down Division Street in the wee dark hours one morning. The pavement looked dry but the frost was invisible. A car ahead stopped for a signal. I stepped on the brake pedal and the frozen brake locked on. The rear wheel was sliding without resistance. I rolled the scooter over on its right side and rode on top of it. The right sheet metal fender was scraping the pavement with the loudest screeching, screaming, wailing ever heard in the quiet hours of the morning! The driver in the car could not see through his frosted window. He opened the door to see what was happening. I was in the lane beside him picking up the scooter. "Was that you making all that racket?" Yep!

In March 1948 I had vacation time coming and it was time for the first trip back to Butler County since getting married and leaving the Air Corp. Keda Britt had moved to Portland and she rode with us to Morgantown to stay a while with her folks. Her brother, Dan, came back with us. He was impressed that the Oregon State police were driving Buicks.

My low seniority rated only a springtime slot on the vacation list. The car had a primitive heater for the cold spring weather. A cover over the manifold captured heat from the motor and funneled it into the car.

The national speed limit was 35 miles per hour and most of the time that was too fast for the road full of potholes left from the winter weather. The trip took 5 hard days of driving each way. That seems primitive but we accepted it as normal for that time and enjoyed our visit with family and friends. The Morgantown merchant, Carl Nietzsche, scolded me for not coming back to Morgantown after my discharge from the Air Corp. He had planned to buy an airplane and put me in business! What a *What If* that was!

I had a life out west awaiting me so we had a most enjoyable Kentucky vacation then made the long drive to our home way out in the West.

## Vanport Flood

That Sunday I reported to the Ankeny car barn to take a streetcar out for a PM run. The clerk yelled, "Grab any bus in the yard and go to Vanport!" There I sat on Interstate 5 that formed a dike or dam on the east edge of Vanport. I watched as apartment buildings floated toward me like huge barges. As they crunched to a stop, refugees would jump from the top to swim or wade to dry ground. One old black man climbed on my bus to watch everything he owned be destroyed. He fingered the lapel on his suit he had worn to church that morning. "This is all I have left," he said wistfully. I took my load of refugees to a school in NE Portland where they could be cared for.

Three of the many buses there were from my division and the drivers were named in the Oregonian. One city bus was lost when a car driver at the head of the line refused to drive through a red light. The passengers had to run for their lives.

18,500 people were left homeless.

## I Become a Builder

After we acquired the double lot in 1946 I had set out to build our home. We bought materials as we had the money. We were 4 blocks from the lumber yard and I carried a lot of small orders of lumber home. Sometimes we had enough to buy a truck load. I built a square flat top building for a bedroom, bathroom and closet. The trailer was still our kitchen. It took 7 years to build the house. Ellen Turcotte moved out from Texas so I took time to build her a 1 room home and later built her a good home on our second lot. I attended every home show to learn my new building trade. Scotty at Demetri's, an electrical supply store on downtown 3rd Avenue, gave me builder's discount on my hardware and electrical supplies. We were quite settled in so it was time to start our family. Charla Kay was born on Sunday morning on February 10, 1949

## Childbirth 1940s Style

We had been married four years and I had been driving Portland's streetcars and buses for three years. Our first vacation in Kentucky was past when Charla Kay was born in February of 1949.

I always knew I wanted to be a family man. We agreed that three children would be the right size family. Since I was the oldest in my family I knew how to take care of babies. You sang and rocked them to sleep and changed their diapers. Mom was a good psychologist. She convinced Wanda and me that washing dirty diapers was good for our hands!

I thought I knew about childbirth. Mom was frequently gone to help deliver babies and would get the Red Cross to help get service men home to be with the mothers giving birth.

I saw women midwives or doctors as most appropriate to help women give birth. Men doctors had dominated the scene for many years. They branded women midwives and home delivery as dangerous and irresponsible. During the Salem witch hunts some doctors declared midwives to be witches and got their business after the women were burned at the stake. In the 1940's women were struggling to get a foothold in the profession. We hired Janet Thayer for our experience. I was running the Council Crest streetcar up Vista Avenue in front of her Victorian home.

On a Saturday night I took Nell to the Emanuel Hospital and by the time of her giving birth on Sunday morning I had had the shock of my life.

I was allowed in the labor room except when a male doctor came in to check the progress. The delivery room was NO MAN'S LAND. The waiting room I considered a nursery for immature fathers not old enough to be with their wives when their babies are born. I could only stand in the hallway and hear my wife scream until they put her out. I saw Charla Kay briefly as she was carried past me to the nursery. I never got to hold her until 8 days later when I took them home.

I had hoped that having a child would bring some closeness into our marriage but the hospital rules had treated me as a useless outsider.

I was shocked to learn they shaved mothers before delivering the baby. Since only a small percent get infected from the razor bumps and only a few die the doctors think that is acceptable. My wife came home with Staph infection. I had never heard of an episiotomy. It was totally unnecessary and left Nell sore for a year. Thus began a decades long love/hate relationship between me and the medical profession. I lost my respect for doctors and would not consider another child being born under these ridiculous circumstances. My experience in youth and the military did not prepare me to challenge authority. I knew the doctors were wrong but I didn't know what to do about it so I would not consider another baby for the next 14 years

I enjoyed my streetcar job and as my house building projects wound down I revived my interest in photography.

**Nancy**
Using the magnetic brake and the old hand crank brake I stopped by the old Portland Hotel that had hosted Kings and Queens and other notables. A little girl, maybe 4 years old, struggled to climb the high step to get aboard. Her impatient mother urged her, "Get on up, Nancy. Hurry!"

Distress showed on the little girl's face as she struggled over the last hurdle and stood up in the vestibule. I said, "Hi. Nancy."

She stopped and looked up with a look of delight and wonder. With a voice filled with amazement and joy she said, "Momma! He knows my name! "Her mother answered with a shove and an order to get to her seat.

I hope I made Nancy's day. I know her sweet smile of delight left a snapshot in my heart that lingers over 60 years later.

## Boogie Woogie and WWII

A driver would pick up bodies at the morgue in downtown Portland and transport them to a facility west of Portland. As he drove past part of the Council Crest route he would stop and chat with his friend, the mail man.

One day the mailman boarded the CC to go up the hill so he could drop off mail as he walked back down and he had something to tell me. He said it never bothered him when his friend was carrying a random body but this day he had Wayne Long. Putting a name he knew on the body gave him the creeps.

Wayne Long was a notorious criminal who finished his sentence and went right to a bank on 82nd Avenue not far from my home, stole money and killed a teller. Then he walked out into the hands of FBI agents who had been following him. This time he got the death sentence.

The mailman carried the mail in a large horsehide leather bag with a shoulder strap. I told him in the Pony Express days the mailman rode a horse. Now the horse rides the mailman!

Not far up the hill Mallory Carter and Marci worked in one of the fine homes. He was chauffeur and maintenance man. She was cook and housekeeper. They met on this job and got married. Soon afterward he was on a ladder cleaning windows when he heard good lively music coming from the house. Curious – he climbed down to investigate. He told me he walked in to see Marci sitting at the piano. He stared in astonishment and exclaimed, "I married me a Boogie Woogie player!"

In the brief rides he had with me we became friends. I was alone one weekend and was invited to their home for dinner. Marcie's boss had shot several wild ducks on the Oregon Coast and shared them. That afternoon she had prepared the ducks and put them in the oven then went upstairs. She heard a loud explosion and went running downstairs and met the cat running in terror up the stairs. The cooking wine had exploded and blown the oven door open! Some of the ducks were sitting out on the open door.

I went over to visit Mallory one evening and he introduced me to his friend. Mr. Green was another black man who had a grandfather who was an Indian Chief. He was a very interesting person. He told of trucking in New York when he was young. Once when going through a tunnel he had been awake for 2 weeks by using pills. The truck drifted toward a pillar. He could see the crash coming but his abused body would no longer respond. It caused horrible damage and a traffic snarl and he was in the hospital a year mending broken bones. Thereafter trucks were forbidden to use the tunnels, only bridges into Manhattan.

During the war he was on a merchant ship going up and down the East coast. It was a handsome freighter with rugged beams and the proud workmanship of an earlier age. One night on his sleep shift he heard voices and the ship wasn't moving. He arose and looked through a porthole. There a few yards away was a German submarine. Above him he could hear his Captain talking to the German Captain. They were old friends! Before the war they had served together in the Consulate in Washington, D. C.

They were asking about each other's families. After a visit the German said, "John, get your crew on lifeboats and get out of danger. I'm sinking your ship."

"You don't have to sink our ship. We are civilians. We're not an armed military ship."

"I know but you have a load of cement. You are taking it to Trinidad where they can build a runway for bombers to sink our submarines. So I have to sink your ship. So get everyone off."

Mr. Green said they all got off and watched as a torpedo sunk their rugged old ship. The sub commander assured them that he had radioed their position and they would be rescued. He was true to his word.

The American public was kept in the dark about the extensive German submarine activity off the East coast. Much is now being told but I learned this firsthand account of it over 60 years ago.

So much for how men's ambitions and politics can make enemies out of friends!

### Tricks

1949. It was the waning years of Portland's old streetcars. Comes Halloween and the affluent youths on Council Crest ruled the night. At the top of Council Crest where the streetcar went through a wooded area one team cut down a 100 foot evergreen tree to fall across the tracks. They misjudged the rate of fall and their targeted streetcar cleared the spot before it crashed. It could have killed the operator and any passengers he may have had aboard and the streetcar would have been destroyed.

Patton Road and Vista was the main rallying point. As I came out of the dark into the wide 3 way lighted intersection I eased slowly through the wild mob. Someone threw a lighted fusee into the rear vestibule of my streetcar. If it had ignited the wooden floor it could have turned the wicker seats and wooden panels of the interior into an inferno. I kept going until I was out of sight around a curve then ran back and threw the burning missile into the street.

At Halloween, cemeteries have been a place of apprehension. Many were lead to believe that the ghosts or spirits of the dead were floating around ready to grab you. I had never felt that way and when I drove a bus past a cemetery I would tell the passengers that, "There are the people who quit smoking." That was true of previous smokers. It was also true that they had quit everything else. When I was in High School, reading lots of books including the Bible, someone pointed out to me what the Bible says, "...as for the dead, they are conscious of nothing at all..., their love and their hate and their jealousy have already perished..." (Ecclesiastes 9:5, 6) They are asleep in the dust awaiting a wonderful Resurrection Day.

I know two guys who quit smoking because of tricks they did to themselves. One night I was having coffee in a truck stop when a driver told me of his woe. His girlfriend had given him an expensive jewel encrusted cigarette lighter. Back down the road he had put a cigarette in his lips, reached over and lit the lighter, lit his cigarette, then, from habit from when he used matches, he tossed the lighter out the window! He said, "I never want to light another cigarette."

The other trick was on a relative. Dad's sister Stella was married to Arthur Dotson. Uncle Dot farmed 300 acres in central Illinois. Ralph Price was his hired man. Ralph later married the boss's daughter, Edna Mae, and they lived in a hired man's house but for now he lived in the basement of the farmhouse. He had to be up about 4 am to milk the dairy cows and do the chores. He had been building a model airplane, one of those made of balsa wood, tissue paper and glue. He was nearly done so he decided to miss some sleep and finish it. It was a nice piece of work. About midnight he was admiring his handiwork and decided to have a cigarette before getting some much needed sleep. As he struck the match it ignited the fumes from the fresh glue and 'poof', in seconds his pretty airplane was a film of ashes on the table. He was so shocked and angered he never smoked another cigarette.

Don't wait for a trick. If you are a smoker, treat yourself to better health and longer life, quit.

## Electric Buses

After the streetcars were gone we had some electric bus routes that delayed pollution for a while. I signed on those routes as long as I could before the oil interests conned the cities into going all oil or diesel for the sake of their bottom line. It would be nearly the end of the century before rail and electric came back. The carbon insert on the shoes that slid on the 2 overhead wires had to be replaced about every day.

With a rush period load I was driving along 42$^{nd}$ avenue when I noticed a regular passenger sleeping past her stop. I pulled into the next stop and awakened her. That evening I told Nell that I had to wake up one of our Christian sisters for her bus stop. She asked, "Did it embarrass her?" I said I couldn't tell if she blushed. She was African-American!

On 42$^{nd}$ Avenue late one evening I stopped for the *Stop* sign at Woodstock. In the old Lutheran Church the Boy Scouts were having their meeting. Some were out playing around and one of them pulled my trolley poles off the wires. I put them back on and got in my seat then jumped up and raced around to the back just as the prankster pulled the poles off again. With me in hot pursuit he ran into the church and up the aisle. I collared him at the front and walked him out to the bus. I made him replace the trolley poles and wrote down the name he gave me which I suspected to be fictitious. I said, "I will call the police and wait for them." He then gave me his right name and address. Armed with that the company's Special Agent had a talk with some parents and Boy Scout nights were tamer after that.

I would drive down Woodstock with my old milk route on the left. On the right at 3203 lie the manicured grounds of Reed College, the little college with the worldwide reputation. On a morning when I would see a bearded professor walking down the sidewalk enjoying the heady atmosphere and preparing his mind to inspire freethinking scholars to use their brains to go out and change the world, I would feel a twinge of envy and momentarily wonder if I had made a mistake in not pursuing the educator's profession. Five years after I left the bus company, Steve Jobs spent one semester at Reed College.

In one last gasp of running electric buses the company bought a few Kenworth electrics. They were equipped with electric brakes that were activated by electricity from the engines that became generators as we braked. A small amount of air in an air brake held the bus when stopped. I did not like the high pitched hum of an electric motor that was on constantly. One cold morning the heater was not working. I was bundled in winter clothing but the load of passengers made the windshield fog over. I called for another bus. They sent me a bottle of glycerin to put on the window!

**Our First TV**
I had 6 passengers when I headed for downtown for a rush period load. I was still in the Industrial area of Southeast Portland on the Sellwood route when a car slowly pulled out from the left and stopped, blocking my lane. You can't detour an electric bus so I pulled up to his right side and sat looking down to see what he was going to do. He just sat there. I stepped out and said, "Why don't you go on and let me take these people to town?"

"What are you going to do about it?"

I stepped back in the bus and picked up a pencil and a transfer envelope to write on and headed for the front of his car. "I'm going to write down your license number so I can report my reason for being late."

He met me at the corner of his car to block my way. I was heavier than him so I walked on crowding him back. He stomped my foot trying to get me to hit him first. I kept my hands down and was soon writing down his number. He jumped in his car and drove into me. I fell across the hood and rolled off on the right side. He roared away hoping I wouldn't have time to get his number. My nose was bleeding and I finished my shift with a bloody shirt. I made out my report and went home to a horrified wife as she saw my shirt.

The next day, after my morning shift the bus company's Special Agent met me and we went to see the DA. He listened to my story and said the car driver and his father had been by and said I had tried to poke his eyes with a pencil and he defended himself. The DA said their story was more believable than the silly story I had just told.

Our Special Agent spoke up. "Wait just a minute! I interviewed the 6 witnesses this morning and they all backed up our driver's story."

The DA was taken aback. He said he could bring charges and get a nominal fine but he suggested a civil case instead. The bus company's lawyer took my case. The opponent's lawyer offered $200.00 to settle out of court. I turned it down but accepted $500.00 and we bought our first TV, a Magnavox Console model.

## Oysters

After we moved back to Butler County in 1934 we sometimes went to Uncle Charlie's in Cleaton for the weekend. We would load into the old Model T Ford and head down through Rochester. The loaded Tin Lizzy couldn't pull the Cleaton hill so we got out and walked while Dad pushed the center pedal which was Reverse on the model T and crawled backwards to the top.

One weekend Dad and Uncle Charlie were hungry for oysters. They bought a gallon of canned ones and Mom and Aunt Violet breaded and fried them. Dad and Uncle Charlie both got sick that night. I had never tasted oysters before. I found them to be delicious and became another fan and lover of fried oysters.

The next time I saw fried oysters was as a Cadet at the Air Corp mess hall in San Angelo, Texas. They were the small ones. I ate 40 of them.

After settling in Portland, Oregon we had access to plenty of sea food. We lived on the east edge of Portland on Lincoln Street. Every Friday evening my wife's folks, Roy and Effie White and the two of us would go about 10 blocks south on 82nd Ave then west on Powell to

Milwaukee Blvd. (about the 12 hundred block) to our meeting at the Kingdom Hall. On the way we passed The Jolly Rodger at 39th. We always stopped and had our sea food dinner. I was the only one who ordered oysters. Since it was always Friday when we ate our fish there I'll bet the management thought we were Catholics!

Sometimes between shifts on the bus I would go there for lunch. If the cook didn't have his deep fryer busy with Halibut I would talk him into battering some oysters and deep frying them. Wow! They were sooooo good.

The ultimate in dining on oysters was at the Dan & Louis Oyster bar in the Old Town part of downtown Portland. Louis Wachsmuth (1877-1958) opened for business in 1907. Now a Portland land landmark and known around the world, five generations have kept the business thriving. After Grandpa Louis died in 1958 Louis A. and Chester ran the business until their sons Louis John and Doug took over in 1977. In 1991 Doug bought full ownership.

In 1997, before moving to Morgantown I went by, took some pictures and said goodbye to Doug and others. I had been a regular customer for 52 years!

One evening after dark I drove a Mt. Tabor bus to the downtown end of the line at 12th and Montgomery. I parked at the curb and had several minutes to wait. I was in front of an old Victorian home with a street level basement with a big glass window. A small restaurant had been opened like a sidewalk café in Europe. I walked in. There were no other customers. The owner was at a table across the room talking with his sweetheart.

He was a younger Wachsmuth sibling not associated with the family business. He came over and took my order from a menu that came from the Oyster bar! He brought my order and returned to his courting. I enjoyed the expertly prepared dinner while listening to "Puff the Magic Dragon" on the Juke Box. It was a magical moment and another memory from old Louis' family.

In Morgantown when I get a yearning for oysters I either do like Dad and Uncle Charlie and open a can and fry them myself or head for Captain D's in Bowling Green.

**Gangsters and Small Cars**
In Illinois I was 9 years old in 1934 as dad prepared to sell his crops and machinery and move back to Butler County. John Dillinger was on the run and until we heard that he was killed by the police we were careful to keep the doors locked.

Al Capone and other gangs ruled Chicago from the 1920s into the 1930s. During that time one of the Portland Traction Company's drivers took a vacation in Chicago. He told me about it after I started work on the buses in 1946.

In Chicago he drove up to the pumps to get gasoline. A car pulled in behind him and the driver told him to get out of the way as he was going to fuel first. The car's occupants confronted him and he got out of their way. He said that the next day a Chicago newspaper made headlines, "Gangsters Knock Westerner's Hat Off."

He said, "They didn't get that right. They didn't knock my hat off. They knocked me out from under my hat!"

In the 1950s the talk was about little foreign cars and good gas mileage. I no longer had my Cushman scooter so maybe it would be good to have a high mileage small car for going to work. My father-in-law, Roy White, soon had a Hillman Minx from England sitting in front of his shoe shop. When the clutch went out and a new one was $900.00 he waited for weeks to get one from England. He went back to Studebakers.

1959 French Renault

My wife and I settled for a little blue French Renault. It was the worst and costliest car I ever bought. I would start to work to run my city bus shift and end up taking a taxi to get there. One day I was waiting for a traffic light on Division Street. In the mirror I could see a large car that was *not* slowing down as he came up behind me. Fortunately, there was no cross traffic as I bounced across the intersection like a cue ball.

My bus driver uniform cap ended up in the back seat. The crash didn't knock my cap off. It knocked me out from under my cap!

I decided right then that the next time I got hit I was going to be in a bigger vehicle than the other driver. The next day I traded in the one year old car on a 1956 Ford Station Wagon.

## Greco

The Portland Traction was bought from the private owners by the City and became The Rose City Transit Company and our black uniforms became powder blue. New electric buses were bought from time to time as well as gas and diesel buses.

Any new models required the drivers to go on training rides with instructors. A dozen or so of us went out for a ride one day with the "Out of Service" sign up front. An old retired driver was seen waiting for a bus so we invited him to join us. He got on along with his cigar. Since we were not in service no one objected. Soon someone noticed Greco sitting by an open window in the rear of the bus. "What's the matter, Greco?"

"I can stand some tobacco smoke but when they smoke horse manure it makes me sick." The old man took the hint and threw out his cigar.

The Portland drivers had the lowest pay scale of any city drivers on the west coast. Most drivers therefore had a second job. Mine was photography. Mr. Greco's was real estate. He was a big lovable bear of a man and well respected.

One day he was driving the Hawthorne line and at 23rd Avenue a passenger was waiting. He was a prosperous looking well-dressed business man with a 50 inch belt line delicately holding his morning cigar between his fingers. He held it at his side as he came aboard. Greco politely asked him to throw it out. He ignored the request and took his seat. It was just a few minutes to downtown so nothing more was said.

Next morning, same time, same stop, same passenger, new cigar. Greco neatly came to a stop in front of him and looked at him a few moments then drove on without opening the door.

Next morning, same time, same stop, same passenger, new cigar. As the bus approached the man held the cigar high in plain sight and for all to see, tossed it into the street. Greco stopped and opened the door. The passenger boarded dropped the token in the fare box and said, "You win," and everyone enjoyed a smoke free ride to work!

## PA

As I drive my bus throughout the town
There is one thing I know for sure.
I must not hit a single thing
To keep my record pure.

So I watch for traffic on my right,
To the left and rear I hunt.
Then I started off with a mighty roar
And hit the car in front.

It was the commonest of accidents. The car ahead would start moving. You would move ahead with the bus. The car would stop and the bus would run into it. The bus driver would get a PA, Preventable Accident, put in his record. The answer? Stay alert and expect the unexpected.

I turned my poem in to the office and it became the only poem ever posted on the Safety Board of the Portland Traction Company which had become the Rose City Transit Company.

As I proceeded north on West 6th Ave. toward downtown Portland in heavy rush period traffic an expensive black auto turned right and deliberately stopped 6 feet back of the stalled traffic ahead of him blocking my lane by just 2 feet. Honking my horn was ignored. I stepped out and kicked the bumper and yelled, "Move up a little."

By the time the spiffy dressed business man got out of his car I was back in my seat. He came to the door of the bus and said, "You drove into my car." I told him that I hadn't but he wanted to make out an accident report. I refused and told him to quit blocking traffic. He drove away.

A well-dressed passenger stepped up and said, "That man may try to cause you trouble. Keep this," and handed me his card. He was a professor at the University of Portland back a few blocks where I had picked him up.

I finished my trip and went to the bus garage. As I checked in, the clerk told me to go see Mr. Woodcock. A man had come in to claim he had a whiplash injury from a rear-ender downtown. Wow! What a kick I have! It was nothing unusual for passengers and motorists to get a lawyer and try to collect from the bus company on flimsy excuses but this man was a lawyer! But my professor's card trumped his fraudulent play and I heard no more of it.

Every Friday I picked up a railroad worker at the Train Depot in NW Portland to ride through downtown and out to his home on the eastside. As I approached downtown a car cut across the corner of my bus and slammed on the brakes in front of the bus. I got stopped after giving him a small bump and got out to make a report. I wasn't worried. A company inspector had seen him deliberately cause the accident. I paid scant attention to 2 men who got out a small truck and came over watching.

A few days later I went in to see what was being done about the incident. The company attorney told me they had paid off the driver. That he had 2 witnesses in a truck that said I was belligerent and careless and had called them G.D. truckers. I interrupted, "Wait just a minute. My father would never allow cursing on our farm and I don't talk like that."

"We have two witnesses who said you did."

The next Friday I told the railroad man what happened. Startled, he exclaimed, "You didn't say that! I did! They were in their truck saying nasty things about bus drivers so I stuck my head out of the window and told them off."

I went back in to our legal office and told them what had happened and that I would appreciate it if the company would back up my side more before paying off crooks.

It was my first experience with the animosity between railroad men and truckers and I had been caught in the middle. I would learn more when I became a trucker.

I did *not* have a PA added to my record.

## His Stamina Dropped

Troutdale, an eastern suburb of Portland, Oregon, is almost the edge of a pristine wilderness. A road lets you drive up Larch Mountain to a parking lot and a trail leads you to the peak at a lookout that has a fence to keep you from falling down the steep side. Looking north the wilderness slopes down until it falls 4000 feet into the Columbia Gorge where the Columbia River and I-84 going east forms the boundary between Oregon and Washington. A picture taken of me in the 1980s shows Mt. St. Helens with the top missing from the 1981 eruption. Following the wilderness to the right Mt. Hood in the Cascades can be seen in the distance. Further to the right is Powell Blvd extending as Route 26 skirting the south edge of Mt. Hood as it goes to central Oregon. It sometimes takes 2 or 3 days to find people who get lost in this wilderness. A protected watershed for Portland's delicious water lies within this wilderness. It was said, also, that it contained the largest concentration of black bears in the U.S.

Mr. Douglas had the distinction of being the first white baby born in Troutdale. He liked to ride the buses and talk to the drivers. Any driver who would, on his day off, drive him to the gravel pit in Oregon City for target shooting would have the guns and ammunition furnished. That was too good an invitation for a Kentucky boy to pass up. My invitation was for the following Thursday, my day off.

As I drove the bus Doug sat by the front door and said, "I should sell some of my guns." I think I was hearing the first admission that he knew he was growing old.

I asked him what guns he would consider selling. When he named a 22 caliber Marlin lever action I asked what he would take for that. He said, "$25.00." I told him to bring that with him on Thursday and if I liked the way it would shoot, I would buy it.

After killing a few random tin cans I handed him the money and said, "The next shot is going to be with *my* gun."

We had set a target at 100 yards for the 30.06 and I decided to try my .22 on that. I flipped up the peep sight and sighted over the top of it to aim high. I lined up on the target and squeezed off the shot. Doug was studying the target through the spotting scope and said nothing. Finally he said, "I don't see any hit."

I took a look. "I think I see something on the border of the center bull's eye." He thought so too. I just had to run down range and retrieve the target. At 100 yards I had nicked the edge of the bull's eye! For years that target was tacked up in my garage.

Since Doug knew the wilderness as well as I knew my old stomping grounds on Dad's 60 acres on Logansport Road with the Romans Bluff, Turkey Rock and Green River, I asked him if he would guide me in some of that bear territory east of Portland. He was delighted with the idea.

With another driver the three of us parked where we could and plunged downhill into a valley. We didn't see a bear but saw numerous signs. They are very elusive.

As we started climbing out of the valley Doug had to stop to rest. Soon he had to again. I saw distress on his face. He had never experienced such a lack of energy. Before we got to the car the other driver and I were almost carrying him.

Jack London writing about a man who had grown old said of him, "His stamina dropped." With his great command of the English language, Jack London had coined a very telling comment. I was seeing it happen to Mr. Douglas. I experienced it myself a few years ago. You gradually slow down. At 85 I still thought I was young. Then one day I could hardly function. Now at 90 I have a measure of strength but where is my stamina? Somewhere back there I dropped it.

## Hazards in Uniform

While in a military uniform you expect your dangerous enemies to be far away, perhaps overseas. But training for assignment can be hazardous as well. I was an aviation cadet in class 45C. That was the first WWII pilot training class to graduate without a fatal accident.

I was casually watching my shadow on the ground one day when I saw the shadow of another Stearman bi-plane on a collision course with mine. I pushed the nose down so I could see straight ahead. I then saw the plane coming head on. I pulled up and went over him. I headed for the airfield and didn't bother to fly a landing pattern. I made my unauthorized first straight in landing, parked the plane, checked in my parachute an hour early, went to the bunkhouse and went to bed. I probably covered up my head! The next day I flew as usual.

As a cadet we had to leave the wire circle we called a grommet in our cap keeping it round and flat. As officers we could remove the grommet and let it droop to give it, what combat pilots had named, 'the fifty mission crease.'

As a Portland Traction Company driver I again, had to keep the grommet in my cap and, when on duty, wear it square on my head. But Portland, Oregon bought the company from the California owners and changed our uniform from black to a powder blue. Again I was permitted to wear my cap with the 50 mission crease.

The hazard in this uniformed occupation was the criminal element in the city.

One summer Saturday night I was working the owl shift on the Broadway route. After midnight the buses left downtown at 32 minutes after the hour and left the end of the line on the hour to go back to town on a different route. My Broadway bus had to cover the Union route on the way back to town. At 1:32 am I left downtown with the usual 15 or 20 passengers and went north on Fourth Ave to Glisan Street turned right and crossed the Steel Bridge to the East Side. Portland's premier shopping center, The Lloyd Center, was eerie and deserted under the street lights as I made my way through to 24$^{th}$ Ave. headed for Dekum where several bus lines terminated. I was letting passengers off in the residential area when I noticed a car would stop 2 blocks back and shut off its lights. Then it would proceed when I did and do the same thing at my next stop. I was being stalked. It appeared that it was my turn to look down the barrel of a gun and hand over the company money.

I didn't want to arrive at Dekum with several minutes to wait for the 2am leaving time so I slowed down so as to arrive there just in time to leave. I picked up a man with a lunch box to go to some early morning job. Good! Now I would not be alone. I would have a witness for whatever good that may do me.

I drove down Dekum to Union (same as 4$^{th}$ Ave), turned south. Soon there was Killingsworth, a prominent street with big stores on every corner. As I waited for a traffic light I saw a police car come to the other side of the intersection. I flashed my lights to get their attention and motioned for them to come to me. I pulled across the intersection and he pulled over to me as the car came up to the intersection behind me. I pointed and said, "That car has been following me since the Lloyd Center. You had better check him out." When the car driver saw me talking to a policeman he turned right and sped away and the police went after him. I never heard any more about them.

As I drove away 2 young men passengers came up and asked, "What's going on?" I explained about the car following me and how I sent the police after them.

"That's interesting. We get off here at this next stop."

As I continued something was rattling under the seats as the bus moved. It was irritating so I stopped and set the brakes to retrieve an empty Coke bottle or whatever. I found a heavy steel bar about 2 feet long, thick in the middle, tapering to about an inch thick at the ends. It was battered as though used as a punch hammered with a sledgehammer. I carried it back to my seat and considered the implications. This thing could have really cracked my skull. It's a good thing I chased away their getaway car before those 2 guys got a chance to make their move!

It's a warm summer night so why am I shivering?!

## Drama on Eighty-Second Avenue

Union Avenue was the 4th Avenue paralleling the east side of the Willamette River. It was lined with used car lots. But business and population was moving to the suburbs. I met Dennis and Delbert Williams because they sponsored a young boxer, Amos Lincoln, to advertise their used car lot. In due time they followed the crowd and moved their business five miles east to the then boundary of Portland, S. E. 82nd Avenue.

Burnside divided NE from SE. My home on Lincoln was S.E. 2100. North of Burnside, on 82nd Ave., I learned to love Fondue at the Mediterranean restaurant. The Montavilla shopping center was at 500 SE. Late one night a police cruiser got a green light and drove on to 82 and was broadsided by a speeder, crushing the 2 officers.

Five of my streetcar and bus routes terminated on or near 82nd. Six blocks from my home was my favorite Chinese restaurant, The New Cathay, with another, The Canton Grill, just across the street. When Colonel Hanks, a look alike and friend of Colonel Sanders, opened a beef sandwich shop on 82nd I covered the grand opening as reporter and photographer for the neighborhood paper, *The Hollywood News*.

At Foster, Wayne Long, recently released from prison robbed the bank and killed the teller. The FBI had been following him so he was immediately arrested. A few weeks later the postman boarded my Council Crest Streetcar. He had just been talking to his friend driving an ambulance. He was hauling Wayne Long's electrocuted body to a west side morgue.

A mall, Eastport Plaza, was built about 10 blocks from home. Keep going south on 82nd past the county line and you find The Clackamas Town Center which was in the national news in December 2012 because of a gunman shooting people.

About 3am I was driving the Powell Bus south on 82. I passed a police patrol shining a flashlight, checking the businesses along the street. Further south a lone northbound car drifted across the street toward my lane. I held my 35 MPH as I studied the situation. Should I speed up? Slow down? Stop? When the car got in my lane a few yards ahead I moved over and passed on the left. The car drifted into the curb and stopped. I knew the police car would be there soon. I turned around at my terminal at Crystal Springs. I stopped and asked the policeman what was going on. The driver had passed out at the wheel and never knew how close she had come to a head on collision with a bus.

I saw Gypsies once in Butler County. They camped for the night in our woods. Dad walked across the field and told them to have a good evening. The next day they were gone. Civilization made their nomadic life impractical so the million of them in the US have settled in cities and become highly intelligent mainstream citizens.

Our friends, the Hamburgs, had a tire shop on 82nd until they sold out to the tire behemoth, Les Schwab. Across the street was the home of a Gypsy family and his used car business was just up the street.

We had friends, Homer and Viola Wood. Viola said she lived with Gypsies for a while when she was young. There are always exceptions to generalities but her observation was that, generally, the Gypsy men were easy going and imperturbable while the women tended to be fiery and feisty. The Hamburgs saw this demonstrated one morning. The Gypsy husband was on his way to work at his car lot. The wife followed, screaming angrily at him. He calmly walked to the street filled with morning traffic. As he walked north she stood at their sidewalk yelling at him until he was far up the street. Then she walked back to her house, seemingly oblivious to the fact that she didn't have on a stitch of clothes!

On Eighty-Second Avenue the drama never ends!

Charles Romans    with Homer and Viola Wood

## Roll up the Wire

When I was born in central Illinois in 1925 the farmers check planted their corn. The rows were 3 feet apart and the hills were 3 feet apart. The cultivator could plow between the hills both north-and-south and east-and-west. How did they do that?

The corn planter planted 2 rows as the horses or tractor took it across the field. A wire stretched across the field had a knot every 3 feet. As the wire dragged through the planter it tripped the release that planted 2 hills of corn every 3 feet. At the end of the row the driver would pull up the stake and move the wire over the designated distance as marked by a marker dragged along on an arm reaching out from the planter. As the last row was planted the wire was rolled up on a geared spool so when you got to the end of the last row your job was done. Years later, after I finished my last trip on a streetcar or bus run I would tell myself. "It's time to roll up the wire." and head for the bus yard.

It was time to "roll up the wire" one morning as I finished my night shift on the Powell bus route. I was at the south border of Portland on 82nd Avenue. I got out of my seat to set the front and side destination sign rollers on "Garage." Before I could shut the door a scruffy character ran to the bus and boarded. I warned him that I wasn't going to town. He ignored me, threw his fare in the box and sat down on the right side where I had a clear view of him until he got off.

I already had a passenger on board. At the Greyhound Bus Depot in town a passenger had asked where to get off for 41st and Holgate. He was from Washington State and was here to visit his sister who lived in an apartment complex on Holgate. I told him there was no need to get off at 41st and Powell and walk 10 blocks. Just stay with me to the end of the line and I would let him off at 41st and Holgate on my way to the bus garage.

As I left the end of the line I didn't go to Holgate. I turned left on Foster Road that angled northwest where it would intersect with westbound Holgate about 50th. Before I could turn off this short cut onto Holgate the character jumped up and wanted off and wanted a transfer, further irritating me. I got my punch and a book of transfers from the pouch and gave him one. At 41st I dropped my other passenger and continued down Holgate, over the rail yards on the overpass, right on 17th, right into the bus yard and parked.

A week or so later 2 detectives stepped on my bus at 50th and Foster and showed me a drawing. "Do you recognize this man?" they asked. Yes! It was the character that got on at the end of the line that morning. He had kidnapped a woman clerk at a hotel and terrorized her into riding a taxi with him to a motel where he abused her all night. Now they had me as an eyewitness putting him at the motel near the end of my route. I also told them about the passenger from Washington. They asked me to come to the police station soon to see some photographs.

The policeman handed me 5 photographs. I said it could be either of two of them. "You need to pick out one." he told me. I still couldn't decide. He called the DA and told him the dilemma and asked if he wanted to do a lineup. While he was waiting for an answer he casually looked at the back of the pictures. Suddenly he looked excited. "Wait! These pictures *are* both him. One was taken in Seattle 3 years ago and one here recently. You have a good witness!

Answering the subpoena I reported to the courthouse for his trial. I was told to wait in the hall until called into the courtroom. There in the hallway was my passenger from Washington. With my information they had found his sister and located him as a second witness.

Lunchtime came and went. We were told we could leave. They had taken this idiot to lunch. He had pilfered a dinner knife and on the way back to court had tried to escape. They subdued him and declared a mistrial. Later I heard they had sent him up for a long time on a series of charges and wouldn't need our testimony. My episode as a witness against a criminal was over.

## 3-D

When Sawyers Viewmaster hit the scene I saw it as a successor to the Stereoscope era, and really it was. I toured their plant and met the photographer that captured many of the Palestinian scenes. I thought I saw a niche for a 3-D photography business. Romans Originals made Viewmaster reels of a few weddings and some children but it really didn't take off.

Duane (Dee) Kinnear in Gresham learned of my interest and experience in Photography and invited me to be his partner in a new studio. I thought about it. I finally told him that the studio would probably support one family very nicely but it would be best if I kept my city bus job and worked for him as needed. He agreed.

For a while his friend Don, managed the darkroom but after a while I took over the photo lab work. Dee kept his hand in the chemicals from time to time. Don's innovations were called BC (Before Charles). My contributions to our routine were AD (After Don)!

Dee's wife, Lee, was receptionist, bookkeeper and helped prepare subjects for their picture session. She did the retouching and coloring. One balmy summer evening she came to the studio to catch up on retouching. I was developing the day's work in the basement lab. She called me on the intercom. "Charles, I am going to leave the front door open for fresh air. I'll leave the intercom on so you can hear if anyone comes in."

"Thanks, Lee. That will give me time to get to my hiding place in the back of the basement."

"*Charlie-e-e!* You're no help!"

## Back to Flying

We got inquiries about aerial pictures. I didn't see any reason to hire a plane and a pilot since I had my Oregon pilot's license. I had not flown for fifteen years so I got a Flight Manual and reviewed the procedures, got my current physical and went to the Troutdale airport and spoke to the manager. "I would like to check out in that plane," pointing to a 4 passenger Skyhawk. He told an instructor to check me out.

I held my altitude on turns like a pro. I performed all the tasks a commercial pilot would have to do on a test. After 3 landings the instructor said, "Let me out. You don't need me. Make your other 2 landings and see me in the office." A pilot has to have made 5 landings in the past month before having a passenger aboard.

After getting listed as a qualified renter of Troutdale Airport's planes I drove to the studio to get Dee and his camera. We took the planned pictures and flew back to the airport. We had a real gusty wind blowing off the Columbia Gorge. The plane flared and tipped and bounced in the gusts. I firmly fought through them and deftly put the wheels on the runway. Dee was so terrified that he never again rode with me!

## Weather

A Canadian company had bought a string of greenhouses stretching along a valley east of Gresham and wanted aerial photos. The Oregon rain was coming down day after day. Checking the Aviation Weather Report one afternoon I learned that a short break in the clouds was predicted to move in from the Pacific and come across the Portland area the next morning.

That night I was printing orders in the darkroom when Dee came by. I told him I had a plane rented for the next morning to take the greenhouse pictures. He gave me a strange look and asked. "It has been raining for two weeks and is pouring down now. What makes you think it will stop tomorrow?

"I was down at the drug store today and saw the Old Farmer's Almanac. It says there will be a brief clearing tomorrow."

"You spent studio money on an airplane on the basis of the Farmer's Almanac?"

The next morning I was watching the western sky when I saw the break in the clouds. I raced to Troutdale and found an available pilot. I grabbed a candy bar from the machine since I had not eaten breakfast and didn't like to fly on an empty stomach. We headed for the greenhouses. I turned the controls over to my hired pilot. I was in the right seat with the door open. The sun was coming through in the rain cleared air. We made a pass west to east. After an east to west pass we made another one west to east just ahead of the clouds moving across. Mission accomplished. I had a perfect set of pictures!

## Huey

At Rose City Transit Company the mechanics in the Maintenance garage kept the buses ready for service. I remember saving them a road call one dark rush period evening. I had a fully loaded Powell Blvd bus headed east on the Ross Island bridge when *all* the dash lights came on. Watching the temperature gauge I kept rolling full speed to 17th Ave then right 10 short blocks to the bus yard. I shut it off and ran into the driver's room and told the clerk I needed a bus pronto. Soon the passengers were on the way home and the mechanics didn't have to make a road call. A fan blade had broken off and sliced through all the accessory belts.

I was known to be a photographer so the company asked me to go to the mechanical department to take some pictures. They had invented a Ring Lapper (or lopper) that honed used rings much like an old time razor strop honed straight razors. It stood to save the industry lots of money and a trade magazine wanted photos for a story.

I don't know if the head mechanic was involved with the invention. That was Huey Roberts. If you went to the shop, over the clash of tools and hum of machinery you would hear Huey's infectious laugh or loud Irish voice giving instructions or spinning a yarn. Soon I would be making a trip to Michigan with Huey.

Usually when the company bought new buses the factory delivered them. But this particular year when they bought 15 new Fageol Twin Coaches they decided to bring them home with their own employees.

Excitement was running high. Who would get to make this rare trip? My record and experience qualified me so I put my name in for the drawing. Two caravans were planned. 7 buses would leave Pontiac, Michigan the first day and 8 more on the next day.

I was assigned to the first group. An inspector would drive the lead bus. I was to drive the next to last in line with Huey Roberts in the last bus, the one behind me. The inspector in the lead was responsible for schedules, fueling and paying for our rooms and meals. The mechanic in the rear had to see that an engine failure didn't leave one stranded without help.

The big day arrived and since the airlines did not yet have jet planes we boarded a propeller driven plane. As we neared Chicago there was a concern that a snowstorm in Detroit may close the airport. We almost had to take a bus the rest of the way. The pilots were cleared to try for Detroit and we made it O.K.

A shuttle bus took us to a truck stop at Pontiac and as we waited for the limousine service to the hotel some truck drivers across the room were making some good natured remarks about amateur drivers which they thought all bus drivers were. A very popular song on the radio at that time was about an inept trucker that couldn't get turned around so I went along with the fun and banter by singing out the title of the song: "Give me forty acres and I'll turn this rig around."

Soon we were at the hotel and dressed for dinner and sitting at a long table prepared to order the tastiest and costliest meals at company expense.

Huey was sitting two seats over from me. While waiting for our food he was staring at his plate and not saying anything. That was so uncharacteristic of him that I leaned over and asked, "Huey, what's wrong?"

"Well, this is our wedding anniversary. My wife is in Oregon and I'm way out here in Michigan." I quietly got the attention of a waitress and explained the situation. She disappeared into the kitchen.

Soon two pretty waitresses came out; they set a small cake with a lighted candle in front of Huey. Standing behind him they sang the Happy Anniversary song. Then, simultaneously, they planted a big kiss on each cheek. We clapped and cheered.

Now Huey was *really* speechless!

### West to Omaha

I flew twin-engine airplanes during WWII. Now I was driving a twin-engine city bus – almost. The Fageol Twin Coach was designed to have twin engines, one on each side at mid bus. But the management of Rose City Transit thought one was enough power for Portland's routes.

We left Pontiac, Michigan early and went west on icy roads that had been graded. I had a portable radio and after we passed Chicago I heard interviews of motorists who had been stranded on the road and spent the night in farmhouses along Interstate I-90 just north of us. We spent our first night in Peru, Illinois. We learned from our Portland dispatcher that the other team was grounded in Chicago by the winter storm that was now hitting Detroit. They were being bussed to Pontiac thus losing out on rest and the leisure dinner we had enjoyed the night before.

We left Peru early, head on into a fierce west wind sweeping across the open prairie for Chicago to keep its reputation as the Windy City. Now it was buffeting our buses requiring constant tiring attention to hold them steady. The constant wind drag made it hard to maintain speed and was consuming extra diesel fuel. Omaha was our destination this evening. What a relief when we arrived at the eastern end of this sprawling city.

Did our inspector driving the lead bus know where we were going? We went on and on and on until it seemed we would leave the city behind us. Finally in the western suburb he turned off to the scheduled motel. We stopped in the lot while the inspector went in to pay for our reserved rooms and ask where they wanted us to park. While we waited my bus stopped running and wouldn't start. I set the brake and went to find Huey. Then I heard 2 more buses stop. We had run out of fuel after barely arriving at our destination. Fuel tanker trucks were scheduled to rendezvous with us at the end of each day. This night that fuel truck had some empty tanks to fill!

When a diesel engine runs dry and fuel is added it has to be primed to get started again. Our mechanic, Huey Roberts had not brought a primer with him. He took a taxi to the shops of the Omaha city bus company. They had no sympathy for their visiting Sister company from Oregon. Huey went back to the motel and took the inspector back to the Omaha company. Reluctantly, after a hefty deposit they let Huey borrow their primer. He eventually got our buses running and parked.

Were we glad to sit down to our evening meal!

My friend in Portland, Norman Larson, had recently visited France. He told me how they pronounced the name of their famous boulevard, The Champs Elysees. He said it was Shomps ee Lee Zay. On our menu in Omaha there was listed a side of Baked Potato Champs Elysee. I had no idea what a baked potato Champs Elysees was but I knew right then I was going to order one loud enough for all to hear.

"I'll have the Baked Potato Shomps ee Lee Zay."

## The stranger on my bus

Owen Wister lived in the Virginian Hotel in Medicine Bow, Wyoming

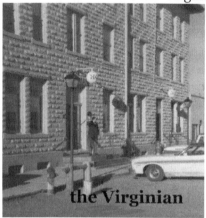

the Virginian

for a while as he wrote *The Virginian*. On every truck trip or vacation I stopped here. Twice I borrowed the key and visited Wister's room with its red wallpaper and red velvet Victorian furniture. I hoped to spend the night in that room. It was available to tourists for a premium price. But it never worked out for me to be there at the right time. But this site was where I prepared one of my funniest pranks. Read on!

Our seven new city buses bound for Portland, Oregon approached Medicine bow about 4pm. Our buses were supposed to be governed at 50 MPH and mine was. The five buses ahead of my bus #549 could do about 52 and often pulled far ahead of me but Hughie had to stay behind me. He could go 51 MPH and he would sometime stop to photograph something like the antelope then use his 1 MPH edge to catch up. Now we were pleased when the Inspector driving the lead bus pulled off alongside the road in front of the Virginian Hotel for a coffee break, more to ease the boredom than anything.

We were soon seated at the counter where I quickly drank half of my coffee and headed for the door. Hughie noticed. "Where are you going?" I told him I was going to wait in the bus. "Not me. I'm going to drink coffee as long as anybody drinks coffee." That's fine. That suited my purpose.

## The Passenger

I backed up a few yards and hurried in to the towns 'Super Market' and bought a ball of twine and a clothes line rope. I found a 2 foot stick to make a coat hanger for my heavy wool overcoat. A large ball of newspaper made a head for my puppet. A leather glove tied on the end of a coat sleeve made a hand. By the rear exit door the rope went from the coat hanger, up through the overhead bar then up to the front door and around the fare box post by my driver's seat. The twine tied to the glove went up across the aisle to the overhead bar then through the seats to the left side of my driver's seat.

The other drivers finished their coffee break and we were soon headed west. The 5 buses up ahead were getting farther ahead and Hughie was hanging way back. I was getting the giggles anticipating

Hughie's reaction when he sees a stranger stand up in my bus. I let things become routine for about 15 minutes. Then, as I topped a rise and my bus was lighted through by the late afternoon sun I reached over with my right hand and pulled the rope over and held it with my left hand with the steering wheel. Then a second hitch and my dummy stood full height in the aisle by the rear door.

Hughie was alarmed. "What is Romans doing with a passenger? Doesn't he know we have orders that no passengers are allowed on this trip?" Then the 'passenger' drops down out of sight. "I'll bet he doesn't know he is back there." The puppet stands up. I hold the rope and the steering wheel with my left hand. I reach to the left with my right hand and grasping the twine I seesaw it back and forth. The dummy's hand waves up and down at Hughie. "Now he has him wiping off the back window!" The dummy would peep over the edge at him or stand up and prop his arm across the aisle or wave again. Hughie didn't know what to think but that 1 MPH advantage was slowly but surely closing the distance between us. He didn't see anything the last few yards but he was soon about 10 feet behind my bus motioning desperately for me to stop. Finally I leaned over and looked at him in the passenger mirror then over to the left in the rear view mirror as though just now noticing him. His quiet motions to STOP become frantic. Then the dummy stood up! Hughie stared in open mouthed astonishment for a moment then swung his arm in a sweeping 'put down' motion and backed way off.

That evening as we dined in Rock Springs Hughie told the story from his viewpoint as only an Irishman could tell it. The driver ahead of me said he thought he saw me stand in the aisle to stretch my legs while driving with one hand so he tried it!

For the next two days, the excitement of getting home to our families was enough to keep us awake and alert. But no one ever forgot the hitchhiker that got on Romans' bus #549 at The Virginian Hotel in Medicine Bow, Wyoming.

## Minnie Pearl

The 1949 Nash was showing lots of miles on the odometer. So in 1954 there was a new deluxe Nash, the Ambassador, sitting by the house on Lincoln Street. Now here is a car you can go to the opera in. Let us make that The Grand Ole Opry!

Nashville was 2500 miles away but the Grand Ole Opry was coming to the Portland Auditorium on 3rd Avenue just 5 miles from our Portland home. I got tickets for the family and we went early. Back stage I asked Minnie Pearl if it was OK to take flash pictures during the show. "If no one was taking pictures we would think you didn't like us." Minnie was a gracious lady. She bought a viewer and Viewmaster Reel of the 3D pictures I took. When I got her check I learned she was Mrs. Henry Cannon.

Minnie had us concerned when she told of an experience she had.

Cowboy Copas

(Photo by Charles E Romans)

On a late evening walk when she heard footsteps she saw this man so she walked faster. Every time she walked faster, he walked faster. Pretty soon she was almost running and he was almost running. Everyone's concern dissolved into laughter when she concluded by declaring, "If that train hadn't come between us I'd have caught him, too!"

After the show they were looking for rides to the Division Street Corral. That was a night club about 80 blocks past our 84th street home near Division Street. I said I had room for 3 passengers so soon had Cowboy Copas between 2 young lady fans in the back seat. As I drove east the girls asked if he was married. He cooled what hopes they may have had when he answered, "Yes."

But his boldest fan was in the front seat. Five year old Charla Kay stood facing back. This was before seat belts and child seats. Copas had been singing to her on stage, now she sang to him. *Shrimp Boats are Coming* was popular on the radio and she had learned it.

Sadly, in 1963 our newfound friend was killed in Tennessee in an airplane piloted by his son-in-law, Randy Hughes who was also Patsy Cline's manager. Cowboy Copas, Patsy Cline, Randy Hughes and Hawkshaw Hawkins were all killed in the crash.

Note on the private aviation of that time: Those of us who were thoroughly trained in the military had a healthy respect for bad weather. We would decline to fly if the weather was too dangerous for our experience and ability. But others felt they were invincible. We noted that doctors seemed to be the most vulnerable. Many had become affluent and were able to buy their own airplane. In those days they tended to give orders instead of information and were too egotistical to take advice. We noted that there seemed to be an inordinate number of doctors among private pilot accidents and causalities. Things got better. Better weather science and reporting has made pilots more wary. But that came too late to save Randy Hughes and his precious and distinguished passengers.

**Captain Eloff**

With my photography I became the Public Relations Representative for the Aircraft Owners and Pilots Association of Oregon. I was the official photographer for the Northwest Rodeo Association and I was the photographer for the Portland Boxing Club owned by Tom Moyer. Through the boxing club I met Captain Eloff.

Captain Johann Eloff brought his boxer friend, Ewart Potgieter (Edward Waterbucket in English) over from South Africa to get treatment for his growth gland. He was 7'3" the same as the ceilings in my home in SE Portland. He had to stoop when he visited me.

Capt. Eloff was a nephew of President Kruger after whom the Kruger Park and game reserve was named. Captain Eloff, like his Uncle, was associating with the Potgieter family. And here I was associating with them in Portland, Oregon.

The Potgieters had large farmlands and hired Zulu tribesmen to work them. Ewart told me that two groups shared by rotating every 6 months.

Apartheid had a tight grip on the country in the 1950s. Capt. Eloff sat with me in a coffee shop window seat on Yamhill one day. As we had coffee we saw some black people walk by. The Captain remarked that they looked like their black people but seemed different. I doubt if he lived to see one of their black prisoners, Nelson Mandela, become their president.

John wanted a portrait so I had him out to my basement studio at my home on 84th & Lincoln. With his white butch cut hair, black formal "tails" suit and a chest full of ribbons he looked quite intimidating. He said, "Don't make me smile. I don't look good that way."

I took several poses as he asked. Then I deliberately ask him about his grandchildren. A twinkle came into his eyes. His stern face melted into a soft smile – not too much. It was much like he smiled as he hugged my daughter, Charla Kay. That is the pose he chose.

I like to think that the 16X20 hand colored portrait I made for him is hanging somewhere in Pretoria now.

### Me and Joe Louis

It was June 1938. School was out and I was spending the summer on Grandpa Vincent's farm in Muhlenberg County, working and visiting my numerous cousins.  I would become a teenager in two months when I turned 13 in August.

A mild interest and excitement was building.

On Wednesday, June 22 a special event was scheduled for a radio broadcast. Several of us would go visit a neighbor who had a reliable 12 volt radio and a reliable wind charger to keep it playing.

Joe Louis was scheduled for a rematch with the German heavyweight boxer Max Schmeling. Max had beaten Joe in a previous match of several rounds. This time Joe took the training very seriously and just knew he could beat Max and even predicted a first round knockout. Our host didn't think so. He was listening to hear this upstart black boy get another beating.

When Joe floored Max early in the first round the neighbor was out of his chair in alarm. When Joe knocked him down a second time the neighbor was screaming for him to get up and win this fight. Max got up again alright and still in the first round Joe knocked him down for the count. The neighbor was enraged. I thought he was going to destroy his own radio!

Joe went on to become America's beloved champion and sportsman. He and Max became lifelong friends.

In the 1960s I was doing publicity photography for the Portland Boxing Club owned by Tom Moyer, a former Golden Gloves Champion. He scheduled a match for Bobo Olsen to defend his Middle Weight title on the stage of the Portland auditorium. Visitors were in town for the event. Once, behind the scenes where business was being discussed, I met the then retired Joe Louis. I chatted with him for a few minutes.

The night of the match I was through with my publicity photography. I am not a fan of the brutal sport of boxing but I decided to use my free access to the show to take some 3-D personal pictures with my Viewmaster camera. I took a power cord so as to not depend on batteries for my flash. I lay almost under the  ropes taking pictures with other photographers.

I detected a loose connection on my flash. Where the short cord from the camera plugged into the long cord from the wall outlet there was a loose wire. I was gripping the metal camera with my right hand. With my left hand I reached back to see if I could reconnect the wires. Suddenly electricity was pulsing through my arms. My right hand tightened on the camera and my left hand got an unrelenting grip on the naked connection.

The roar of the crowd drowned my voice and those beside me had their attention riveted on the action in the ring. I would have to save myself. From a squatting position I did a backflip that pulled me loose from the wires.

The next night I worked a night shift on the bus. After midnight I picked up the taxi driver that often caught my bus home after his shift. I started telling him about my experience with the electricity. "Was that you?" He had been sitting high up in a back row watching the fight. He and his friends had laughed when they saw my bout with the hot wire.

Joe Louis died in Las Vegas in 1981 the same year that I got married in Las Vegas and began my happy life with my Janie.

## Ten Dollars and a Bus Ticket

Before he left for his home in South Africa the 7 foot 3 inch Ewart Potgieter was booked for a bout with the 6 foot 4 inch heavyweight contender, John Holman from Chicago. It was more comedy than a boxing match. Ewart's long arms kept John at a distance and Ewart's lumbering bulk wasn't fast enough to nail John.

Holman was popular in Portland so promoter Tom Moyer brought him back for a lively match with the 4th ranked Eddie Machen. At the Portland Airport I took publicity pictures of Holman arriving and later took my Speed Graphic to the fight hoping to get some salable

pictures. As I built our new home, Nellroy and I were spending our money as fast as we made it,. So I found myself with vacation time and very little cash. I bought a round trip Greyhound bus ticket and with ten dollars in my pocket I headed for Kentucky.

I went to a family gathering in Muhlenberg County where I used my speed graphic to take a lot of pictures. It was a very opportune time for picture taking. It was the last time I could take a picture of Mom's parents, John and Maude Vincent, with all 10 of their children. That picture has been displayed at many funerals since then. Sue is the only one left. She was the only one younger than me.

Aunt Nell was the first to die. Cancer was the cause. I took a nice portrait of her and over half a century later at our Vincent family reunion in 2011 I met her grey haired daughters. They learned of that picture I had taken of their mother and they asked for copies.

When I took those original pictures I assured the relatives that I would produce some good professional pictures from that film. I took several orders. What was left of that ten dollars began to grow. I wasn't through yet. I had John Holman's Chicago address.

I had a short layover in Chicago. I left the bus depot in downtown Chicago. I caught a streetcar for south Chicago where Holman lived. I transferred to a bus for his neighborhood. I ran 2 blocks from the bus stop to his house. Fortunately, he was home. I showed him the photos of his Eddie Machen fight. He bought $25.00 worth. I ran back to the bus route. One came right away. I got off at the streetcar transfer point and watched anxiously down the track wondering if I should spend some of my money on a cab. Soon a streetcar arrived. Downtown I ran for the Greyhound station. The passengers were loaded and the driver was filling out his paper work at a stand. A minute later we both got aboard and I was headed west for Portland Oregon with a lot more money than when I left!

When trucking years later I was in Chicago waiting for my dispatch. I visited John again at his home. He had become a Christian and as one of Jehovah's Witnesses never again pursued the violent game of boxing. He graciously offered for me to stay at his home if I should have a long enough layover. That opportunity never materialized but I would have liked that.

## Dr. Irwin Ladd

When Woodland Park Hospital opened in SE Portland Dr. Irwin Ladd was the first administrator. In his maternity cases he had husbands support their wives in the delivery room. That became the policy in his hospital. So this "plague" would not spread, hospitals, doctors and associations proposed a law against "visitors" in the delivery room. There had to be a public hearing before this law could be rubber stamped by the legislature. Doug Baker, the local columnist, learned of this and mentioned the time and place of the hearing. Dr. Ladd was called before the medical board because he got his name in the paper but he had nothing to do with it and they could not muzzle individuals such as me and Doug Baker.

One item I presented at the hearing was from an Encyclopedia Britannica report that quoted a Texas doctor who said, "There is too much togetherness with laymen. We don't want them in the delivery room." Since when do we have a caste system in this country?

Dr. Moore, representing Emmanuel Hospital where my daughter was born in 1949, wasn't pleased with my half hour presentation. After the hearing he and I had a face to face confrontation in the lobby as a crowd gathered around to listen. "We are not concerned with our status. We are afraid of infections," he asserted.

"That is no real concern. In thousands of cases there has been *no* evidence of increased infections when husbands were allowed in the delivery room." I had prepared my facts and arguments well for this hearing.

Dr. Moore: "Another reason we don't want the husband present is because one man poked the doctor in the nose when he took the blades (forceps) to his wife."

My answer: "I kept quiet when the doctor used forceps on my son. But the next doctor who reaches for the forceps had better give me a good medical reason for doing so or I may poke him in the nose!"

We engaged Woodland Park Hospital and Dr. Ladd for our next baby. Vincent Kendall Romans was born there on September 4, 1965 just 20 years since we planned in 1945 to have 3 children. The birth was easier for my wife as she was reclining rather than lying awkwardly and painfully flat. Dr. Ladd did everything our way. He was surprised that a third birth, a large one at that, (10 lbs. 11 oz.) could go so smoothly with no shaving, cutting or forceps.

"Bring him along." he invited. So I picked up my son and carried him to the nursery.

Four days later I took him by Dee's studio where I worked. I photographed 2 year old Henry Kent holding his 4 day old brother, Vincent Kendall.

Women were calling me about getting their husbands in the delivery room. I advised them to change doctors and go to Woodland

Park. The other hospitals didn't like losing the business. Within 2 years every major hospital in Portland had a family birthing room.

Dr. Ladd went to Japan as a medical missionary for his church. Later I learned he had died of cancer.

Doctors who will defy their system over archaic rules and risk their profession are rare and worth their weight in gold. Dr. Ladd was one of those rare individuals.

### Dr. Robert A. Bradley

As we planned for our third child I continued to learn all I could about doctors and hospitals. It came to my attention that Dr. Robert A. Bradley at the Porter Hospital in Denver had been delivering babies with the father present since 1947 with 7000 experiences on record. He was preparing a book, *Husband Coached Childbirth,* for publication in 1965. I drove to Denver to meet him.

Dr. Bradley was as interested in my story as I was in his. He took me out to dinner and we talked and talked. Later he spoke at the ICEA (International Childbirth Education Association) meeting in Montreal, Canada. In addressing the group he told of me and my experiences. He sent me a copy of their report.

As a doctor, he was restricted in what he could say about change. He encouraged me to write my book. My 600 page manuscript never made it to print. It was old news. We had won our battle and it was no longer a big issue.

Dr. Bradley's book has been a huge success. In 1996 an up-to-date edition was published. Dr. Bradley died in 1998 so I can share with you his experience with the opposition.

Dr. Robert A. Bradley was another great fighter for the rights of patients.

### Me and General MacArthur's Aid

Doug Baker was the columnist for the Oregon Journal. He was an Aid to General Douglas McArthur during WWII. I worked with Doug on a number of stories, medical, sports, etc. After the Board of Health hearing on husbands in the delivery room he called me. "You seem well versed on that subject. How about being on my TV talk show next tuesday night." I accepted. I traded runs and days off with another bus driver and fielded questions from viewers for a half hour. I castigated doctors for interfering in a family event. Later one of the drivers who saw the show said, "I would hate to have you mad at me!"

As Public Relations Rep for the Oregon Aircraft Owners and Pilots Association I invited Doug and his wife (a certain party) to take a night ride with me. We would take off from Troutdale and immediately land at Portland International as though we were travelers from far away and making a convenient stop for dinner. Then after dark we would see Portland from the air. By taking a Troutdale Skyways instructor with me the publicity for Skyways rated me the use of the Cessna for free! Here is what Mr. Baker wrote. I thanked him for the promotion! I was never a Major!

~

### Portland by Starlight
### From defunct Oregon Journal
## Long Pageant of Beauty by Doug Baker

There are many ways to look at a city. In a way, it's like looking at a woman. You can take a Gray-lines rubberneck and ogle the main attractions. You can walk slowly about the town and study it thoughtfully with more serious intentions. You can gaze fondly the way a father does at a daughter in a school play. Or you can cast a critical eye at the old gal's blemishes.

Portland's a pretty gal and needn't worry too much about the camera angles in any perspective. But her best profile is the one she presents skywards — particularly in the hours after dark.

Last Friday night I saw her at her best. Charles Romans, a former Army Air Corps major, and Bill Kullman, a Skyways flight instructor, took A Certain Party and me aloft to see the city from the air.

We boarded a Cessna Skyhawk at Troutdale airport just as night was falling and scurried along the Columbia River to Portland International where Romans put the sleek little airplane down for an hour while we had dinner at the Zodiac Room.

By the time we were back in the air again, the city was a jeweler's showcase, lighted only by the lamp of Venus, a thousand lesser stars and its own incomparable luminescence. At 1500 feet we drifted along the blaze of Sandy Boulevard for a while, then cut across the slash of light that is Powell. We saw Eastport Plaza, a fairy-sized town and the dark, mysterious blob that is Mount Tabor. Flying westward, we crossed the velvety, brooding depths of the Willamette and I saw for the first time, from the night sky, the new freeway approaches, looking ever so much like blue satin ribbons sprawled under the starlight.

For more than 30 minutes, we explored the city's nocturnal face, drinking in the beauty of million myriad pinpoints of light and picking out familiar objects wearing unfamiliar garb. The TV antennas near Council Crest became spires lighted with flaming rubies. Memorial Coliseum, its parking lots jammed with cars, resembled an aquamarine brooch. Barbour Boulevard revealed a hitherto unknown brilliance. The buses at Rose City Transit sheds and the trains of the Brooklyn railway yard took on the look of Christmas toys. Lloyd Center looked even brighter than it does by day and the autos on its exposed parking tarmac resembled those little ceramic tiles women buy to make mosaics. The downtown area, the brightest of all, burned with a friendly incandescence. The parking lots at Portland Zoo were lighted, but empty and lonesome looking. Most lonely sight of all was a single light burning in the middle of the Gresham dog track.

Particularly impressive from the air were the buildings on Medical Center Hill, looking like storied cave dwellings. The Willamette's bridges took on a new stateliness with their pinpoint lamps, only firefly size. Swan Island's ship repair facilities reflected an impression of a river port — an illusion of dynamic industry where you knew there was only night's somnolence.

After three or four passes over the city, the wine of all its beauty becomes a little heady and you're happy to find the flashing green and white beacon that takes you to Troutdale Airport again and the split-second thrill that comes when your pilot searches for the unseen runway with the plane's wheels in the half-dark.

And after it's all over and you compare notes with A Certain Party about the flight there's a bonus. Portland has a new convert. "I've never seen anything quite as beautiful," says A Certain Party. "After 10 years I think I'm beginning to understand why you love this town."

~

### Night Flight over Mount St. Helens

I love to fly at night. My daughter, Charla Kay, was dating James Robinson from England. I invited him and 2 others for a night ride over Mount St. Helens. I reserved a Beechcraft Musketeer and we took off on a night lighted by a full moon. Climbing steadily we were a few hundred feet above the peak when we arrived. We enjoyed the scene and the shadow of the plane on the moonlit snow field below us.

Maintaining 10,000 ft. I headed for Portland where her gem like image would grow larger and larger as I spiraled down and she spread out for miles below our wings before landing at Portland. It was an exciting 1 hour adventure before Mount St. Helens exploded.

On the way south I asked my passengers if they could stand a stall. It suited them fine. After the 2nd stall and recovery I held the right wing level which made the left wing look tilted up.

I looked over my shoulder and asked James if that last stall had bent the wing. Comparing wings he looked as if he were watching a ping pong match!!!

Later I said I thought I had scared him off from marrying Charla Kay. By then she had married Daniel. His comment was, "Why didn't you scare me off."

## Melba and Stubby Staubitz

Melba and Stubby came to town to do a photo session for the Austin Studios. After Austin left town Stubby and Melba stayed and opened their own studio, Aragon Studios, on the second floor at downtown 10th and Washington. When not busy at Dee's I photographed children and families for them.

Melba had dated George Wallace when they were younger when he had not become a governor notorious for blocking black kids from white schools. Melba and Stubby made friends. Old Charlie who lived nearby was one. He would sit on the davenport across the room and watch them conduct their business. I hurried in one day to pick up film and get my instructions. "Shoot the kids together, shoot the grandparents separately, etc." Sounded like I was working for the Mafia! I grabbed my gear then hurried down the hall. I stopped and hurried back and peeped around the door. "Oh, Charlie." Charlie took the cigar out of his teeth and with an expectant look says, "Yeah?"

"Hi!" He returned the greeting. Everyone was laughing as I hurried away. You don't want to ignore an old friend of the company!

## Foggy Flight

Every year two friends of Melba and Stubby came to town. Hal Fowler and Bruce Frazier signed up merchants for a book full of coupons. The books were popular and sold easily. I was introduced to the guys as someone who knew the city, since I was a bus driver, and could efficiently deliver and collect for the books. I had an English made Matchless lightweight motorcycle. I could start at 9 am and deliver 60 coupon books, turn in the money and report for my 3-11 pm bus job.

Bruce owned an airplane, an Aeronca Champ. He gave me keys for it to use anytime. One day Charla Kay and I flew down to the coast to have lunch in a small town. As I tried to turn at the end of my landing roll a brake cable broke. In the strong crosswind off the ocean I could only spin around and around. So I walked to the office and the owner was gone. His son was minding the store. He said no one but his Dad flew on windy days like this. But he is an old WWII pilot he told me. "So am I," I answered.

He spliced the brake cable and since no restaurant was nearby Charla and I went to a grocery store and had bananas for lunch before returning to the Hillsboro airport where Bruce kept his plane.

Bruce invited me to go with him on Sunday to the Olympic Peninsula in Washington to pick up a tie down he had left there. The weather forecast was for heavy morning fog. Bruce drove me to Hillsboro and I flew the plane to a runway on top of Mt. Scott in SE Portland. The next morning we drove through heavy fog to the runway which was above the fog.

He asked me to take the left seat and do the flying while he played with a new portable radio with aviation channels. There was no radio on the plane and only a compass to navigate by. I watched my compass heading carefully. Mount Hood protruded above the clouds and fog some 50 miles east.

Some 30 or 40 minutes passed and I felt something was wrong. Mount Hood kept moving around until it was almost behind the plane. I asked Bruce about it. He took a look around then grabbed his radio which was sitting by the compass in the window. The magnets in the radio were pulling the compass way off. It swung around to its proper position but now - where were we?

Seeing a clear patch we flew over it. There was a distinctive coastline that we found on the chart to be near Astoria. We had been heading out over the Pacific Ocean!

We plotted a new heading and arrived at our fog free destination OK. We retrieved the tie down then flew to the coast where there was an FAA approved landing area on the beach. With the prevailing wind off the ocean you could land north or south – your choice. The wide beach allowed planes going opposite directions to pass safely.

Some movie star had a fine restaurant nearby where we dined in style. Then back to the beach where we dug some clams to take home in the bucket Bruce had brought for that purpose.

We flew to Mt Scott. Bruce retrieved his car. I flew the plane to Hillsboro. Bruce picked me up and we went home after a very eventful day. It was great to be home and not floating out in the Pacific Ocean hoping someone would find us.

## Conquering Mount Hood

I had never climbed Mount Hood. It would be dangerous unless one had experience or a competent guide. I had neither until I met Phil Pyshny.

Phil was a member of the Mazamas, a mountain climbing club. It is named after the imploded volcano that formed Crater Lake in Southern Oregon. It's an Aztec name that means mountain goat.

Phil agreed to accompany me to the top of Mt. Hood. Our young lady friend and neighbor, Sherry Akin, would be the third climber in our party.

On September 7 we were at Timberline Lodge early. We rented crampons for our shoes, ice axes and whatever climbing gear we needed and we were well on our way above timberline when the sun came up on our right. One mile above the lodge we passed the Silcox Hut at the 7000 foot level. During the day that was the terminal for the ski lift.

At 8000 feet the climb was getting steeper, the air thinner and breathing harder. We would lunge and gain 10 feet or so and stand, breathing hard, to get enough oxygen for another few feet.

After the sun came up a wind began rising from the west. It was getting harder and harder. Without the winter coat of snow there was a lot of exposed sand. The wind was picking it up to our west and slamming us with stinging force. At the 9000 foot level Sherry said, "I don't think I can go on." I was hoping she would call it quits but I was within minutes of being the one to call it off.

A few days later I went to Troutdale to rent a plane. I usually took a 4 passenger Skyhawk 172 but this time I rented a 6 passenger 206 Cessna. I didn't need the seats but I wanted the powerful 285 HP engine to take me over the 11,000 foot Mt. Hood. With two neighbors as passengers I approached the top from the west with a strong tail wind. As I passed a few feet above the peak I looked down and said, "Now I'm at the top of Mount Hood!"

On the east side the down slope was sucking the wind down and the plane plummeted down with it. I quickly peeled off to the left to get out of line with the top and headed for Troutdale. It was a turbulent ride so I slowed down for the sake of the wings and our queasy tummies.

I checked the plane in at the airport. Mission accomplished!

Phil Pyshny footnote: Phil had been in a bad accident and barely survived. He remained sickly. He would ride in cars but never would he be the driver.

I was reading a two volume English novel, *The Tontines*. It followed two English families through a generation of experience with this investment scheme which was sort of a combo of annuity and lottery. It is a fascinating story with a setting during Industrial Revolution and the rise of railroads in England. Phil borrowed the books from me and when he succumbed to his illness I never got my books back.

Recently I got to thinking about my friend Phil and the books. On the Internet I found the books on eBay so now I have read the interesting story again. The internet helps your past catch up to you.

## Our Mary Worth

During the great depression a comic strip was born. Apple Mary was a street person who sold apples to eke out her existence. When times got better she became Mary Worth, a lady who made a difference as she stayed with those who needed her help. Readers, such as me, looked forward to each subsequent adventure of this lovable motherly lady.

In Portland we had our own Mary Worth. Mary Ellen (Kendall) Turcotte had joined us. I built us a house on a double lot on 84th Avenue and Lincoln Street. On the other half of the lot I built Aunt Ellen a house. Soon she was a working woman, hiring out to stay with families who had a new baby or an elderly person who needed a helper and companion. On weekends or between assignments we looked forward to hearing the experiences of Auntie, our Mary Worth. She even looked like the Mary Worth of the comic strip! The 2 former Kendalls, the sisters, Effie Winifred and Mary Ellen, lived only 4 blocks apart.

Mary Ellen has long since passed away and my number 2 son has the house. Vince is a finish carpenter and an artist with wood. He remodeled and enlarged the house into a fine home where he lives with his wife, Danielle.

The Kendall sisters are long gone but the Kendall name lingers as my son Vincent Kendall Romans lives in the home I built for Mary Ellen (Kendall) Turcotte, our Mary Worth, over six decades ago.

## A Mary Worth Episode by 'Auntie'

'Auntie' Mary Ellen was off on another Mary Worth experience. General Rilea engaged her services to be a live-in companion and helper for his ageing mother.

During the early part of WWII Thomas E. Rilea was Commanding Officer of the 82nd Brigade as Brigadier General. He was awarded the Army Distinguished Service Medal.

Camp Clatsop occupied 3 miles of Oregon coast. It was federalized during the war. In 1946 it was returned to Oregon control and made a National Guard training facility. The now Major General Rilea was put in charge and made Adjutant General of Oregon. No one else had ever attained such rank and position without going through the military academy at West Point. In his honor, Camp Clatsop was renamed Camp Rilea.

He came up through the ranks. Where did he get so much energy and drive? I'll bet it was from his mother! I took her picture as her granddaughter held the Oregon flag presented to her by the Governor as he made her an Honorary Oregon Colonel. (Take a bucket of Kentucky Fried Chicken and move over, Colonel Sanders – Kentucky isn't the only state with Honorary Colonels.)

Part of Auntie's duty was to give Mrs. Rilea her medications at the time and in the sequence strictly prescribed by the doctor. A wrong combination at the wrong time could have dire results. Sometimes this ageing warrior would want to take charge and make changes. She would berate Auntie for not letting her have her way. When the atmosphere got too hot Auntie would go off to another room to let Mrs. Rilea cool off for a while then go back and firmly administer the pills as prescribed.

Finally Auntie Mary Ellen, alias Mary Worth, was given a weekend off. We were enjoying her company and stories when the phone rang. Lively old Mrs. Rilea had gotten into her pills and had taken them *her* way. They stopped her heart.

Auntie grieved over the loss. "If only I had not taken that week end off I could have saved her life," she lamented. We told her it wasn't her fault and she had been a good and faithful companion for Mrs. Rilea's last days. It had been a difficult assignment and I think *she* had earned a Distinguished Service Medal!

## The Sunday Drive

Remember the Sunday drive? The family would pile in the car and go to a park or zoo or just go for a drive. Gas was cheap and the roads weren't crowded.

In Illinois our destination was often the Bloomington Zoo where I favored the Monkey House. On the next farm was Dad's sister, Stella. In Minier 9 miles away was Dad's brother, Bill and Uncle, Wesley Romans. It wasn't just relatives we visited. We often enjoyed Sunday dinner with the Morton Meeks family. Morton had married Dolly whom Dad had dated a few times when they were single. Then there was the Sunday visit to Mrs. Allen who had dated Buffalo Bill. That old Model T Ford really got us around.

It eventually brought Dad and Mom back to Butler County. We often visited Mom's folks in Muhlenberg County. The old Ford could climb the Cleaton Hill only in reverse. We walked up while Dad backed it to the top. We really got modern when Dad bought Grandma's Model A Ford.

## NellRoy, Effie,Roy, Auntie
## 1936 Ford Columbia Gorge

From Portland, Oregon we had lots of places to see. We could drive along the Columbia River east in the Columbia Gorge. The Pacific Ocean beaches were less than 2 hours away. Mount Hood was just an hour away. For a 10 hour drive we could go to southern Oregon and see Crater Lake. It was a deep lake sitting in the top of a volcanic mountain called Mount Mazama. That is where the Mazamas, a mountain climbing club, got their name.

One weekend my family of 3 and my in-laws, Roy and Effie White, drove down and enjoyed the sites, the lodge and the chipmunks that would eat out of your hand.

After the open road began to get crowded it was still fun to rent a plane and enjoy the open sky.

On December 29, 1963 I rented a Beechcraft low wing airplane. At 12:10, 14 year old Charla Kay and I took off from PDX (Portland International Airport) for Crater Lake.

The site could be hard to spot in Oregon's massive green forest. I flew to Eugene and took up a heading of 125 degrees. That dead reckoning plotting brought me dead center over the lake at its Northwest side. I dived down to a few feet above the water and flew across then up over the far rim. I crossed the lake from different sides then climbed to cruising altitude. We had seen Crater Lake from a perspective that most never experience.

At Albany I made a touch and go landing just to break the monotony.

After exploring the local area for a while we landed at PDX at 3:10, just 3 hours after leaving.

The Sunday drive was becoming a thing of the past. What would spoil the fun flight?

After the Arab oil embargo the hourly rental for a 4 passenger plane jumped from $16.00 per hour to $67.00 per hour. Ouch!

## Shuttle across the Pacific from Seattle

My twin brother, Duane joined the navy. I had a twin brother? Yes, two of them. Did that make us triplets? No. Henry Duane and Harold Wayne were twin brothers born in 1934 and I was their older brother 9 years older. They had one twin brother each but I had two! I've had a lot of fun with that scenario.

Henry Duane was on the troop carrier, the USS General W. A. Mann making regular Pacific crossings between Seattle, Washington and Yokohama, Japan. It was a regular commuter run taking personnel to and fro.

When they had shore leave he and his fellow sailors would browse and shop in downtown Yokohama. They had a favorite street with a Japanese name they couldn't pronounce so they called it Itchy-Scratchy Street! I had him buy me an Earth clock. It was a popular glass domed clock that had four balls on a vertical arm that would rotate one way then back, a sort of horizontal pendulum. The clock had to be set on a brick mantle anchored in the ground and then it would be extremely accurate. A fellow bus driver admired it so that I sold it to him for a small profit.

When Duane arrived in Seattle with a day or more before leaving on his next voyage we would drive up to visit him for a few hours. Mom and Dad were always glad to hear that their far away sons got to visit each other.

I enjoyed visiting Seattle from time to time. My favorite New England clam chowder was and is at *Digger O'Dells* on Union Avenue in Eastside Portland. In Seattle the waterfront restaurant, *The Pier Four,* had clam chowder about as good but with a slightly different seasoning. In Morgantown I settle for a can of Progresso clam chowder which is not bad after I add my own seasoning. My first World Fair was the one in Seattle. The Space Needle is a remaining relic of that fair and an interesting place to dine. The last time I ate there was when my #2 son, Vincent was 6 years old and taking everything apart. When he went over to inspect the barrel size bolts that hold the Space Needle to its platform I ordered him away from them. It's dangerous to underestimate the power of a kid!

My second World Fair was in Spokane, Washington and my third and last one was in Knoxville, Tennessee.

When visiting Duane in Seattle it was cheaper to eat with him aboard ship than to eat at the nearby Space Needle. After a visit that ended all too soon it was time to go back to Portland to get ready for my next bus shift.

**Dry Dock**

In the winter of 1957 Duane's ship dry docked for a month in Portland. It was a great month of visiting and the most time that I had spent with one of my younger brothers since I left for the Army Air Corps in 1943.

When Duane wasn't sitting at our table at meal time we were on his ship eating Navy food. All too soon the month was over and the General W. A. Mann prepared to go back to Japan by way of San Diego, California. On the day it was preparing to leave I went aboard and posed the Captain reading a book about famous admirals. I was welcome because the ship captains were always glad to get publicity. It was good for recruiting men for the Navy.

Although Portland is over 80 miles from the ocean it is a sea port. Ships can come up the Mighty Columbia from Astoria and turn into the Willamette River in North Portland and stop at the Swan Island shipyards or come on to the center of downtown. During the Rose Festival several Navy ships dock along the waterfront.

So routine coming and going of ships is not usually newsworthy to the Portland news media. My promise that I could probably get pictures in the paper was of interest to the Captain.

After the picture taking was over I hurried to my car and hurried to North Portland's St. John's Bridge. It is a beautiful big suspension bridge designed by the same man who designed the Golden Gate Bridge in San Francisco. I hired a taxi to take me to the center of the bridge and drop me off with instructions to pick me up in 15 minutes. The center is arched high above the Willamette so huge ships can pass beneath on their way to the Columbia. I hurried to the upriver side just in time. The General Mann was really moving. I hurriedly took a few shots and hurried across the roadway to the downriver side to shoot another two or three pictures and watch the ship carry my brother off to distant lands. In just a minute or two they were out of sight.

Did I tell that taxi driver 15 minutes? I have 12 minutes to wait. I am exposed to the winter wind high above the river and snow is swirling around me. I hunkered down for about the longest 12 minutes of my life!

The Oregonian published the story and 2 of the photographs. I mailed a set to the Captain and to Duane. Sometime later Duane sent me a list. His shipmates wanted 200 copies! They were as excited as the Captain to have their ship featured in the paper and they wanted copies of the photos. The cold day's work was worth it to make all those sailors happy!

I enjoyed driving the vehicles. I enjoyed the passengers. I suffered from the effects of pollution. I detested the attitude of the drivers competing for space on the streets. It was time to try being a full time photographer.

**BOOK 5**

**Photog-rapher**

## James and Jane Caine

I saw Jim's ad in the Oregonian. He was preparing to build and publish *Boaters/Pilots Hi-Lites,* featuring fly-ins and fun spots. It had the potential to be a popular guide book for those seeking recreation facilities near air strips. He wanted an assistant with a pilot's license. I deemed the project had a fair chance for success so decided here was my chance to resign from bus driving. I could practice my photography, writing and flying with Jim's Cessna 210 airplane with the retractable landing gear.

**A Busy Afternoon**

Jim had some paperwork for his lawyer in Seattle. I flew the Cessna while Jim worked on his papers. I landed on Boeing Field and while Jim met with his lawyer I wandered over and looked inside Frank Sinatra's Lear Jet.

We left Seattle and I dropped Jim off at Troutdale, Oregon where his Lincoln was parked. Then I took off for Moscow, Idaho. There I was met by an associate and I gave him the paper work from Jim. We chatted a few minutes and I took off as the sun was setting and the evening sky soon turned into the dark of night. My next stop was in Walla Walla, Washington. I dialed the radio to the airport transmitter. The runway angled a little left from my flight path. I moved a few miles to the right where my flight was in line with the runway. When the lights of Walla Walla came in view, I lowered the landing gear, reduced the throttle, lowered some flaps and went straight in for my landing.

My contact had nothing for me and we agreed that he didn't need to come out to the airport so I took off for home. As I approached the Columbia River the moonlight revealed a huge grey cliff extending maybe 2 miles high. A thick layer of clouds lay between me and Troutdale. That didn't worry me. Pilots flying east out of Portland's cloudy weather have an ace-in-the-hole. I was about to use that hole. Winds in the Columbia Gorge keep the air clear for one to three thousand feet. As I dropped down to enter the gorge and entered that yawning cavern I felt like a bat coming home to roost. Soon the lights of Troutdale came in sight. I landed and tied down the plane. I retrieved my red 1960 Cadillac and went home to my family.

When I thought of all I had done since noon, I marveled at what a time saver an airplane can be.

**Me and Charles Morse**

In 1967 I recruited a young pilot to work with me in getting stories and ads for the Pilots and Boaters Hi-Lites guide book. He had his own airplane. We set out to explore resorts in British Columbia, Canada. Our first stop was on Charlotte Lake. We were there to check out the Rimarko Ranch. We wanted to include it in the aviation guidebook, *Hi-Lites*. The owner, Charles H. Morse, was just preparing to leave for Chicago.

Mr. Morse was the grandson of the founder of the manufacturing company, Fairbanks Morse. Who hasn't heard of the Fairbanks Morse scales? This third generation Morse had served his time as president.

Now he divided his time between working for the company and enjoying his ranch on Charlotte Lake. I don't know if Charlotte Lake was named after his daughter or his mother, maybe both. His daughter wrote a poem about the pristine land in which the lake was found. Here is a quote,

Here is flung defiant challenge
From a land so wild and vast
Time and men have yet to spoil it,
And it stands as in the past.

From a poem by Charlotte Lee Morse

Charles had only a few minutes to talk with me but he liked the idea of his resort being featured in the guide book. He furnished me pictures and asked if I could include his daughter Charlotte's poem in the book. Then he boarded the small private plane that would fly him to Vancouver, Canada where he would catch an airliner for Chicago. Like me he was born in Illinois. He was maintaining a home in the ritzy suburb of Forest Hills just north of Chicago.

As he left, Mr. Morse invited us to look around. As we walked around the buildings I noticed several bear skins of all sizes nailed to trees and walls. I asked about them. One of the staff said that one long-time hired man was a Canadian Indian. When he was young his father was killed by a grizzly Bear and since then he had killed every grizzly he could.

The resort welcomed pilots. The hunter's cabins had modern bathrooms with hot and cold running water and electric heaters. So much for roughing it!

Charlotte Lake is 14 miles long and 7 miles wide and over 250 feet deep. Trout are plentiful in the lake and the surrounding land had plenty of moose, mountain goat and deer.

Months later I heard from Mr. Morse. He called me from Illinois. He had lost contact with a pilot friend and asked if I would see if he could be found in the Portland area.

When Mr. Morse came to Portland he was staying in the Penthouse Suite on the top floor of the Benson Hotel. I had not located his friend. He introduced me to the several guests that were with him. I don't remember if his daughter Charlotte was one of them.

In May of 1988 the Chicago Tribune carried the obituary of Mr. Morse. Among his survivors was his daughter who had become Charlotte Thomas.

Mr. Morse was referred to as a former resident of Lake Forest but he had died in his last home at Pasadena, California.

I enjoyed my brief association with Mr. Morse. He was a congenial man and he did well in carrying on the name of his illustrious family.

We explored the grounds, got our story and took off for further adventure.

## 11 Sisters

On the British Columbia, Canada air chart we saw a landing strip up north that might be a little known place of interest. We decided to check it out. Bad choice! The runway was covered with boulders and a big X declared it to be a CLOSED airstrip.

Where would we go? In Canada you can't legally fly after dark unless you are on an instrument flight plan. Far to the south was a fishing camp named *11 Sisters* with a 3000 ft. runway.

Using the Dead Reckoning navigation skills I learned in Butler County High School I gave the pilot a heading. At the planes airspeed my Estimated Time of Arrival was dangerously close to sundown. Halfway there I said, "The chart shows a small lake about here." Looking about we spotted it just left of the plane's nose almost directly below us. So far we were right on the right track..

As we neared our ETA and the sun neared the western horizon we looked for the runway. The evergreen trees were a solid carpet of green, darkening in the evening light. From the safe and rather high altitude where we were we could see a darker streak like a pencil mark at a diagonal across the landscape. That had to be our landing strip. As we dropped to a lower altitude it widened into a narrow half mile long clearing among the tall trees. The pilot skillfully landed his plane and taxied over near the lodge to tie down. We were barely in time. The hostess met us with a lighted lantern to show us to a cabin!

The setting was rustic. The bunk beds had springs but no bedding. We unrolled our sleeping bags and started a fire in the wood stove. That was cozy in the cool of the evening. We soon had a pot of boiling water on the stove. When we checked into Canada we showed the officer that we had the 2 week supply of emergency rations required by Canadian law. Our tummies told us this was an emergency, so I broke open a package of freeze dried chili to dump in the boiling water. Did it taste good! If any wolves howled or bears sniffed around that night we didn't hear a thing. We slept like logs.

The next morning I interviewed the owners for our book project. The resort was called *11 Sisters* after the 11 lakes nearby. Their fishermen guests were driven to the lake of each one's choice every morning and picked up each evening. They told of one guest from Chicago who flew in for a week or two each year that didn't care about fishing. The least productive lake for fishing was the one called Loon Lake. That is where he wanted dropped off each day where he spent the day talking to the loons!

As we climbed into the sky to leave the untamed wilderness of British Columbia I was leaving the nearest thing to a Jack London story filled with danger and adventure that I would ever live. Out West and the Great Northwest had proved to be closer to my Butler County, Kentucky home than I had ever imagined.

## A Drawer Full of Money and a Glass of Milk

I planned to drive to Ellensburg, Washington and stay 2 weeks. Cle Elm and Ellensburg had airports and pilots and businesses I wanted to consult about our Aviation Guidebook. My teenage neighbor, Charles Hammon, asked if he could go along. I was glad to have his company.

Charles was a remarkable young man. His mother was alarmed when she found a drawer full of money in his bedroom. But he was a meticulous book keeper and showed where he had earned every dollar by selling pen and pencil sets. His folks showed him about banking and he became the only senior to drive his own car to school – one he had paid for himself. He was making them so much money that the pencil company flew him to the east coast to tour the plant.

On our way through Seattle and east on I-90 through Cle Elm to Ellensburg Charles was selling pen sets at every stop. At service stations he would set up a display and sell the business a supply at wholesale. Every individual he met was a potential personal sale. Before I got to where I set up business he was making money.

On Friday I called my manager, Jim Cain, to come and take us to Portland for the weekend and I would leave my car at the airport for use on Monday. He soon arrived in the 200 MPH Cessna 210 that we used for business. As he approached to land it was hard to see the spring steel and black tires of the landing gear against the leaden sky. Charles asked me, "Does he have the wheels down?" The air traffic controller nearby heard that and grabbed the radio and asked Jim if his landing gear was lowered. It was.

Soon we were back in Oregon and preparing to land at the Troutdale Airport east of Portland. Jim was flying the standard approach pattern downwind along the south side of the airport. At a strategic point you cut back the throttle, glide past the field, make 2 left turns to align with the runway upwind for landing. Charles has seen the airport to our left but is puzzled. Why are we flying east toward Mt. Hood? He leaned over from the back seat and asked me, "Does he see the airport over here?"

I laughed and said, "Jim, your flying is sure being questioned today."

Charles is one of those fortunate individuals that look young for their age. He looked as if he would stay 12 years old forever. He told me about his 18th birthday. He had loaded his car with pen sets and headed for Texas. Passing a tavern where the legal drinking age was 18 he decided to go in and see what it was like beyond those previously forbidden doors. As he entered, the bartender yelled, "Get out of here, kid" He protested that he was 18. Another yell, "Get out of here." Finally a still skeptical bartender said, "Sit over there," indicating a far corner of the dining room. After a long delay he came over and examined his driver's license. "What'll you have?"

Charles said the look he got was almost enough to kill as he ordered, "A glass of milk."

**Basque Country**
My next assignment was Nevada. I wasn't a gambler but the hotels with casinos served outstanding food at low prices. In Elko I got a room at the Stockman's Hotel and Casino and marveled at the huge mounted bear towering on his rear legs just inside the entrance. Elko was the site of an annual Basque Festival. At the Portland boxing club I had heard mention of a Basque boxer that had made a name for himself. Now that little raveling of information was about to turn into a full sized thread through the fabric of my life. I read the brochures and was fascinated by these people who celebrated their roots that originated in a small country between Spain and France.

On the way to Reno I stopped for the night in Winnemucca. For economy I got a room in the old Winnemucca Hotel. For the evening meal the guests were gathering in the lobby. One wall was lined with a massive wood bar backed by a large mirror. It had been brought across the plains by wagon train.

At 6:15 sharp the dining room doors were opened and each one took his seat at a long table. Bowls of food were passed family style. When bowls were partly empty, waitresses would replace them with full ones. Glasses, filled with your drink of choice, were kept full. I was being introduced to traditional Basque dining.

The main boarders in the hotel were railroad workers. The bedrooms on the second floor were unheated. When I got up in the middle of the night to use the common rest room the window was open at the end of the hall and I walked barefooted on snow. But the heavy covers and cold air made it great for sleeping. In fact, I overslept the next morning and the workers had dined and left for work when I went down for breakfast. This posed no problem. I was invited to sit at a table in the kitchen. While chatting with the friendly help, I was served anything I wanted, deliciously prepared just for me!

Nevada was the home to many Basque because of the flocks of sheep. Their primary traditional occupation was herding sheep. Later while trucking through Las Vegas I regularly stopped for an excellent Lamb Chop dinner. I could enjoy being a Basque. The Basque thread had been introduced into the fabric of my life and would appear later in a most solid and interesting way.

Next I went to Reno and stayed in the Ponderosa, a base for my writing and photography. Next I covered the capitol at Carson City and then the historic gold rush town of Virginia City. My red 1960 Cadillac with the company logo on the side made a good prop for many of the pictures.

I joined Jim and Jane in Sacramento to organize our material for publication. I headed for Oregon to pursue my photography and get regular income coming in.

The guide book proved to be a fiasco financially but it had been a rich experience for advancing my skills in writing and photography.

## Harlen and Lou Rice

Back at Dee's Distinguished Portraits in Gresham, Oregon, Harlen Rice was helping while I was on the road with the book project. Now we worked together in the darkroom, photographing weddings, school children and doing whatever Dee and Lee needed. I learned from Harlen and he learned from me. When color photography was becoming more prominent Harlen and I went to San Francisco to scout for a quality color lab to print the studio's color orders. We became lifelong friends. He eventually opened his own studio next to his home in Raleigh Hills on Portland's West Side. In the 1980s, when he and his wife, Lou, went on a vacation in Tahiti, Janie and I house-sat for them. Rice's Raleigh Hills Studio is a beautiful page in Portland's history.

When we had an overload of weddings on a weekend Dee enlisted the help of a freelance photographer whose name slips my mind. I'll call him Gary. The Multnomah County Fair was open and Gary and Dee were browsing the extensive photography display. Sexy pictures of women showing lots of leg was often called 'cheesecake'. Gary told Dee, "I heard that Charles got second prize for his cheesecake but I don't see any pictures with his name on them."

Dee Laughed. "You'll have to go over in the Baked Goods department to see Charlie's cheesecake." I had won second prize for a cheesecake I had baked!

Gary later moved to Arizona and had pictures in the Arizona Highways magazine. When Janie and I had our reception in Phoenix in 1981 he came by and took some of our treasured pictures of that event.

### Dee's Distinguished portraits
Now that the guide book had weaned me away from bus driving I was free to make my mark on the Portland photography scene. My basement studio was convenient for some private sittings. I called the business Romans Originals, a name my daughter, Charla Kay, has used for her E-Mail ever since. The darkroom was convenient for my freelance work.

I was soon working for 4 major Portland studios besides my own contacts for freelance work. Memorable experiences from all of them have left snapshots of memory in my mind and heart.

### The Wedding Photographer
There is joy and beauty at weddings and a good photographer captures the beauty and the story. Brides have told me they saw their wedding for the first time when they saw the photos. They had been so involved they could not stand back and see the overall scene.

Having photographed hundreds of weddings I can say that each one is unique. Some are traditional as practiced by the ethnic group or religion. Sometimes the families had no idea of what was proper and some would ask me how to proceed. I would authoritatively direct them to do what I thought they would do if they knew what they were doing. It worked!

Some brides told me how the pressure had everyone tense until I arrived and that my friendly confidence made everyone relax.

Some things that happened stand out in my memory. Like the time I saw the bride before the groom did. She had come from an Arab country and when the wedding march played and she came up the aisle her husband on the stage with the minister saw her for the first time in his life. They say that those arranged marriages have a better lasting record than ours where our young people choose their own mate.

Then there was the time that the groom was so nervous that he was about to pass out. Since this was a Seventh Day Adventist wedding there was a nurse among the guest so she gave him a shot to help him make it through the ceremony.

One of the perks for the photographer is an invitation to enjoy the food at the reception. I especially enjoyed the Philippine receptions. They usually had a 10 or 12 pound piglet roasted whole. Wow! Was it good along with other delicious dishes.

The going away pictures end the photographer's duties. One couple had their wedding at the Quay in Vancouver, Washington. It was a beautiful setting on the Columbia River. I was a showman as usual with my black suit and red brocade vest and gold watch chain. The Speed Graphic camera added to the old fashioned look. The father of the bride came up to me and said, "You look like someone who knows how to take pictures."

When it was time for the couple to leave we went out on the dock where they boarded a waiting helicopter that leaped them across the river to the Portland Heliport where their car was parked. They sure gave everyone the slip on their getaway!

My happiest after wedding dinner was on May 11, 1981 in Las Vegas, Nevada. Janie, a widow for 11 years, was living in Phoenix, Arizona and I was living in Portland, Oregon. We decided to meet half way and get married in Las Vegas between my truck trips. I flew down and she drove up with her daughter, Melinda and granddaughter, Sunny. At 9:30 after the wedding we had dinner together. My new bride was on my left and Melinda was across from me. I first met Melinda when she was one day old 31 years earlier.

Dee had a problem. He came to me and said, "Charlie, we have a wedding Saturday at the Lutheran Church on Woodstock. The preacher has the reputation of eating photographers alive. I don't know how to deal with someone like that. Would you take this one?"

"Sure."

After taking the ceremony photos and the couple coming down the aisle I followed them down stairs and took their pictures cutting the cake. They had just poured the punch when the pastor sat at a nearby table and laid out the papers for them to sign then impatiently tapped the table with his pencil. I used another minute or so to picture them serving each other the punch and directed them to join their minister to sign papers. I photographed the signing then trailed behind the crowd as we went back upstairs for group photos. The minister came up beside me and in a firm low voice said, "If there is anything I hate it is someone who comes to a wedding as a guest and acts as if he owns the place."

"Well," I replied. "I am a professional and I can do the job however it needs to be done." I could see his temperature rising. I went on to say, "If anyone wants it done a certain way I can sure do it that way. All they have to do is tell me." I guess he couldn't think of any suggestions. He never said another word to me!

## Ilse's Hollywood Studio

Ilse Borenstein had a portrait studio in the Hollywood district on Sandy Boulevard in Northeast Portland. The Hollywood Movie Theatre was next door. Since Dee's in Gresham didn't take all my time I did Ilse's darkroom work as well. I was available for Weddings and outside photo shoots as well. The Hollywood News was published nearby and I wrote a small story to go with Ilse's weekly ad. One lady said she got the paper just to read our story. When Colonel Hanks, a lookalike of Colonel Sanders, opened a sandwich shop on 82 Avenue I represented the paper as a reporter.

Ilse was a teen age survivor of the fall of Berlin. She studied photography in Germany. She mastered the art of portraiture, retouching and oil coloring. If the customer chose a picture with the eyes shut she could retouch them open on the negative! She was amazing. When I heard her book a sitting for a lady's pet wolf I also heard that the wolf didn't like men. I made it a point to be elsewhere at the time of that sitting!

I did none of the photography in Ilse's studio, and Ilse had two ladies who were full time colorists. When a friend brought her young grown daughter in with a high hairdo and an old fashioned red velvet dress I knew I wanted to use my talent for oil coloring on her picture. Ilse gave me permission and I made the 16 x 20 brown toned print and took it home with me.

Red velvet in a photograph is black and absorbs the highlights. I varied the shades of dark red as I applied the color to the velvet dress giving shape to herbosom. Healthy flesh tones in her youthful face and highlights in her auburn hair made the portrait seem alive. As a fill I painted a vase of colored flowers over her shoulder. I finished at 4 am. Mother and daughter loved the picture and Ilse sold a rich, old fashioned oval frame with the picture. One of the colorist asked if I had taken lessons in an art school. No I hadn't. She said I had painted everything just as I would have been taught. I still leaned toward photography as my preferred way of making works of art.

## Portland Rose Festival

Melba and Stubby Staubitz Came to Portland and decided to stay. They opened the Aragon Studio on the second floor of an old time building at South West 10th and Washington. By working with them and for them I dug deeper into old Portland's past. They were two outgoing enjoyable people. She had dated George Wallace in their younger days before he became the fiery Governor of Alabama.

The second floor windows gave us a view of 10th Ave on one side and Washington Street on the other side. Bus traffic had replaced streetcars.

The annual Rose Festival Parade was a beautiful event but difficult for transportation schedules. I viewed my first Rose Parade when my streetcar was blocked at the route. I viewed the whole parade from my seat in the driver's vestibule.

The next time I was involved I had a bus. I brought to town another packed load of spectators for the parade and headed back for the east side to get another load. I turned right on Burnside toward the bridge. When I got to 3rd Ave. a policeman stepped out and stopped me and turned the crowd loose to line the street to watch the parade. I stepped out and asked if he could get me through and the answer was "No."

Soon a bus company inspector came up to the door and wanted to know if I had managed this front row seat on purpose. I said, "Sure." Well that got me a "See me" in my driver's box. A few days later I went to Mr. Woodcock's office to answer it. He said he had an inspector's report saying that I had stopped service on purpose to watch the parade. I explained about the policeman. "Why did you tell him you did it on purpose?"

"He asked a stupid question. I gave him a stupid answer."

He grinned and waved me out of his office.

In 1960 the city was excited. Paladin was to be the Grand Marshal of the Rose Parade and Jayne Mansfield was the star on one of the floats. The town was packed and I would have a grand view from the second floor of the Aragon Studio. The parade would come down Washington and turn on 10th just below our windows. I got excellent photos with my Viewmaster camera.

One year at Ilse's Hollywood Studio we had the school photo and yearbook contract for Grant High School. So when they chose their school's princess for the Rose Festival she was one of our customers. Ilse sent me down to the coliseum when the Rose Festival Queen was to be chosen from among the princesses from all the schools. Our Grant High girl was chosen! Now we had a celebrity on our hands. I politely stood aside as the press and other photographers took lots of pictures of the new queen on the posing stand. Then I stepped forward and raised my camera. I caught her attention and she recognized me from the studio. Her face blossomed into a radiant smile which I captured.

She and her mother looked through hundreds of photos and that was their favorite. Ilse produced for them a large hand colored portrait for their home to remember the year she was the Queen. I was happy to have made a contribution to her happy day in the sun!

## Grant High School Wedding

He worked as janitor and she worked in the office. These two school employees were highly visible and very popular with the students. So when they fell in love and planned to get married there was only one place big enough for the wedding – the Grant High School auditorium. Ilse was asked to supply the photo coverage. She asked me to be the photographer at the wedding. She would do the formal portraits in the studio.

The two were from Haiti and very black. His mother made the trip from Haiti for the wedding but the bride had no relatives present. She boarded with a white family and the husband was chosen to give her away. When the wedding march began this balding business man escorted on his arm this lovely black bride down the aisle and up on the stage. There were 3 blacks and 3 whites in each group to the left and right of the couple standing in alternating black and white. The audience of some 500 watched in hushed awe at the beautiful ceremony and this spectacular display of racial harmony.

After the ceremony it was time for the photographers to direct the show. This big wedding had attracted the attention of the media so the

Oregonian had a photographer there. I posed some appropriate groups for his news photos. He took his pictures and left. Now the show was in my hands.

I photographed the large group then dismissed all except his mother, the best man and the bridesmaid. His mother was posed with the couple. The best man and bridesmaid were dismissed after the picture of the four. Now it was just me with the bride and groom.

I put them through several loving poses called misties, teardrops and other intimate names. Ilse was in the audience with her husband, Isaac Borenstein. She said the audience was mesmerized by the show I was performing on the stage.

Downstairs I shot photos of cake cutting, punch pouring, certificate signing and many other candid and posed scenes. But I could not leave until hours later. This was a Haitian wedding. As midnight approached we along with the remaining guests gathered again in the auditorium. On a table in front of the stage sat a black cake heavy with rum. As the clock struck midnight, a knife gripped by the bride and groom, sliced into the cake. On this Haitian moment the wedding festival ended.

## The Myna Bird

Isaac Borenstein was a tailor in the Meier & Frank department store. On the second floor you had to walk through the pet shop to get to his work room. He said that when he took a break he often talked with the Myna bird. I was on my way to visit Isaac one day when I stopped by the tall cage. I looked at the Myna bird. He looked at me. I whistled at him. No response. I tried another whistle. Still no response. For a few minutes I tried various whistles and warbles and got only a curious stare. I was about to give up when he asked, "Can't you talk?"

Whoops! I looked over my shoulder hoping no one was looking. Who was the bird brain in this exchange?

## Yuen Lui Studios

Just as the bus driving in Portland paid the lowest on the west coast, photography didn't pay well either. For weddings I was paid $15.00 and all expenses where the same event would pay $75.00 in San Francisco. One weekend I made $75.00 by covering one wedding on Friday evening, three on Saturday and one on Sunday. In San Francisco that would have paid $375.00. So I made myself available to yet another major studio. In addition to Dee's in Gresham and Ilse's in the Hollywood district I did a lot for Yuen Lui's Studio in the Lloyd

Center. I did occasional work for my friend Harlen Rice and his thriving studio on the west side. I also had a number of freelance accounts of my own.

I was honing my technique for weddings at every opportunity. In 1962 I went to the Winona School of Photography in Indiana where I picked up some ideas. The big change came in 1969 when Bill Stockwell from Oklahoma City taught at a 3 day paid seminar. Dee and I and a few Portland photographers attended. The poses were called 'casuals' belying the fact that they were carefully posed by the photographer. "See the wedding through the misty eyes of the bride," was a key theme. Some were taken by aiming the flash at the ceiling. The soft yellow glow made it appear as though the candles had lighted the intimate scene.

I wrote an account *'The Revolution in Wedding Photography'* and it was published in the *Bride and Groom* supplement of the Press.

Stacy Wong had a fine studio in Portland. He stopped by Ilse's one day and as we stood on the street he was looking at the window display of a wedding set I had taken. "You pretty good at that stuff."

Not many liked this break with tradition. Mr. Lui would send his Portland manager, Boyd Halloway, notes saying, "Tell Romans to keep his light on the camera. Our lab can't get flesh tones in his pictures." I told Boyd I was taking the pictures for the bride, not Mr. Lui."

A young lady from Seattle saw the display of one of my weddings in Ilse's window and said I had to be her photographer. So Mr. Lui had to pay for me to spend a weekend in Seattle and take her pictures. After he died his son, Wah Lui had all their photographers take wedding pictures the Stockwell way.

As an appropriate prop for my growing reputation as a wedding photographer I grew sideburns and a handlebar mustache. For weddings I dressed in a black suit with a red brocade vest and with a speed graphic camera I looked like someone from 1880. It prompted one father of the bride to comment, "You look like someone who knows how to take pictures."

Yuen Lui studio had a thriving business in child photography taken at scheduled sittings in the home. Sometimes, before weekend weddings, I would take the proof prints out to the homes where the children had been photographed by the Yuen Lui Photographer. I went up to one door and a young boy announced, "The president is here." I don't know which historic president he thought I was.

Another young boy let me in then ran off. A week later the mother came in to pick up her order. She told the manager, "When I bought the coupon I was determined to take only my free picture. But when your salesman came with that beard and mustache my son ran off to the other room. I thought he was scared of him. But he came right back with a comb, hopped up on Mr. Romans' knee and spent the whole time combing his beard. They got along fine. I was so flabbergasted I sat there and picked out this big order."

At another home I arrived with my sport coat bulging with proofs and sales pads. The little twin girls played and didn't pay us much attention as their mother and I made out the order. As I was leaving one of the girls said something to me. I didn't understand her baby talk so she repeated it for me. I still didn't understand. I asked her mother, "What did she say?"

"I didn't understand it either. What did you say, Judy?" Judy repeated for her and a strange look came over her mother's face.

"Well. What did she say?"

"Oh! I hate to tell you."

"Oh go ahead. I like to hear what the kids say."

"Well, OK."

"Goodbye, Captain Kangaroo."

## Bob, Child Photographer Extraordinaire

Weekends could keep me busy with weddings, beauty pageants, proms and other interesting events. On weekdays I would sometimes take a photography route scheduled from certificates that had been sold. It was grueling work and I usually avoided it. Every half hour you had to set up at a different home, quickly set up a battery pack, lights, tripod and a heavy camera loaded with a long roll of 70MM film. I loved taking the pictures. I would be on the floor or high up as excited eyes followed this clown photographer and the hand held trigger kept the camera clicking. I got scolded for using so much film but big orders often came from my shoots.

I preferred to spend the afternoon and evening returning with the proof prints and taking orders. But 2 salesmen consistently outsold me. Bob I could understand. He was a quiet, shy person that was comfortable with kids. He was their perpetual playmate. He was the Pied Piper of Hamlin when it came to leading kids into the most delightful of poses. The parents liked this quiet man who had mesmerized their little ones into posing for delightful poses. They bought big orders.

But Jerry was something else. He would bring in big orders but he was so befuddled that someone in the studio would have to help him make out his run report. How did he ever make a presentation to sell a big order?

I found out the next year when he was no longer with the Yuen Lui Studio. I went to some of the same yearly customers. Several told me, "That man who came here last year didn't know anything. We had to make out the orders for him."

Ah, ha! He hadn't sold them anything. They had to sell themselves!

I came back to the studio about 9PM one night and Bob had just dropped off some orders. We agreed to go downtown to have a bite to eat at the Greek restaurant. There was a lively crowd but the hostess found us a table in the middle of the room by a platform stage which, as we sat, came to the top of our heads. Bob was across from me and the stage was at his right shoulder. We ordered salads with Blue Cheese which in the dim light looked like a dish of ice cream. Nothing was happening on the stage until we got our salads.

Suddenly the stage lit up and a plump lively lady proceeded to perform a vigorous belly dance as she whirled around the stage. Nothing detracts me from my food but Bob sat with his hands in his lap and stared over his right shoulder. It was obvious that Bob would prefer to be somewhere else. Then she addressed the crowd. "For this next act I need a volunteer."

She walked to the edge of the stage and invited Bob. Bob stiffened and looked straight ahead. "Come on up, Pooh, Pooh." The crowd yelled for him to join her. She pleaded. "You don't prefer that cold ice cream to me, do you?" Bob looked right through me. He looked like a deer hypnotized by a pair of headlights, waiting to be slaughtered. She finally gave up on him and got someone more willing.

I finished my salad and we left. He hadn't touched his!

I got to the studio early the next morning but he was already leaving with his gear. He didn't want to be there when I told the crew about the night before.

When we *Romans* dine with the *Greeks* you never know what may happen!

## Paul Harvey

I am not an early to work person if I can help it. I put off getting into the harness until I listened to the 15 minute Paul Harvey news cast at noon. My favorite Paul Harvey story was about the butcher. The lady customer came in and wanted a chicken. The butcher brought one out of the cooler, headless and dressed. She looked it over and said, "I had in mind one a little more plump." The butcher went back in the cooler and learned he didn't have another chicken so he brought out the same one. The lady studied it. That's a little better. I'll take it." The butcher was pleased. Then she added, "In fact, I'll take both of them." Uh Oh!

## The Case of the Pancake House

I was 'passing proofs' in Vancouver, Washington. It was 9PM - time to make one more picture sale. As I parked in front of the address a car parked behind me. I prepared to go in with my picture proofs and two men got out of the car and asked, "How long will you be here?" I gave them an estimate and they said they wanted to talk to me when I got out.

I told my Yuen Lui customer that 2 men were waiting for me so I'll go see what they want. The men asked a few questions and looked at each other. "I think this is our man." They told me to follow them to the Vancouver, Washington police station.

I sure was wondering what this was all about on this late night drive.

After some more questions I was told the problem and locked up.

A week or so earlier a pad of checks was stolen from a home. The thief then cashed forged checks at 5 banks and a second check at 3 of them for a total of 8. Since I had been in that home selling pictures I was a suspect.

To get a peddlers license in Vancouver you are put through the same routine as a criminal. So my picture and fingerprints were on record. My picture was shown to the 5 tellers and 2 of them said, "Yes, I remember him." I had gone to those drive-through windows to get change for doing business. With my wedding photographer guise of mutton chop whiskers and handlebar mustache and driving a 1960 red Cadillac I had expected to be unforgettable. It was part of my business persona. The other 3 tellers did not recognize my photo because I had not been to their banks.

I called my wife and we planned to pay the $500 bail as soon as they arranged the booking, etc. I spent 2 nights in their jail and hired a lawyer I knew about. Mom was visiting from Butler County so we visited the lawyer together. He had been studying the situation and said to us, "I advise that you plead 'Guilty' and I'll get you the lightest sentence possible."

"Whoa! I won't plead guilty to something I didn't do."

Mom said, "If Charles needed money he would not have stolen it. He has a family that would have helped him out."

The lawyer said, "Well, you are closing some doors but I will do the best I can." He assigned me his investigator to interview my customers of that day. I had checked in at the studio at 8am then dawdled at the nearby pancake house with other sales men until after 11:45. At 12 noon I had got my change at the bank and drove to the first customer. She was walking her dog so I sat in the car and listened to the last of Paul Harvey news and then started my 8 hours of work. The sales receipts I had turned in at the office confirmed my whereabouts for all afternoon. The DA contended that I had time to pass those bad checks that morning before starting my work.

For 3 months I went over and over the evidence. On a poster board I made a map of the bank locations. Could they be paid 8 visits in about 3 hours? Not likely but I was wondering what it would be like in the Walla Walla prison for 20 years.

One day I decided to look at the sales slips for the *day before* all this happened. There it was! The evidence I needed! I had turned in a check for an order but part had been paid with cash which I forgot to include. Manager Boyd had made a note on the order to see me the next morning. Then about 11 am he came around to the Pancake House and found me still there. So I went to the office and settled with him.

This solid evidence proved that I was in Portland that morning. The case was dropped.

In January I applied for my new license. Detective Shipley grabbed the application and headed down the hall. After a while he came back.

"We have decided to let you have the license but what happened last year better not happen again."

"Mr. Shipley, I didn't have anything to do with it happening last year." Well, yeah. I took the license to my lawyer's office and had him copy it for my file. My new picture did not have the beard and mustache. I decided I didn't want to be so unforgettable

## Aircraft Owners and Pilots Association

As Public Relations rep for the local pilots association I arranged a crop dusting demonstration for the upcoming Air Show at the Troutdale airport. I gave one of the central Oregon farmers a quart of men's cologne. He loaded his chemical tank with plain water and added the cologne. At the precise scheduled minute he appeared at the Troutdale Airport and sprayed the runway with a fake fertilizer that smelled much better than the real thing. He climbed off to the south to return to his farm work. The crowd was awed as most had never seen a crop duster in action.

Before getting permission for this stunt I got some static. "What if some spectator goes home with strange perfume on his clothes and he gets divorced? We may get sued." Well that never happened.

For our next association meeting I hitched a ride to Klamath Falls with one of the pilots in his Piper Cherokee. As we landed on this high desert airport I saw a coyote posed regally atop a mound watching this large bird land in his domain.

While we were eating lunch a call came in for one of the local pilots. Lightening had set a dead tree afire and he was dispatched to drop water on it before it became a major forest fire. His mechanic went along for the ride. After dousing the fire the old WWII bomber was not able to clear the ridge. Before we finished our lunch we were told that both men had died in the crash.

## Slot Cars

Dee was impatient. He was realizing his goal to be a first rate photographer. We both produced blue ribbon photographs but the financial returns were meager. Business was good but his other goal of being wealthy by the time he was 40 was not materializing. Then the slot car craze hit. Here was his opportunity. Dee and Lee rented a large room on busy 182nd Avenue and set up multiple 60 foot six lane tracks and soon had a busy business. He left it up to me to run the studio.

## Studio Manager

For six months the studio was mine to run. In the ever changing front window display I placed Mom's stereoscope and some stereoviews for

historical interest and plenty of samples of our artistic portrait output. I enjoyed working with the various models who posed for the camera. Each one is a unique challenge. One young lad about 7 years old came in with his mother and with defiant pout and a firmly planted foot announced, "I ain't smiling for nobody." I rubbed my hands in glee. "Oh! Goody. I don't have to give a nickel to those who don't smile." Needless to say, the smile never left his face and the nickel landed in his pocket. The pictures were great and landed a large order.

The studio was busy but with prices that fit the market it seemed we were treading water. The future seemed flat. I told Dee that he was wasting great talent by not producing great pictures. I gave him an ultimatum. Sell the slot car business and get back in the studio that bore his name. At a certain time I was going trucking. Now it was his turn to say I would be wasting my talent driving a truck. I heard it takes a certain kind of man to drive a truck. I wanted to prove that I was one of that special kind of man.

BOOK

6

Truck

Driver

**Learning from the Corn Flakers**

When I decided to go back to driving it was going to be trucks, not buses. Now I found a roadblock to my plans. Truck drivers and trucking companies had a negative opinion of bus drivers. Every application was turned down. Joe Exley, who had 50 trucks and 100 trailers running the west coast, told me plainly that no amount of bus driving experience could make a trucker. I didn't agree with him but I saw I would have to go through the Truck Driver School to be considered for a job. So I **borrowed** $500.00 from my mother-in-law and applied for the two week training course.

Swan Island in the North Portland Willamette River bottoms was an industrial area below a nice residential area on the high cliff. Consolidated Freightways had their headquarters and truck yard on Swan Island. Founded in 1929 they became the largest freight hauling trucking company in the country. In 1939 they formed the Freightliner Corporation to build the famous Freightliner trucks with CF as their main customer. Truckers on the road seeing these CF trucks nicknamed them the 'Corn Flakers'.

Now they had a trucking company and a company to build trucks. One of the employees saw a need for trained drivers. He formed a driver school in North Portland near the stockyards. The popular Stockyards Restaurant was conveniently nearby. Ex CF drivers and other experienced drivers were the instructors. With my farm background I was more interested in hauling food than freight but I learned a lot from these freight haulers. One trainer, we will call him Jim, gave us an insight on the company drivers. The old timers, the million milers with good records, were the most cautious when in a yard or busy traffic. But when they hit the open road they lost no time getting up to the speed limit and holding it for hours. They did not spend excessive time at the truck stops. They were real professionals.

Gregg, one of the trainers thought he had to act like an army Sargent which irritated the students. The previous class had rebelled and threatened to quit if they didn't fire him. The school agreed to find a replacement after they used him for one more class. Now this one last class was about to quit ahead of time. In my mid-forties I was the old man of the group. I told the young trainees that I could see that Gregg was a very good and experienced driver and they could learn a lot from him if they could ignore his personality. After all I was the one he rode on the hardest since he didn't like bus drivers. They decided to follow my advice. Later I was driving close to the curb carefully centered in my lane. One of the students asked if I wasn't too close to the curb. Gregg said, "He's OK." That was the nearest he ever came to a compliment.

We took a coffee break in east county after which I was to drive up a steep hill. As the momentum rapidly dissipated the trick was to depress the clutch, put the range selector in neutral, put the gear selector in a low gear, then the first selector back in gear in the low range and let the clutch out, doing all of that almost instantaneously.

I sipped a little coffee then went to the truck. I practiced the movements of the double down shift in the parked truck. The crew came out and boarded, 3 in the bunk and Gary in the right seat. I hit the hill at full speed and as the speed rapidly fell toward zero I shoved the clutch with my left foot, flipped through the gear downshift, tapped the accelerator to sync the motor with the gear and let out the clutch. We were still in gear and climbing. "You've got it. You've got it," they all shouted. My practice had paid off.

One student was a Native American. His training was paid for by a government job training program for minorities. He was a rough Charles Bronson kind of fellow. I won his friendship by treating him as a fellow member of the human race, which he was. He once confided in me that he sometimes brooded over what the Europeans had done to his people and land until he had trouble sleeping and wanted to get a gun and see how many whites he could kill. He wished the Indians would rise up and retake the land and kill every white man. I asked him, "What about Jehovah's Witnesses? They have no prejudice against you or anyone and never kill anyone."

"We might let them live but they will have to stay on their reservation," was his answer.

I hope he finally made peace with the modern world and got a good job with the training furnished him by his 'Great White Father.'

To complete our training two small Portland trucking companies let us go as second driver on a California trip (without pay). On the way back, my trainer met a southbound trainer at a truck stop. I heard the other driver say to mine, "I thought we agreed not to sleep while the student was driving."

"I know. But his driving didn't make me nervous so I just relaxed and got some sleep."

That comment presaged for me a successful trucking career!

## Hired by Exley

It was Saturday and I was visiting my friends, Homer and Viola Wood. We were having a lively Bible discussion when the phone rang. Homer's dispatcher, Martha Carlson, told him that his partner, Mr. Roper, had called in and left for another job. She didn't have a driver available. Did he know of anyone who could go on his Los Angeles trip tonight? "Why yes. My neighbor, Charles Romans is here now. He recently went through the Truck Driver's School and is looking for a job."

"Take him with you and when you get back check with Joe to see if he will hire him."

So that evening I left Portland on my first trip with Joe Exley's *Exley Express* trucking Company.

There are various ways to manage the driving hours to stay legal. Homer showed me the way most Exley drivers managed it. One driver drives 5 hours. Then they spend an hour at a truck stop while they freshen up, relax and eat then the other one drives 5 hours.

Homer told me of an interesting psychological quirk. He said when a new driver stops for a break, there may be several truck stops in that vicinity, but the one he chooses will almost invariably be the one he stops at every time he runs that route. With 50 trucks on the road with 100 drivers it wasn't unusual for several drivers to show up at one restaurant. One waitress directed us to a large table. She said, "You Exley drivers are like rabbits. Two of you will stop in and soon 10 more will join you!"

We got unloaded in L. A. on Monday, picked up a load of produce and headed for Oregon. We got to the company yard at night. Homer checked his mailbox and our dispatch said to take the load on to Seattle. Then go to Kennewick, Washington and get a load and bring it to Portland.

When we arrived back in the yard Martha told Joe to go out and check Homer's partner. When he saw me recognition slowly dawned. He said, "You ugh, ugh."

"Yes, I was here a few weeks ago."

"You were a bus driver."

He looked dismayed that a former bus driver had been driving one of his trucks all over the west.

"Since then I went through The Truck Driver School." He had hired others from the school so he looked more at ease.

"I'll check with Homer and if he says 'OK' I'll hire you as his partner."

So by sort of slipping in the back door that's how I started my trucking career with one of the best driving jobs on the west coast.

## Cowboys and Indians

Homer Wood was a cowboy in his younger days. My father-in-law, a shoemaker, made boots and saddles for the cowboys in his younger days. Now I had a former cowboy for a trucking partner.

Homer told of using his saddle for a pillow some nights where there was no shelter and only his slicker between him and any rain.

Once while riding down a trail he saw off in the distance, a wild stallion with his harem of mares. The stallion took Homer's horse for an intruder in his territory. He came racing to intercept them. Homer's cow pony was no match for the wild one. The distance was closing fast. Homer took his right foot out of the stirrup and drew his leg up for a kick for whatever good it would do. Would the wild horse break his horse's neck?

Racing in fast, the stallion took a fast warning nip at the top of his opponents neck, then veered off and raced back to his mares much to the relief of Homer and I'm sure to his horse as well.

Homer's grandmother came to Oregon via the Oregon Trail. The trip left from St. Louis, Missouri the city known as the gateway to the west as now commemorated by the famous Gateway Arch.

Her wagon train was organized and ready to hit the months-long trail when another man joined the group. So and So was not a colonizer. He was, "Going out west to kill 'engines'" his slang word for 'Indians'.

The long days of travel began. Way out west of St. Louis a group of Indians were foraging. The grandmother in the party became tired so she stopped to rest under a shade tree while the others went looking for more berries. As the wagon train slowly passed by, So and So saw his first chance to kill an 'engine'. He goes over and shoots her dead.

When the hunting party came back for Grandmother it was obvious to them what had happened. Enraged, they followed the trail of the wagon train. When So and So saw such a large number of his enemy he was soon trying to hide among the barrels and furniture of the wagons. The tribesmen told the Wagon Master to hand over the murderer and they would not bother any of the rest of the trekkers. They were glad to comply.

"Leave," they were told. As the wagon train slowly moved down the trail they saw the murderer stripped and spread eagled on the ground as they proceeded to skin him alive. Did he feel his life's purpose of ethnic cleansing was fulfilled since he got one of them before they got him?

The young pioneer who became Homer's grandmother followed the Oregon Trail all the way to Oregon. Somewhere down the family line someone with Indian ancestry married into the family. Homer was proud to be part Native American.

During WWII he served in the Merchant Marines.

## Martha and Common Sense

Joe Exley had built a trucking company but he almost lost it. There may have been more than one reason but one was: Joe liked to be extravagant. Martha Carlson, who worked in the office, went to Joe and said, "I can make this company work if you put me in charge." Joe had nothing to lose so he gave her the 'go ahead.'

No one could challenge Martha, not even Joe himself. Joe's brother was manager of the Los Angeles office. Another brother was manager in name only at the Richmond yard. She even sent them the work orders for their local drivers. They only handed them out. A driver from that period told me of the orders she gave him.

" 'When you get your load to Pacific Fruit in Seattle, go to the office and get the check, put it in this stamped envelope and mail it to this office.'

"As I walked out to look for a mailbox, there was Joe. 'Do you have the check?'

"Yes."

" 'Give it to me.'

"Martha was furious. 'Don't ever give him the check.'

"The next time, I hurried to get the check. I sealed it as I ran to the mailbox and threw it in. When I got back to the dock, Joe walked up. 'Have you got the check?' Yes, but I just mailed it."

Joe left disappointed but Martha had another check to keep the company afloat."

Some drivers hated her iron hand but wouldn't quit for anything. They loved fighting with her and trying to see who could outwit whom.

Martha had two interests. One was the rodeo where it was said she went to root for the animals. Billy wanted to ride in the upcoming Molalla Buckaroo but Martha told him he couldn't have the time off. So he called in sick. He rode the bull out of the chute, bailed off, landed on his feet and slammed spread eagled on the fence, face to face with a spectator on the front seat, Martha. "Good ride, Billy." That was all that was ever said.

One Saturday evening I went down early to get the truck ready. The dispatch in the box said to leave at 8am. That didn't make sense. That must be a typo. I called Homer and read it to him. He told me to go home. He went down to see that it said am and not pm. I didn't catch on that he was taking advantage of Martha's typo to get some extra time at home. When we reported for work the next morning she looked up and said, "You know better than that," Then her attention went back to business.

Her second dedicated life interest was running the company. She insisted on making all decisions. If there was trouble on the road, you called her even if it was 2am. One driver had a problem and the next day told her how he had resolved it without calling her. She wasn't pleased. "Why did you do that?" she demanded.

"It seemed like the common sense thing to do."

"Common sense doesn't have anything to do with this business."

Whoop-te-do! What a profound thought! I have seen many places where it can be applied. How about the way our elected officials run the government?

## Cowboy Hats and Asparagus

We had just gotten unloaded in Phoenix, Arizona and Homer was checking the dispatch for our return load. It warned too watch out for the asparagus. I wondered why.

"Asparagus is a funny vegetable," Homer explained. "If it is warm it can grow 2 or 3 inches between here and Portland. That makes it tough and ruins it. The reefer can hold a cool temperature but it can't bring down a warm temperature. The asparagus has to be chilled before loading. One of the drivers brought a load in the other day and it was ruined at a big loss to Exley. Martha was furious. She warned me on this dispatch to watch the temperature on the asparagus."

We proceeded to this plant in California where we were to load, among other things, 4 pallets of asparagus. We got in a line of trucks to await our turn to load. Floodlights brightened the area for this all night operation. We watched as trucks came in from the fields and the produce was bundled, palletized, and then drenched with icy water to chill it to the safe temperature. Most of our trailer was already loaded when the forklift placed the asparagus on the back. Everything seemed so efficient we were sure they did it right so we hurried out of there to the first truck stop for coffee. Homer climbed up and stuck his thermometer in the asparagus. Oh no! It was dangerously warm.

When it was my turn to drive we entered Oregon. As the truck crawled to the peak of the Siskiyou's I stuck my thermometer out of the window. Good! It was almost freezing at midnight. At the top I pulled over in the brake check area. I opened the side door and the rear doors. A cold breeze blew through the pallets gathering heat from the asparagus as it poured out the side door. The temperature was coming down fast! Homer stuck his head out of the bunk and saw me reading instead of driving. "What's going on?"

"I'm chilling the asparagus."

"I hope it works." He went back to sleep.

When I shut the doors and drove down the mountain, the temperature was just right and got that way in time to save the asparagus and we rolled in with a fine load.

When we parked Scotty was at his truck at the far side of the lot. He came running over and shook my hand like I was an old friend. From then on I was.

Scotty was the only black driver at Exley's. He was also the only one who wore a cowboy hat - until then. When he saw me wearing one he knew he had found a kindred spirit. I lost a friend when he passed away.

Scotty brought a load in from the south. It was scheduled to be delivered to Seattle. Scotty told Martha he was too sick to go any farther. "Please, get another driver." After Seattle the trip was to reload in Kennewick. Martha begged him to do the Seattle part and come back and she would send someone else for the Kennewick load.

"I can't do it," Scotty stated firmly then went home and died.

Martha was trying to get one more trip out a dying man!

## Asleep at the Wheel

Homer drove in from California, pulled into our Portland yard and refueled. I had been in the bunk since leaving Medford in southern Oregon. I still felt a little sleepy but now it was my turn to drive. Our load of produce had to go to Seattle.

I drove across the Columbia River and I was about an hour north of Vancouver, Washington when I became aware that the white stripe at the right of the road was under my steering wheel. The right wheels were almost in the ditch! In a panic I started yanking on the steering wheel but wasn't getting results. Perhaps centrifugal force on a curve was pulling me right. About then I see a power pole in my path straight ahead! I just about put my foot through the floor stomping on the brake. If I had not had my seat belt on I would have been bouncing off the ceiling!

Now, fully awake I looked around in disbelief and considerable relief. The truck wasn't moving. I had pulled over and laid over the steering wheel for a fresh-up nap and woke up thinking I was going off the road.

I was wide awake the rest of the way to Seattle!

## Kid Talk and Salty Language

I was preparing to leave on another trip to California. I overheard 4 year old Vince ask 6 year old Henry, "Is Daddy going to Lost Angeles again?" Henry assured him that I was.

Vince had another question for his wiser older brother. "Why do they call it Lost Angeles? Do people get lost there?"

"Yes. They get lost there all the time."

As I was leaving I said, "Goodbye. I am leaving for Lost Angeles." Their parting advice was, "Don't get lost."

Of Exley's 50 trucks and 100 trailers a goodly number of loaded ones would leave on Saturday so the LA local drivers would have them to unload on Monday morning. By Sunday morning Homer and I would be well into California. Homer would have his usual breakfast of grapefruit slices and we would push on in to the Exley yard east of downtown LA. With a lot of night ahead of us and a long wait on Monday as our trucks were unloaded we looked for one of the all night movies. They were always cheap old movies but good killers of time.

Now and then a movie would come on with some pretty strong cursing. Now Homer had been a cowboy and had sailed in the Merchant Marines and I'm pretty sure he had been around a lot of salty language. But on these R movies he would walk out. He said, "Those silly actors don't know how to cuss. I can't stand their stupid talk." Hollywood could probably have used Homer to teach their cowboys how to curse!

## Boats

Homer had a boat but its engine had a broken block. The water was not thoroughly drained one winter and it froze. Their boats were the number one subject of discussion when Exley drivers got together at meal breaks. I asked Homer why so many drivers had boats since they seldom had more than 4 hours off between trips. He said, "You have to have something besides this monotonous road to think about.

Joe Exley's new yacht was the main conversation for days. Every time the subject was discussed Joe's yacht got longer and longer. Finally I spoke up. "If we don't quit making Joe's boat longer and longer we will have it too long to come up the Columbia River."

As the drivers talked about their own boats none could outtalk Frank Wickam. Frank, with his red turkey neck and ever present cigar was the biggest talker. His was the biggest boat. His was the fastest and fanciest. His was also the most expensive yet the most affordable of any of the driver's boats. How could that be? Because his was not a boat Frank had; it was the one he was always going to get!

## Pollard Flat

Running north through northern California I-5 is one curve after another. Homer said we would eat at Pollard Flat, a restaurant popular with truckers. It was literally in the middle of nowhere. There were no public facilities for miles ahead or behind. I had never stopped there before but Homer said the food was very good. I pulled in as he had directed and woke him up. We went in and I headed for the men's room completely oblivious to the fact that the few other truckers in the room and Homer were watching me with interest. I didn't disappoint them. I opened the door and started in when suddenly I jumped back in alarm. It took a few seconds for me to realize that the naked woman in the bathtub was a mannequin!

Homer was right. The food was excellent.

## Home on the Road

I enjoyed being a dressed up trucker. I would wear silk shirts and a bow tie. Sometimes I would wear a black velvet vest.

I was sitting at a table in the truck stop with my partner, Homer Wood, when a grey haired waitress came over to wait on us. She admired my fancy attire including the vest. "I had a husband that I dressed up nice to send him out on his truck trips and some waitress stole him from me." How sad.

As second driver to Homer Wood on his Exley Express truck I was experiencing my first trucking job. I was learning about life on the road. Homer set a good example for staying clean and fresh. Indeed all the Exley drivers appeared to take pride in looking good on the job.

Truck stops are equipped to serve the truckers needs. When in need of a shower you could check out a towel and soap and use the next available shower stall. Sometimes you had to wait in line.

The union had negotiated in the contract that we had to have a minimum of 4 hours at our home yard before going out on our next run. I told Homer that the fast paced routine reminded me of the three R's in school. "How's that?" he asked.

"Here we have the 3 shishes. We just have time to SHave, SHower and SHove off."

Not far away in the same Southeast Portland neighborhood was a competitor to Exley named Coast Transport. Their drivers were friendly but just didn't seem to have the polish of the Exley drivers. Their trucks were a drab dark blue or black compared to the red Exley trucks. In other words we at Exley were the ones with the pizazz.

I came in from a California run and as my wife was at work I was in no hurry to go home so I went to a neighborhood restaurant for lunch. I spotted a Coast Transport driver and joined him at a table. We chatted and he asked about Exley's new trucks. Joe Exley had bought several new trucks for his fleet and they had been sitting in the yard, unused, for several days. Of course, the Coast Transport drivers would be noticing what was going on in the rival's yard.

"Why isn't Joe using those new trucks?"

I had not the least idea about the reason for the delay in using those trucks but that didn't keep me from engaging in a little tomfoolery. "Well, he's got to get some drivers qualified to drive those nice new trucks."

He was incredulous. "Exley doesn't have qualified drivers for his new trucks?!"

"You'd be surprised how many of those drivers don't have white shirts and ties."

He exploded and sputtered, "When I can't drive in these blue jeans and work shirt I'll quit driving!"

## Old 97

I soon completed my first year of trucking and was eligible to be a first driver. I was assigned to truck 97. An old thread was again weaving through the fabric of my life. The ballad, *The Wreck of Old 97,* was about a real train wreck that occurred in 1903. The ballad became the first million seller in recording history. Mom had learned that song and sung it to her babies. When I had a trip off, my truck was sent south with another driver. It got in a minor accident and ruined the corner where the number *97* was painted. It was in the repair shop when I headed for L.A.   On the next trip my truck was repaired but had been sent south with another driver. So I head south with his truck. We meet at the Fowler truck stop as he was headed north. He wanted his truck back. I called Martha to ok the switch. Her answer was, "Absolutely *not*."

He angrily stated, "That will cost her another side of beef." It probably did, too. He was notorious for taking part of the load home with him. The company and the law were on to him but had not been able to catch him in the act.

My truck number had not yet been painted on the front corner. When I bought services such as ice for my load the supplier asked for the truck ID. After a few trips I decided to take care of the problem my way. I got some yellow tape and formed the number in Roman numerals. 97 was now truck number XCVII. Soon the bills came in for truck number XCVII. Martha noticed. Soon I was using a substitute truck while mine was in the paint shop.

Newly hired, Ernie was dispatched to be my second driver. He was an experienced trucker and everything went well until one night he was trying to sleep while I negotiated the curves in northern California. He came climbing out of the bunk to sit in the right seat. "I may as well drive and let you sleep. These curves scare me to death and I can't sleep." Then he told me his story.

"I was bringing a loaded log truck down a mountain trail when the brakes failed. Finally I failed to make a curve and the truck turned over and the logs broke loose. I was knocked out and came to over beyond the pile of scattered logs. Later my wrist watch was found in the middle of the pile of logs. These curves are making me relive that nightmare of a ride."

I understood that. I told him to relax and in a few minutes we would be at a truck stop where we could take a break and change seats if he stilled wanted to. As I drove along I showed him how I negotiated curves. If the curve was to the left I hugged the middle line making more space on the right before the right wheels could drift off the pavement. On a curve to the right I stayed on the edge of the road making it farther away from the center and oncoming traffic. Study the curve and back off 2 or 3 MPH, then as you enter the curve apply slight acceleration. The driver wheels put pressure on the front or steering wheels and you have a stronger hold on the road, giving you better control. About then the truck obediently wheeled into the

Pollard Flat Truck Stop and parked like a team of mules coming home to their barn.

We entered the restaurant and I guided us to a table with a good view of the Men's room. Before he could sit down I hinted, "Over there is the Men's Room." He went right over and opened the door then almost tripped over his own feet stumbling back. Looking over at me he could see that I knew about the nude mannequin sitting in a bathtub. He laughed and was soon at the table for coffee and pie.

When we were ready to go he said, "After that prank and hearing you talk about driving I think I can sleep." And he did. Hey! Maybe I should have been a psychiatrist!

Hank Meaders was assigned to go to L.A. with me while his truck was in the shop. He called me on Saturday. "My sister lives in Salem and our Mom is visiting from Arkansas. If we leave early this evening and stop off in Salem they will feed us." That sounded like a good plan to me.

That evening we went to the kitchen where the food was waiting. I took a plate and went to the stove where a big pot of beans was hot. Hank's sister was loading her plate and told me to help myself. "Go ahead," she invited. I waited until she left for the dining room then loaded the center of my plate with cornbread. When she returned I was stacking the beans high. She yelled, "Oh! Momma! Come here. We've got us an Okie!"

I had noticed Gene. When we were lying around a motel in San Ysidro waiting for our loaded trailers to come out of Mexico, he would be playing cards, talking about girls or drinking beer with the other drivers. Gene noticed me too. I would be quietly resting or reading. So when Martha called him at home to go on an LA trip with me he later told me that his first impression was, "I don't want to run with that square," but decided he could stand me for one trip. So we loaded in Kennewick, Washington and headed down through Klamath Falls for California. Gene had grown up in Tennessee but didn't know I was from Kentucky where we as boys usually had a gun in our hands just as the Tennessee boys had. When we got in the mountains of southern Oregon he suggested we do some target shooting. A convenient roadside dump had plenty of tin cans. He pulled his ever present .22 revolver from under the army blanket spread over the doghouse. I took it and walked across the highway as he set up some target cans. "You're getting pretty far away for a pistol aren't you?" He was surprised at the distance I was putting between us and the targets.

Our expertise was quite the same until I asked him to throw a can up in the air. "That wouldn't do any good."

"Go on. Throw one up for me."

"That would be wasting a bullet."

I insisted and he finally threw one out across from us, an easy flat arch to lock in on and I put the bullet through it. He had never tried to hit moving targets and he was amazed at the ease with which I picked them off.

We stopped at the Fowler truck stop and after eating he invited me to play pool with him. I beat him two games. He was beginning to think I wasn't such a square after all. When we got back to Portland he asked to be my regular partner.

I eventually learned that he was addicted to gambling. We would get to Reno and he would gamble until his money was gone and I would have to buy his meals the rest of the trip. He told me of losing all his money once and called his folks to send him ten dollars for food. He got the telegraphed money and went back in the restaurant where the gambling machines were. The next thing he could remember was standing out on the sidewalk. He still hadn't eaten but the ten dollars was gone.

When we had an Arizona load I would borrow twenty dollars from him. At Reno I would see that he ate before gambling. At Las Vegas we would eat and he would ask if I had his money yet. My answer was, "No." Then sometime later as we neared the Arizona border past the gambling parlors I would say, "Oh. Gene, I have that 20 for you." as I handed it to him. He never asked where I got it.

From me he learned to respect women as intelligent fellow humans. If it was my turn to drive I would watch as he had 2 beers and then insist we leave. He would reluctantly leave without a third beer, "Alright old Mother Hen." His family and mine became friends until we changed jobs and lost track of each other.

## El Camino Real

I was discharged in Amarillo, Texas in November 1945 and soon headed for Oregon with my Texas bride, Nell Roy and her folks, Roy and Effie White. I would sing bits of a song *Along the Oregon Trail* well knowing that *the* Oregon Trail was up north starting at St. Louis, Missouri. And the song I was mimicking was *Along the Navaho Trail*.

When we got to Los Angeles, California we headed north on another famous trail.

Russia had colonized Alaska and made Juneau its capitol. Spain was concerned that they may expand south. They laid claim to the California coast by establishing a series of missions along the coast starting at San Diego and on above San Francisco. These missions named after Catholic Saints were connected by a highway named El Camino Real (The King's Highway or The Royal Road). Highway 101 parallels or is on stretches of that historic highway.

On my first trucking job I made 2 trips a week from Portland south and became quite familiar with several of these settlements as I picked up loads of produce in or near these towns. Ones I called on several times were, San Diego, Santa Barbara, San Luis Obispo, Santa Cruz, San Jose, San Francisco and San Rafael. San Juan Capistrano fascinated me because of the popular song, *When the Swallows come back to Capistrano*. Those migrating birds always came back to Capistrano on the same day every spring inspiring a celebration as well as the song.

Spain finally yielded her colonies to the independent Mexicans and when gold was discovered the Forty-Niners overwhelmed California and brought it into the English speaking fold and it became our West Coast state.

The huge sprawling Spanish city of Los Angeles (The Angels) was Portland's largest trading partner. Exley maintained a terminal east of downtown. While we waited for the locals to unload our trailers we could walk downtown to the Pantry where older waiters dressed in their suits and dignity served us and many movie stars that came there for the most delicious and perfectly prepared T-Bone steaks to be found anywhere.

My favorite of all the cities though was San Francisco with the cable cars. There I found the tops in sea food at Fisherman's Wharf.

Downtown dining at the Top O' the Mark (Mark Hopkins Hotel) gave one a great view of the historic city. But when, on Market Street, I sat down in the beautiful dining room of the Omar Khayyam Restaurant and dined on a most deliciously prepared dish of calf brains, what more could a Kentucky farm boy wish for? I might say like the popular song, *I Left My Heart in San Francisco*.

A favorite joke: Cisco had a band that was getting raves and was invited to perform in Hong Kong. The boys had a free afternoon before their performance so they went sightseeing with strict orders from Cisco to be back on time. Pedro caught a taxi boat, a Sampan, and went across the bay to browse. When he realized he was close to being late he ran down to the waterfront and caught a boat and as he approached the shore he saw Cisco pacing along the dock looking for him.

He leaped ashore and as the boat pulled away they headed for the theater.

"Where's your harp?" he asked Pedro.

"Oh no!

"I left my harp in Sampan, Cisco."

## Obituary on the World Wide Web

Joseph Milton Exley died March 1, 2007, at age 97

Joe Exley was born June 22, 1912, in Gresham, Oregon. He graduated from Gresham High School and served in the U. S. Navy during World War II. He owned Exley Express Trucking and lived in the Portland area all his life.

## Where Are Your Big Trees?

I had been trucking for Exley on the west coast for two years. With a good record I could now get a trucking job about anywhere. My heart was set on driving the Oregon Trail. I would be going home both east and west. I soon got my chance.

The wage contract had expired and the Exley trucks were parked waiting for a settlement. My partner, Gene Jenkins and I were at the meeting room at the Union Hall one day waiting around when someone came in. "Who wants to go to Iowa?"

My hand went up as I yelled, "I do." My partner Gene followed suit.

Two men had pooled their capital, bought two trucks and had a driver on each. They needed two co-drivers. I was assigned to Art Bartlett's truck. We would haul Apples to Iowa and meat back to Oregon. I asked Art if he was married. He was. I told him, "The day you got married you turned into a Bartlett pair (pear)!

It is a wonder that I didn't get thrown off the truck right then. He had only two jokes and they were worse than mine. At every truck stop restaurant, the waitress would bring a glass of water. He would take a sip and remark, "I see you got the mouse out of the well." I could relate to his joke since we sometimes had a mouse drown in our well on the farm. Now Art reminded of that every day.

Next the waitress would ask, "Coffee?" That was rather a superfluous question. I've never seen a trucker sit down to the table without ordering coffee. But she was polite to ask. And every time we were asked if we wanted coffee Art would ask, "Is the pope a Catholic?"

Art was an experienced driver. He was also an experienced butcher. If he ordered a T-bone steak and they brought a Rib-Eye he might comment to me how they got it wrong but he never complained about any meal and some were really tasteless. I asked him about that. He philosophically said, "It will fill an empty place."

I liked his attitude. I, too, ate some fuel when my body needed it but I enjoy *good* food when I get it. Junior Phelps thinks Captain D's is the ultimate in fine dining. I still keep beans and cornbread at the top of the list with lobster, catfish, T-Bone steaks etc. on down the list. Some people live to eat and others eat to live. I combine a little of both.

Art had never been to the Midwest so when we got to the deciduous forests it was a strange sight to him. The oaks, walnuts, hickory, maples, etc. looking like 60 to 80 foot high lawns mowed to even heights it was a great contrast to the 100 feet plus  evergreens of the west. He asked, "Where are your big trees." I explained that the western soft woods, pine, cedar, red wood, Sequoia, etc. made low cost building materials while the hardwoods of the Midwest and East made fine furniture and ornaments. The Japanese were paying $2000.00 for a black walnut tree at that time.

I enjoyed working with Art. I learned from him and he learned from me. I made a few trips with him before being put on Charlie Jones' truck.

Charlie Jones was a real grump. He preferred to drive solo. He would sleep only an hour then sit in the right seat and read until time to drive again. He was a chain smoker so for fresh air I rolled open my window. The frigid outside air mostly went behind me and my rolled up sleeves and across to Charlie. He kept reading. He finally looked up long enough to say, "They've got me running with a danged Eskimo!" Then he went on reading.

While lunching at the Pocatello, Idaho truck stop he talked about cars. He loved cars. But he hated the cream pitchers that looked like a cow. So I said, "Charlie, I'm going to invent a cream pitcher just for you." He didn't show interest or even a sign he had heard me. "It will be a car and the spare tire will be the handle. The cream will pour out of the radiator." Still no response showed. "I don't know what it will look like but I've got a name for it."

He half turned and put his crossed arms on the back of his seat. "Alright, alright, what's the name?"

"The *Stanley Creamer* I announced."

The Stanley Creamer," he sputtered as if it was the most ridiculous thing he had ever heard.

He finished his favorite meal, a bowl of oyster stew and we headed east.

Once Charlie run solo to the east coast and picked up a load of expensive fine moldings. It was a rush load for Portland and against Charlie's protest the boss flew a second driver to Montana to spell Charlie on the driving. Charlie retired to the sleeper which was not a part of the cab but a unit, sometimes called a coffin, set on the frame behind the cab. The other driver drove an hour down road and went to sleep at the wheel, ran off the road and turned over, spilling molding down the hillside. The sleeper cab with Charlie in it tumbled and rolled way down the hill. Charlie climbed out and clambered up the snow covered hill and leveled the driver with a punch to the chin. When the police came later one asked Charlie, "Shouldn't you get on some clothes?" Charlie was so angry he was hardly aware that he was out in the cold in only his underclothes!

Charlie had all his teeth pulled. He had to wait for his mouth to heal before getting a set of false teeth. At Storm Lake, Iowa we had to spend the night before loading at a local meat packer plant. We drove out to Christopher Jay's restaurant on Storm Lake for his excellent T-bone steaks. When we turned in our meal tickets for reimbursement the boss said, "I don't see how anyone without teeth can eat a T-bone steak."

Charlie said, "When the boss is paying for it I'll eat it if I have to stomp it tender."

An old fellow, another Charlie, was dispatcher. I got orders to go solo to the Tacoma, Washington docks. After loading I called the office. The boss answered. I said to him, "Do you know what that Charlie did?"

"What?"

'He sent me to the Tacoma dock just for the Halibut." (Say it rather of fast.)

"Didn't you get any fish?"

"Yes, I got the Halibut."

When this little company went out of business I was without a job. I wasn't worried. There were plenty of good paying jobs for the middle class. With most everyone working the government got plenty of taxes. The world was mostly beautiful.

**Casual Driver**

I had quit the Exley Express trucking company and Joe Exley never rehired a former driver. My next job driving to the Midwest lasted a few weeks and went out of business. The word around was that the new trucking division at North Pacific Canners and Packers was *the* driving job to have and they were adding trucks to their fleet. But I was planning a trip with my sons when school was out in 1973 and didn't want to get a good job and ask for a three month leave right away. So I made myself available as a casual driver.

Soon the word was around that a good driver was available for trips as needed. I was soon making trips for Trans-Western, Garrett and others. Even Exley called me for a run now and then. Most of the jobs were for hauling freight which usually was by doubles instead of one trailer.

Doubles consisted then of a tractor and two 26 foot trailers. Doubles were tricky to drive and many times when driving north in a California storm of blowing snow I would drive my Exley semi past doubles grounded by the California Highway patrol since they easily jackknifed on icy roads and tied up traffic.

In my casual work I pulled a trip to Klamath Falls. For the trip back to Portland I was pulling two trailers loaded with freight. The back trailer contained a drop shipment for Madras. As I drove up through Central Oregon I contemplated my problem. When I arrived at the trucking yard just west of Madras I would have to drop the back trailer, drive up and drop the front trailer, then hook up to the back trailer and back it up to the dock.

Backing up a set of doubles is very tricky. A regular driver for a freight company is expected to develop the skill to do so. But for me to back up that rear trailer in a straight line would go against all my instincts of backing up a semi. Every move of that trailer, second back in my side view mirror, would require an opposite move on the steering wheel from my trained habits. But when I arrived at that yard an hour before their opening time I decided to give it a try.

I swung in front of the dock and drove away from it until I was lined up. It didn't stay lined up. As I backed up the trailer immediately jackknifed. I pulled up to get it lined up. Another failure. I pulled up again and this time I was getting dangerously close to the fence. With no more pull up space I used my bare clearance to pull away from the fence, circle the building and start over. I circled that building several times. It was getting close to opening time. I would try once more then

I had better start dropping trailers and do it the amateur way. This time the trailers stayed lined up. I kept a light hold on the steering wheel and the rear trailer bumped solidly against the dock. In a few minutes the crews arrived and unloaded their freight, signed the delivery papers and I was ready to drive over the south edge of Mount Hood and go to Portland. I had successfully backed up a set of doubles for the first and only time.

On a cold day in Roseburg, Oregon I stayed by the heater in the office while a hostler dropped my 2 loaded trailers and hooked up 2 empties for me to take back to Portland. I pulled out of the yard and a little way down the road detected that my rear set of wheels were not turning but sliding on the ice. I couldn't see anything wrong so I assumed that an airline to that set of wheels was frozen so I got a wrench and backed off the spring brake so the wheels could roll but with no brake available on those wheels.

At Portland I told the manager in the office about the trouble. The local hostler was standing by and heard my report. He suddenly hurried out and was soon back. "The hostler in Roseburg hooked the air hoses backward. You didn't have any brakes at all on the two trailers."

I had driven a set of doubles 200 miles on icy slick roads and they had stayed perfectly lined up.

Talk about a steady hand on the steering wheel and a light foot on the brake!

**American Made**

I was leaving the house with the family one Sunday morning when the telephone rang. I turned back and answered it. A Portlander, let's call him Roger, had a small fleet of flatbed semis. I had never heard of him but he learned that I had been driving as a casual driver and I may be available. One of his trucks had been loaded with lumber in Bangor, Washington. The driver brought the load to Portland and quit. Would I take the load to Detroit, Michigan? I would and I was soon on my way. Floods were ravaging upper Michigan and the army wanted that lumber at the Detroit dock as soon as possible.

After getting unloaded I called for a westbound dispatch. I went to Ohio to pick up a large machine at a big cavernous shop. While waiting for it to be loaded I walked out to a back fence. I was looking in the open side of a steel foundry. Men were pouring molten metal in a very hot atmosphere. Big slabs of red hot metal were dragged onto a block or anvil. A huge heavy block was mechanically raised above it then released to come down like a heavy hammer to pound flat the red hot slab. Again and again it slammed down shaking the ground several yards away where I was standing. I was watching industrial America at work before it and its jobs were moved out of the country.

From there I went to a brickyard for 4 pallets of bricks. There I saw a blocks long Kiln where bricks slowly progressed through and came out baked hard.

On the way west I stopped at the Laramie, Wyoming truck stop. A company truck was there. I met the drivers. They were brothers hired to drive as a team. They were 2 small guys and their last name was Green.

Back in Portland the boss's wife came out to the parking lot to get my papers. I told her I had met those Martians they had just hired. "Martians?" she asked.

"Yes, those two little Green men."

I agreed to continue working for Roger. It was a good filler job until school was out and I could take the long vacation trip with my sons.

The second trip was another load of lumber for Detroit. This time I saw posted in a truck stop that a truck was needed to take a load of fabricated steel to Paige, Arizona. The boss said, "Take it." I worked my way west and south and arrived in Flagstaff, Arizona on Friday. The load was to be delivered on Monday. I enjoyed a weekend in Flagstaff. On Sunday I went to meeting.

Early Monday morning I skirted the east end of the Grand Canyon and drove on into Paige, Arizona. I asked what the steel units were for. They were building a big facility to process coal from that area. I told them they were wasting their time. Looking at this rugged red land I said it was obvious that the Indians had strip-mined the area long ago!

After getting unloaded the dispatcher told me to head for Los Angeles. I was to pick up a load of wavy plastic panels in Venice on the coast. From a truck stop in L.A. it was 5pm when I called the plant in Venice. I asked the manager if I could get loaded that day if I could be there at 5:30 pm. He said yes. I took off for the coast looking for every opening in the rush period traffic. I was in every lane, even the left lane, until the traffic peeled off at the next exit. At 5:30 sharp I stopped in front of the office window. I went in and asked, "Are you ready to load me." He said it would be tomorrow morning. "But you said..."

Sheepishly he said, "I didn't think you could do it."

The next morning I watched as a thin liquid was spread over a wavy moving bed. The liquid hardened and cooked into hard plastic. This moving sheet never stopped but as it left the oven a saw cut it into 10 foot or 12 foot or whatever lengths of sheets were on order.

The material was light so the load was piled high and tightly strapped.

After taking the long way home Portland looked mighty good.

## Wolf Creek Pass

I called for a dispatch from the Midwest. My truck was needed in Colorado Springs, Colorado ASAP to pick up a load of iron. The iron was in the form of 4 foot high rolls of wire. The forklifts loaded 2 rolls side by side which just fit the 8 foot wide truck bed. My truck looked as though it was loaded with 2 truck long slinky toys!

I crawled through the center tunnels and secured a cable through each stack. The tie down bands coming across the top I pulled as tight as I could with the ratchet tighteners mounted along the truck bed. The individual rolls were standing up and leaning slightly forward. If they flopped back they would give the truck a hard jolt. I was determined that they never flop.

The load was for Tarzana, California about 10 miles south of San Fernando north of Los Angeles. I headed south. I could go south to Albuquerque, N.M. and use the freeway to Los Angeles. Looking at the map it appeared that going west on Route 160 could cut off a few miles so I turned west. Some miles went by and the road became a gentle climb. This went on and on. Then a sign said so many miles to Wolf Creek Pass.

I had often heard a popular song by C.W. McCall about a wild truck ride over Wolf Creek Pass. Even the song could make a trucker feel fear. Now, what was I, an amateur freight hauler, doing at 10,000 feet on Wolf Creek Pass?

The sign at the top didn't help. It warned truckers to gear down. It said there was 6 or 7 miles of 7% grade followed by miles more of 6% grade. 6% can be a challenge as on California's Grapevine Hill north of L.A. or eastern Oregon's Cabbage Hill. Hot brakes expand and no longer grip the wheel. The trick is to have the right gear, the right speed, and a light pressure on the brakes and they will not get too hot.

I fearfully put the truck in second gear and started crawling down and down. It was reassuring to have the mountain side on my right. But that was about to change. I came to this hairpin curve switchback that put me on the right edge of the road by a fearsome drop-off. A small area of space had a warning sign, "Do not park or stand in this area. Scene of numerous accidents of trucks and other vehicles out of control."

What a relief to arrive at the bottom with the brakes still functional. At Pergosa Springs I pulled in to the lot at the Truck Stop/Restaurant. Another company truck was already there. I joined our veteran driver, Cletus Jones, at a table and ordered a much needed cup of coffee. We discussed the mountain. "If one flew off the road at that switchback it looks to be about a thousand feet before you smash."

"No," he said, "It's 2 thousand feet."

The rest of the way to Tarzana was anti-climactic.

The rolls of wire were unloaded and I learned that I would be reloaded here with their product: burning bar.

A Mexican/American crew was taking what appeared to be lengths of galvanized water pipe and stuffing them with 7 strands of iron wire. With special threads and fittings, pure oxygen was fed through and ignited resulting in a 4000 degree cutting torch that would slice through metal or concrete. The operator wore asbestos clothing and/or worked through a hole in a metal shield. Industrial USA was full of surprising and interesting things to keep us busy and prosperous.

It looked like a load of 3/4 inch galvanized water pipe. It was a load of Burning Bar in bundles of 25. It was to be dropped off at 8 destinations from coast to coast. The appropriate bundles had to be dropped off at each place or the customer's equipment wouldn't work with the threads on the pipe. My first drop was to correct just such a mistake. I was to trade 2 right bundles for the 2 wrong ones that had been left. This first drop was in central Illinois where I was born in 1925. General Motors had a plant east of Bloomington and used burning bar to slice up rejected auto bodies. My next drop was in Tennessee below Nashville. This gave me the only opportunity to cross Kentucky in my whole career of trucking.

Next to the Science Hill where I attended grades 4 through 8 was the Martin family home. Hannah Mae was a schoolmate. Her older brother, Clyde later married Dad's sister Stella after she was widowed in Illinois. After Hannah Mae, Clyde, and Lora Clay grew up and the family scattered, the house was acquired by our local Lawyer, Walter Kyle. He moved the house toward town near the bottom of Big Hill and built himself a brick home on the vacated lot. Mom acquired the home on Big Hill and was living there when I drove the truck to Kentucky.

In Oregon I was a subscriber of The Green River Republican and was aware of a rivalry between the Morgantown police and truckers. They caught every overloaded truck they could. I arrived in Morgantown at 2:00 a.m. I drove slowly through town until I attracted the attention of a deputy. I identified myself as a local boy intending to visit my mother. "Where can I drop this loaded trailer for a few hours?" He obligingly directed me to the fairgrounds. I dropped the trailer and drove the tractor (it's called bobtailing) to Mom's house on Logansport Road. I left the headlights shining on her living room window as I awakened her by knocking persistently.

She looked at me and the front end of the semi in astonishment. "How did you get that truck in the yard? Jerry (my cousin) tried to get his truck in here for over an hour and gave up." A left turn into that grassy driveway from such a narrow roadway would pull the rear wheels of the trailer right into the deep ditch at the end of the culvert. But I didn't bring my trailer with me.

We visited. I had been on the road for over 2 weeks. She washed my clothes while I slept a while. She fed me a home cooked breakfast and saw me off to my next stop south of Nashville. That part of the trip was uneventful but when I got in sight of my next drop in Radford, Virginia I saw pickets patrolling the gate. I went into a neighboring business. They offered to unload the burning bar order and have it there for their neighbor.

Between there and the next delivery at Charleston, West Virginia I negotiated some of the crookest roads I have ever seen. I had to start on the wrong side of the road to get the trailer around some hairpin switchbacks. No one was around when I arrived at the yard in Charleston. I cut the wire holding their bundle and one by one I shoved the hefty pipes through the fence onto the ground beyond the gate. I rolled up the paper work and left it in the gate by the lock and headed north.

Next, I unloaded an order in Northeast, Pennsylvania. The name of the town is misleading. In extreme northwestern Pennsylvania is a small panhandle. In the northeastern corner of this panhandle is the town of Northeast on Lake Erie. It was after dark when I left Northeast in northwest Pennsylvania. The next day I was to make my last 3 deliveries. I would go east a ways and stop for the night.

I didn't get far. The clutch quit working. Using the accelerator to synch the RPM of the engine with the speed I shifted the gears without the clutch. Rain was pouring down and I was ready to call it a day. I saw a truck stop and found my way to a parking spot in the downpour. Just as I stopped all the lights went out on the truck. The clutch cable was broken and as I stopped it fell across the battery wires and burned out all the truck's wiring.

I would not be completing my eastbound trip tomorrow (Friday). The truck would be in the shop all day. I opted to spend the weekend in Albany and unload east to west on Monday. On that rainy Friday night I drove the repaired truck to Albany and rented a room for the weekend.

The highlight of my weekend was dining at the nearby restaurant. It had a primitive name, The Cranberry Bog. Dining in the rather dimly lighted low ceilinged room and served by waiters in page boy outfits I felt like I was in

Medieval England. I ordered the *duck a L'Orange*. It was cooked to perfection and served with elegance. I had never tasted anything better.

While working at Ilse's Hollywood portrait studio in Portland. Oregon, Stanley Kubrick's movie *2001: A Space Odyssey* was playing next door in the Hollywood Theatre. I saw the movie several times. It is a great show. In Albany, New York Kubrick's latest movie was showing. I went to see Clockwork Orange and wished I hadn't!

On Monday morning I drove to the address of my Albany delivery. It was in a cul-de-sac in a residential neighborhood. The Burning Bar dealer was selling these pipes out of his garage! Curtains fluttered as I maneuvered the semi to back into his driveway. I was careful not to touch a single lawn. Nearly half the load was for here and my 2 other drops of 2 bundles each were on top of 2 4x4s on top of the load. There was no forklift so the dealer and I cut the wires on each bundle and carried the bars into his garage one at a time. We got the right side of the trailer unloaded and he had to get breakfast for his 2 children and take them to school. I told him to get me his handsaw. While he was gone I sawed off the 4x4s that extended over the empty right side of the trailer. The exposed side of the lower load sagged a little. With a little nudging the remaining halves of the 4x4s tilted and the 4 heavy top bundles rolled off and stopped neatly on the right half of the trailer. When the dad came out to drive his kids to school he stopped in astonishment. "How in the world did you do that?"

I had to engage in a little tomfoolery so I told him. "We Romans learned a lot about engineering when we helped the Egyptians build the pyramids."

Next I went to Oswego on the shore of Lake Ontario. After unloading I drove down to Interstate 90 and headed west. It was getting late. I would have to unload in Buffalo on the shore of Lake Erie on Tuesday.

After dropping my last two bundles in Buffalo, New York, I was ready to call for a dispatch and hoped it would be for home. I had been on the road for over 3 weeks.

From Buffalo, New York I called Portland for my dispatch. It was for a Portland load. I was going home at last! I was to pick up two log skidders at St. Thomas, Ontario, Canada. First I had to get my truck into Canada. I caught a taxi and crossed into Canada as a tourist would who wanted to view Niagara Falls from the Canadian side. At the Port of Entry I purchased a permit, a temporary license to drive a truck in Canada. The taxi took me back to my truck in Buffalo.

Now I entered Canada legally. The permit saved me from an arrest and fine. I proceeded along the north side of Lake Erie to St. Thomas about halfway to Detroit. There the two big log skidders were loaded on my flatbed trailer.

I crossed the bridge into Detroit to enter the United States. It was dark when I arrived at the first toll booth west of town. If my load was a wide load and extended even one inch wider than the trailer I would have to park at night and drive in the daylight only. But the log skidders were exactly eight feet wide, the same as the trailer. As the lady at the toll booth took my money she kept glancing at the big tires on the log skidders. They looked like they should bulge wider than the trailer. But did they? Finally as she handed me my receipt she asked, "Is that a legal load?" I laughed and assured her that it was and headed west.

I had one more hurdle before getting home. In eastern Oregon at La Grande the state police had a training school. The numerous patrolmen liked to practice on trucks. So one of them stopped me and inspected the rig to see what violation he could find.

My paperwork was in order, the brakes were in good adjustment, all lights worked, but I got a ticket for "inadequate fire extinguisher." The needle on the pressure gauge was barely in the red zone. When I got to the delivery yard on 82nd Avenue in Portland I asked for a Xerox copy of the import papers. I sent a copy to the judge in La Grande and wrote, "It is not true that I had 'inadequate fire extinguisher.' As you can see from the import paper, 2 fire extinguishers were included. As stated, they were in the step well of each log skidder easily accessible if needed."

I got my ten dollars back by mail!

My freight hauling days were over. It had been fun and a good experience but now school was out and I was ready to make the 11 week tour of the country with my 8 and 10 year old boys. When that trip was over I would seek a job hauling my favorite load — food.

## 1973 USA Trip

The Toyota was small and economical. I could almost reach the back window from the driver's seat. Ten year old Henry Kent and eight year old Vincent Kendall took turns riding in the front seat. We headed east for Kentucky to visit their Grandma Romans.

Soon we left for New York City. A three day Watchtower Convention was scheduled for Yankee Stadium. It was a good opportunity to see the stadium before the extensive remodeling would soon change the old historic Yankee ball park. The boys' sister, Charla Kay, had been baptized in the ocean when we attended the 1958 convention here. The boys and I stayed with a family, the Johnsons, in Queens and volunteered to provide the ride to the stadium each day for 2 German delegates, Johann Frank and his English speaking niece, Honee Fiedler. One morning I had Vince to meet them as they came out of their lodging and say, "Guten Morgen." At first Johann returned the Good Morning greeting, then he realized that Vince had greeted him in German; he grabbed him up in a big bear hug and exclaimed, "Oh! Sprechen die deutsch!"

We continued to chauffeur them as they stayed an extra day for sightseeing on Monday. They asked about our beer. I asked a local business man where I could find a good bar for them. My 2 underage boys and I visited a nearby park while they tried American beer and declared it to be way too weak compared to their German beer! On Tuesday I rode along as Ernest Johnson used the family Lincoln to drive them to the airport. While Ernest went in to check on their flight I turned to our guests in the back seat and on my fingers on top of the seat back I counted to four as we did in an old army marching song, "Eins, Zwei, Drei, Vier."

As I had secretly arranged with Honee, she asked, in German, "Can't you count higher than that?"

"Ja." With my hand against the ceiling I again counted on my fingers, "Eins, Zwei, Drei, Vier." Johann liked our joke.

I had the Toyota serviced and late that day we left New York. By driving all night we could be in Louisville for breakfast. After daybreak we were just east of Louisville. I called my sister Velma for directions. She and her husband, Clifford, owned 40 acres just south of the Jefferson County border in Bullitt County. She told me, "Hurry on out and after breakfast you can stack bales of hay for Cliff." I said I had been awake for 24 hours but let me sleep an hour and I would stack bales all day if needed.

Clifford drove the tractor and as the bales of hay came out the back of the bailer onto the front of the flatbed wagon I would stack them until they were higher than my head. Velma came out and stopped Cliff. "A 100 pound bale would be easy for Charles but he is struggling. You had better check those bales." Sure enough they were about 150 pounds each. Since they sold them as 100 pounds of hay they would be giving away 50 pounds of hay. Clifford adjusted the machine and I had an easy job after that.

Down state in Morgantown we spent another month catching up on family history and renewing old acquaintances. My close cousin, Robert Dotson from Illinois, now lived in Ville Platte, Louisiana. Bobby and Marianna's would be the next major stop on our tour. So I donned my pith helmet and hit the road. Pith helmets were common in Butler County when I was growing up there on the farm. In Portland I wore one when not wearing my bus driver's uniform. They were not uncommon in Portland since the Oregon mail carriers wore blue ones as part of their uniform.

In 1963 Bobby was living in Oxford, Mississippi. He and Marianna drove to California to attend an event in Pasadena. I took my family there from Portland. Bobby was sitting high up on the south side of the Rose Bowl when I walked in with my family, Nell Roy, 14 year old Charla Kay and 11 week old Henry. We found seats high up on the north side. The pith helmet helped in the California sun. Bobby nudged Marianna. He couldn't recognize faces at such a distance but he said, "The one in that hat couldn't be anyone but my cousin Charles Romans." Soon I was surprised to find them sitting behind us.

We spent the following afternoons and evenings at the Rose Bowl and every morning watching the weather. I wanted to rent a plane and fly over to Catalina Island but the morning fog just wouldn't burn off until it was too late.

Now, in 1973, I was going to see Bobby again. We went straight south to the panhandle of Florida before heading west. We arrived in Ville Platte about 11:00pm. No lights were on in Bobby's house. The boys were asleep in the car so I rolled the sleeping bag out on the lawn and went to sleep. The next morning I slipped on my shoes and knocked on the door. I said to Bobby, "Is this a good place to get some breakfast?"

"Well, yes. But I don't think I know who you are." Wow! He had recognized me all the way across the Rose Bowl. But here I had left my hat in the car!

Mom had said that cousin, Norma from Indianapolis, was living in Houston, Texas. I called her as we approached and she gave me directions to her home in Katy a west Houston suburb. She had married the Air Corp captain and he, also, had left the service in 1945. He became a well-known artist in Houston but he was married to his work so they had become divorced. Their 2 children were grown and Norma's daughter had given her her first grandchild. I met Norma's daughter later but now she was meeting my boys, who were 2 of her forth cousins. Norma told me that her brother, Ron was raising his family in Minneapolis. Mom sure did keep up with family. I got a weekly letter from her while I lived in Oregon.

On our next stop in Pampa, Texas my boys met Molly McGee, my dear friend from Air Corp days. They took to each other immediately. Molly was delighted to meet the two sons of her old friend, Nell Roy, who had been the playmate of her daughter, Doris, when they were growing up in Pampa.

By touching base with Bobby, Norma and Molly I was strengthening threads that had been weaving through the fabric of my life for decades and would be prominent during the next decade.

We had one last memorable event. In Arizona I bought children's admission tickets to the massive crater formed by a meteorite striking the earth. To conserve our dwindling cash I waited for them in the car.

The boys were getting excited about seeing their mother again. Although I had them talk to her on the phone almost every day, in Kentucky Vince had said on the phone, "Momma, I'm forgetting what you look like." So now, except for restaurant and rest area stops we saw the rest of the cross country trip through the windows of our moving car. Now the boys had a great experience in their memory and I felt refreshed and ready for my best and last trucking job.

### North Pacific Canners and Packers (FLAV-R-PAC foods)

Mr. Ragner (Hokie) Hokanson managed the trucking division for NORPAC. He owned the trucks and leased them to NORPAC. He looked over my application. "H-m-m. No accidents and no tickets. That's the kind of drivers we like to hire. I am adding another truck soon but it is promised to a friend in Texas. You can have the next one after that."

While I was waiting for the job I was home alone one day when I got a call from a dear friend. When we moved to Oregon in 1945, Burl and Jane Borden and daughter Joan moved there from Arizona. We were almost next door for a while. They became good friends of my in-laws, Roy and Effie White and I was just sort of around. Burl was a really nice guy and I liked having him around as a casual friend. I observed Jane's industrious ways and Christian devotion. When their daughter, Melinda Lou was born in 1950, Nell Roy and I visited her at the hospital and I signed one day old Melinda's guest book. Later they moved back to Phoenix. Now 24 years later I get a call. Jane is on a brief vacation in Oregon and calling old friends. She was now a widow. I told her of my prospective trucking job and got her phone number in case I ever trucked through Phoenix.

A few days later Hokie called me, "My friend went skating with his kids and broke his ankle. So the first new job is yours." A senior driver gets the new truck and the new driver gets the hand me down. That's how I started out on NORPAC truck number 3. It was a Freightliner with a 350 HP Caterpillar diesel engine that wouldn't get over 45 MPH when bucking a headwind. I was as excited as a kid with a new toy as I made a 5000 mile round trip to the Midwest every 2 weeks. On a rare exception I would get a trip to Texas, Arizona or California.

### Going Home

I was always going home. Every other Friday I would leave Portland for a 5000 mile trip. Going east I was on my way home in the Midwest. I often saw cousins in Illinois, Indiana, Ohio, Michigan and Wisconsin. In

Armington, Illinois I once stopped and got a haircut by Bob Mobley who had given me my first haircut over a half century earlier. Only Kentucky was left out, much to the irritation of my sisters. NorPac had an enormous customer base. Seldom did I go to the same city or company two trips in a row. The return trip going home to my Portland family was almost as varied. The Ness Company on Swan Island received products for several Portland Stores. The product was mostly meat and cheese. We unloaded at their warehouse; their trucks delivered the orders to the stores. Wisconsin is one big cheese factory dominated by Green Bay. Many of my dispatches said to load in Green Bay. I would spend the night in the Union Truck Stop in Oshkosh, freshen up, have breakfast and call in before proceeding to my Green Bay appointment. Many times I would call the dispatcher and announce, "This is Charlie in Oshkosh."

Another frequent pickup was at the Land-O-Frost freezer in Calumet City just south of Chicago. When they moved their operation to Searcy,

Arkansas, Hokie said he hoped I wouldn't be too disappointed to be going

to Arkansas instead of visiting my Illinois cousins. I said, "Mom will tell me who to see in Arkansas." It proved to be Aunt Mamie, Uncle Ollie Andrew's ex-wife who lived about 30 miles north of Searcy! Her son, my cousin Ollie Newman, was a chief deputy with the Little Rock Police and frequently flew to distant places to bring back prisoners.

Besides the joy of trucking to my Midwest home territory I delighted in living the history of the Oregon Trail. I sometimes bought a buffalo steak in Portland and stashed it in the trailer with my frozen load. In Wyoming I would find a wide siding along the road to park the truck. I would set up my grass-hopper, a 3 legged propane stove, and soon have buffalo meat pan broiling while watching the antelope graze beyond the roadside fence and think of Buffalo Bill whose museum lay up ahead, and remember that, as a small boy in Armington, Illinois, I had known old lady Allen who had been one of Bill Cody's young girlfriends.

## Blizzard

The blizzard was fierce as I left Montana. I stopped at the all night truck stop in Beach, North Dakota. I ate a hot meal, topped off the two 150 gallon diesel tanks after putting 3 cans of Heet in each tank to keep the diesel from freezing. Someone said it was 60 below zero that night.

With food, fuel and a snug truck I headed east in the blowing snow and bitter wind. Miles later I was climbing a long grade and watching my gauges when I detected the fuel indicator going down. Was the cold affecting the reading or was I losing vital fuel? The truck struggled to the top of the grade. Not until the road levelled did I pull over and park. I put on a down-filled jacket over my down-filled vest. Over that I put on a long wool overcoat. Flaps came down over my ears from the fleece lined cap and a fiber face mask and heavy mittens completed my 'space suit' for that unfriendly and dangerous wind howling outside my driver's door.

A crossover between the fuel tanks had crystalized in the cold and had broken off at the right fuel tank. No shut-off valves had been installed on these tanks on old #3! Back in the truck I whittled the wooden handle of my window scraper to a point. Climbing down again I jammed that stopper into the leak on the right tank. Without the crossover that was the only fuel I could use.

Why not save the other fuel also? I whittled another peg. The end of the flexible hose needed a clamp which I had but I couldn't handle the screwdriver to tighten it. I took my right mitten off and got the job done. My right hand was getting numb fast. I tried to hurry back into the truck but the metal handle felt like a hot stove. I had to struggle the mitten on to handle it.

At Bismarck I parked until the shop opened the next morning. I had the crossover replaced and shut-off valves installed on both tanks. Now number 3 was a little more modern.

I was never afraid of the weather. Someone said, "One's confidence should never exceed their competence." My many winters and years of operating machinery and vehicles had developed considerable competence so I guess my confidence was not misplaced.

The Midwest was my home, my playground, my stomping ground. Born about 100 miles southwest of Chicago, the second half of my childhood was spent in western Kentucky. I literally had cousins by the dozens. At Morgantown, Kentucky, Mom sat in her rocking chair and sent her missiles everywhere by USPS. So it was that I was directed to Cousin Andrea James in Gary, Indiana. Aunt Irene's daughter Andrea was married to Doc James and they operated a used car lot just off I-80. On this one visit I was unloaded and on my way to Michigan. Late after dinner we watched on TV as a powerful storm moved across Lake Michigan. It was a modest and comfortable living room. Across the room from Andrea's chair was a trash can sporting a picture of Elvis Presley. Across from Doc's plush chair was a can with Dolly Parton's picture.

As the storm reached the halfway point crossing the lake I stood up, "Well I have just time to get to the truck stop named Famous. After the storm passes,

I'll be there to pick up my load in the morning."

My timing was right on. My truck was the last vehicle to go up that exit ramp before the storm closed it. I turned left, crossed the overpass and parked in the truck stop. I awoke to the sound of snowplows clearing the roads of a huge snowfall that blanketed the area. No coffee was available; the truck stop management had sent all employees home and left a yard full of truckers to fend for themselves. The interstate north and south was being cleared but the local road eastward was heavy with the new snow that inevitably dragged my empty semi to a stop. After a while the snow plow came down this road, swinging over to pass a few feet to my left, piling snow against the side of my truck to the level of my driver's window. The snow plow driver worked his way back to my side of the road several yards ahead leaving an impassable barrier between me and the cleared road ahead.

The radio was reporting about people helping people just as the young couple in the nearby farmhouse and the older couple near my destination warehouse, would be helping me. I climbed over the doghouse and exited the truck on the right side. I waded through the deep snow to the farmhouse and asked the young couple if I could borrow a scoop shovel. They were happy to lend me one and graciously offered for me to share meals with them.

The rest of Friday and most of Saturday I was shoveling snow, clearing a path 8 feet wide and 6 feet deep. Late Saturday I returned the shovel and drove out of my trap. About a mile down the road I settled down for the long wait at the dock where I would be loading on Monday. Soon the middle aged couple from across the road knocked on my door. They had an empty nest. Their only daughter had married last summer and the empty bedroom reminded them of their loss. Would I use their extra room until Monday morning? Michigan hospitality was making my enforced layover a happy one.

On Monday my trailer was loaded with 55 gallon barrels filled with Michigan cherries. Each barrel was on a wheeled platform. I rolled the little pallet in, gripped the far side of the top, jumped up on the side and threw my weight to tip the barrel off of its carrier, then rolled it on its bottom rim and let it fall into its place. I delivered them to North Pacific Canners in time to leave on my next trip. It was the only time I ever got home too late to spend 3 or 4 days with my family.

Hokie said one time he listened to the weather report and became worried for his trucks back east. Then he reminded himself, "I have hired the most professional bunch of drivers I know. I'm sure they can handle any situation." Then he slept well.

My boys had been seeing westerns on TV. Sometime a western show showed bones bleaching along the trail. Once I told of seeing a semi upended in the median about every 10 miles between Chicago and Detroit, Vince asked, "With bones in them?"

**Me and Reser's**

When Reser's started selling potato salad out of their new plant in Beaverton, Oregon just west of Portland they had 2 delivery trucks and 2 drivers who were friends of mine. One was Paul Hammon a former school teacher and father of Charles who once dated my daughter.

Selling Grandma Reser's potato salad, the business grew and grew and became the 7th largest company in Oregon, hiring thousands.

After unloading in Cleveland, Ohio and calling for my return dispatch. I was to pick up 5 tons of mayonnaise there in Cleveland for Reser's. That would be one fourth of my load and the rest would be meat from a packing house in the old stockyards section of Chicago.

It was late in the day when I headed west for Chicago. It would be good to get there before the next morning rush period. But I had trouble making good time. The roads had icy spots and a fierce head wind was buffeting the truck. Having 10,000 pounds of weight in the front of the trailer while empty on the back wheels made the vehicle unstable. Every time I exceeded 40 MPH the trailer would fishtail. I had to stay on high alert to stay between the ditches.

It was about 3 AM when I turned off of I-80 on to I-94 and headed north toward downtown Chicago. I had to go to 39th street which was called Pershing after the WWI General. There I would go west to the old stockyards area which was now dominated by meat packing plants.

To my surprise this highway of many lanes had lots of traffic. Apparently many were going to work early, perhaps because of the weather.

Soon I came upon one of the strangest traffic scenes I have ever seen. Perhaps the open slope tilting slightly toward the north had a little colder temperature and had become coated with black ice. The street lights bathed the scene in an eerie yellow glow glistening off the icy road. Cars breezed by me and when a driver saw the mess ahead he would hit the brakes and spin out of control and slam into the stacks of snow in the median or the shoulder or into each other. It was an impromptu Destruction Derby. I had chosen a lane and stayed with it at a slow steady pace keeping my wheels turning to maintain traction. Up ahead a car spun around a few times and came to a stop squarely across my lane. I wasn't about to touch my brakes. I drifted steadily at him. He got his car in gear and backed out of my lane just in time.

At Pershing I went up the Exit ramp and turned left finding hardly any traffic here. In a short way I came to a Rail Road overpass. The sign on it said clearance was 13 feet and my trailer was the standard 13' 6" high. We veterans of the Chicago scene knew that at this overpass the road was lower on the eastbound side. So I moved over, went under then back to my side. Up ahead I knew there was a 24 hour restaurant for truckers. I could hardly wait. The snow plows had cleared much of the street. Across the intersection was a space along the curb just right for my truck. It was paying off to come here early. I secured the cab, left the diesel running to keep the engine and the cab warm and climbed down from my seat. In mincing steps to keep my feet under me on the icy street I made it to the restaurant. I sat on a stool at the counter and ordered a cup of coffee.

That was the wildest cup of coffee I have ever seen. It bucked and shook and was about to splash the coffee out of the cup. I set it back down. I grabbed onto it with both hands and with trembling arms and shaking hands I brought it up to my mouth. Soon the strain and tension of the last few hours was draining from my body and fatigue was taking over. I ate a plate of ham and eggs and soon parked at the packing plant and got some well-deserved sleep.

Those other 30,000 pounds of weight would stabilize my load so the other 2500 miles to Oregon were routine. I unloaded at the Ness warehouse on Swan Island in North Portland and their local driver took the mayonnaise to Reser's.

When I moved to Morgantown in 1997 I found Reser's potato salad at Save-A-Lot. It is funny (strange, that is) how one's past catches up with you even in Butler County! So during the present you had better build a good past!

That good potato salad still causes me a weight problem. If I eat it too often my belts get too short. So I don't indulge too often. But there is a limit and soon I go get another 2 pound plastic tub of Reser's potato salad. I never sit down to a heapin' helpin' without thinking about that cold day in Chicago.

## A Cup of Coffee

The English enjoy their tea but Americans, along with millions all over the world, choose coffee as their favorite beverage and lift one to a dozen cups of coffee every day. Coffee is the second most traded commodity in the world, topped only by petroleum.

The Starbucks crew at the Bowling Green coffee house were fascinated when I used a gift card from their mother store in Seattle. It was a gift from my good friends, Ross and Susan Retter who can enjoy their morning coffee looking out over the Pacific where they can see whales and ships go by.

For my morning cup of coffee I can choose a cup picturing me standing by the Stearman bi-plane in 1944. One pictures me on top of Steen's Mountain with Wild Horse Lake in the background. It was a gift from the Steens Mountain High Altitude Running Camp where I drove the bus for ten years. One shows a lad in Knickerbocker knee pants like Mom used to dress me for Sunday school in the 1930s. The boy is looking at 3D pictures in a stereoscope like Mom's. I got the cup from Jerry Dene. Like me, Jerry deals in old stereoscopes and stereoviews. He is a friend of mine and of Mr. Giles, our local postmaster. Jerry now lives in Columbia, Kentucky. From his wheel chair Jerry restores old stereoscopes to their original beauty and luster and sells them on eBay. Jerry's talent has preserved the beauty and luster of the 1890s for lots of homes.

When I add the cream and sugar into my morning cup of coffee a tea spoon stirs the coffee and the cups stir old memories. Oh! Why do we have to stir the *coffee* with a *tea* spoon?

My favorite cup is the one I purchased at the gift shop of the Dixie Truck Stop at McLean, Illinois. I was born just 10 miles from there and was three years old when it was built. Now, 90 years later we are both still going strong!

When you see a semi going down the road in a shaky manner it is probably due to the loose nut on the steering wheel. In the parlance of the open road, the loose nut on the steering wheel is the driver. The best grease to smooth out the performance of that nut is a cup of coffee. The coffee can calm the tension of driving on an icy road. A good cup of hot coffee can perk one up from the drowsiness of many monotonous miles.

When I pulled in to the Union 76 Truck Stop at Calumet City just south of Chicago, I was just plain tired. The lot was nearly full but I found a slot and backed the Freightliner and trailer in and secured the cab.

This restaurant was popular with tourist and locals as well as truckers and when I entered the huge dining room it was packed. I finally found a seat in the window farthest from the kitchen. Then I waited for a waitress. I waited and waited and waited. So I decided to use my head. I set my coffee cup on top of my head!

The manager, who was catty-cornered across the room by the kitchen, soon spotted that crazy guy sitting over there with a coffee cup on top of his head. He pointed and loud enough for every waitress (and everyone else) to hear, said, "Give that man a cup of coffee!"

The crowd got a laugh and I got my cup of coffee!

## Train to Chicago

One of my favorite jokes is a railroad story. I had a chance to tell it over the radio in Michigan. I was trucking empty out of Ohio to get a load in Detroit. As I approached the state border a sign on a fencepost told the number for KZOO the radio station up ahead in Kalamazoo, so I dialed it in. A talk show host said, "Let's not be serious today. Let us tell stories and jokes."

So a grandmother came on and told something about a grandchild. A preacher told his funny experience. I thought, "If I can get to a phone in time I'll tell them a funny one." I soon found a mall and parked near a Sears' store. In the entrance was a pay phone. The operator put me on standby. Soon the MC clicked me on the air.

"So you are a trucker?"

"Yes. But this is a train story." So I proceeded to tell it.

This business man in New York needed to go to Detroit for a business meeting. He judged that the best way to be there the next morning was to take the night train for Chicago and get off in Detroit in the middle of the night. He instructed the porter that he would get some sleep and the porter *must* awaken him in Detroit and get him off the train. He emphasized how important it was and for him to use whatever means, just get him off. "I'd better not wake up in Chicago."

Well, he did wake up in Chicago. He was enraged. He cornered the porter and really told him off. He called him every name he could think of. The Porter meekly said nothing. The man finally ran out of vocabulary and went off to make other arrangements.

Another porter heard all this and came over, "Man you take that kind of talk and say nothing. What's the matter with you anyway? Don't you have no gumption?"

"Shucks man. That wasn't nothin'. You should've heard that man that I put off in Detroit last night."

I got back in the truck. Someone was talking. When he got through the MC started laughing. He said, "I'm still putting that man off in Detroit!"

Train travel had been a part of my life. I am glad I lived it. I became a lifelong railroad fan. I was aware of the competition between trucks and trains so I couldn't miss the opportunity for some kidding. I had parked the truck and gone to Sunday meeting with my cousins. The speaker was a black brother from Bloomington whose secular job was with the railroad. We retired to my cousin Ralph Price's home for dinner. As the table was being set I sidled up to the speaker and said, "There is likely some prejudice between you and me." That got everyone's attention.

Surprised, he asked, "Why is that?"

"You being a railroad man and me being a trucker."

Part way through the meal there came a lull in the conversation. He said, "You have to admit that the railroad can haul it cheaper"

"Yeah, if it ever gets there."

Ralph interjected, "There they go," as everyone laughed.

## Dubuque, Iowa Hams and Oregon Strawberries

My dispatch: Pick up a load of meat, including 20 boxes of hams, at the Dubuque Meat Packing Company in Dubuque, a town in northeast Iowa on the west side of the Mississippi River. I had to deliver the hams in Seattle before going home to Portland. In Seattle, when I stacked the 20 boxes on the pallet there were still more hams, 12 more boxes! I called 'Hokie' Hokanson in Portland, Oregon. He made some calls. The hams should have been on a Willy Shaw truck and delivered to a different dock in Seattle. I delivered the 12 cases doing Willy Shaw and the Dubuque Meat Company a favor before going home.

Hokie said we could have had a lot of free ham to eat. I said, "That's true but we don't do business that way." He knew I would say that. He was a strait laced Swede and a good man to work for.

A month later I had a load to deliver to the cafeteria of the Indiana University south of Indianapolis. Six 5 gallon tins of frozen strawberries had dented lids and were turned down by the dock boss. I bought some big black leaf bags and put a can in each one. I called in my report and, again I was dispatched to the Dubuque Meat packing Company.

That Dubuque Company is run like a military unit. You are not allowed to drive on their property. You park in a lot across the street, drop your trailer and one of their tractors hooks to it and takes it to their wash rack then to the dock for loading. After loading it is dropped on your side of the road again but before you hook up you walk across the street and up an outside stairs clinging to the brick wall of the fortress to a tiny landing on the second floor or rather, on the side of the wall at the second floor and reach through a 2 foot sized opening to sign the papers. Then with your copy in hand you can hook up your trailer and head west.

But on this trip their truck driver came over and told me to call the office. The telephone was a phone booth on the street with a pay phone. I made the call. A stern voice informed me that all trucks were to come in here empty and 6 tins of frozen strawberries were found in my trailer. I explained about the refused merchandise that I had to take back with me. I said the plastic bags would protect them and they would not be harmed by their washing the trailer. He said, "We have a lot of thieves around here and we can't be responsible if some of them go missing."

It was my time to be firm. "Listen! A month ago I arrived in Seattle and, by mistake, you had put 12 cases of hams on my truck. I delivered them for you at our expense. When I get to Portland and find that even one can of strawberries is missing, you had better not ever *ever* again put an extra box of hams on my truck by mistake." With that I slammed down the receiver!

When I got to Portland all six tins of strawberries were undisturbed!

## Guns

What is all this fuss of wanting access to assault rifles? Do those who want that kind of gun think their home will be attacked by a whole pack of criminals? Do they think there is a legitimate need for a gun that throws out bullets like a water hose wetting down the side of the barn. I grew up on Dad's 60 acres in Butler County, Kentucky using a Stevens Favorite single shot .22 caliber rifle. I never once failed to get my game with the one shot. I hunted squirrels, rabbits and birds. In the Air Corp I won the 'Expert' wreath and tags for Rifle, Pistol and Carbine.

While trucking for Flavor Pac Foods the freight haulers called a strike which did not involve our food haulers Teamsters Local 81. But things were getting a little tense on the road. The boss warned us to be cautious. He was worried for us.

Joe Haines had a load for Texas and on the way he parked out back of a truck stop and prepared to go in and eat. A car load of strikers saw him park and drove over by his truck. They told him to shut down and stay parked. "I can't do that," he told them. "It's not my strike."

"Well if that door wasn't locked we would pull you out of that truck and teach you a lesson."

"The door is not locked."

They piled out of the car and went up to Joe's door. One of them grabbed the handle. Sure enough, Joe didn't have it locked. The striker yanked the door open and they were staring into the barrel of Joe's six shooter!

They threw up their hands and said, "No! No! Don't shoot! We don't want any trouble." They piled in the car and sped away.

I was up in Montana when I stopped for a break. I parked way back in the lot but I had been seen and here came 4 men in front of that long line of trucks, striding purposefully my way. I climbed down from my seat to meet them.

I explained that if this was a food hauler's strike I would not have left the company yard. Now I have 40,000 pounds of perishable food and it is my Christian responsibility to take care of the boss's interest and not waste this food. I quoted scriptures to prove my point. They left shaking their heads.

Part way to the restaurant one of them turned back. "You make me ashamed of myself. I used to be a practicing Christian. But I have neglected that for a while. You handled that real well a while ago" I thanked him and we shook hands. It was time to eat and head for Chicago.

No gun needed.

### The Spokane World's Fair

For two years I tried to make full time photography my career. It wasn't working. Portland would not pay enough for good photography to make it pay well.

I was missing the feel of the steering wheel so I went trucking.

Five years later things changed; greater appreciation for art was growing in the Northwest.

I was rolling west with a loaded semi when I stopped at a truck stop in Montana and found my cousin, Homer Price, from Armington, Illinois. He owned his own truck and he too had a load for the west coast. Sometimes this large United States is part of a small world! We rolled west together until we got to Spokane, Washington on Saturday evening. We slept in a truck stop. Sunday morning we had breakfast and then dressed up for a Sunday morning meeting.

Charles Romans & Homer Price
In Spokane, Washington

That afternoon we spent at the 1974 Spokane World's Fair. Spokane is the smallest city ever to host a World's Fair but over the 6 months 5 million visitors came. The theme was the environment and to many of us it seemed that it was a turning point, the time when the Northwest awakened to the beauty of art and the beauty in our environment. We had lunch at the German restaurant where I enjoyed, for the first time, Beef Stroganoff. It became one of my favorite dinners.

We left that evening with plenty of time to deliver our loads on Monday morning.

Some months later I stopped in at the Gresham studio for a visit. Dee told me, "Charlie, when you were here and a local factory owner came in and wanted a machine photographed we would bid $30.00 and hoped to get the job for we needed the money. Now if a job like that comes in I say,'$300' and hope he will go away but he says to do it."

I was happy for Dee but I was still enjoying the open road.

## A Big Bouquet of Roses

Roy and Effie White's daughter, Nell Roy, became my wife on July 7, 1945. She had just completed a course in a business college in Oklahoma City. She found good opportunities to practice her new skills after we moved to Portland, Oregon that winter.

Her first job in Portland was with the Loose-Wiles Biscuit Company, later named Sunshine Biscuits. Not a lot later she got a chance to move to a better job at the Paget Mortgage Company. She enjoyed being downtown. During her noon hour she would eat her sandwich then walk off the calories while window shopping. She often found and bought stylish clothes. She was 'a real dresser.' She never did become overweight. A new job opened up for Nell Roy.

A local man perfected the Code-A-Phone. Wealthy Mr. Ford of the Roseburg Lumber Company bought his patent and built a factory in Portland. The inventor worked for him in the development department. Nell Roy was hired as a bookkeeper in the office. The company was called Ford Industries. The company prospered.

Nell Roy was a payroll specialist. She would go throughout the factory to deal with foremen in the various departments. She became well known by all the employees. So one day when she was in the factory on business she was paged to return to the office pronto. Everyone was curious about this strange event. Well, it was caused by me!

A former city bus driver I knew had opened a flower shop on Hawthorne Boulevard. Our 25th wedding anniversary was coming up. I was going to be on the road trucking. I made a deal with my florist friend to deliver a bouquet of 25 roses to Nell Roy in her office. The delivery man arrived while she was down on the factory floor.

The word about the roses spread through the company like wildfire. "What a day!" she said to me later. All the rest of the day a steady stream of employees came through the office to count the roses. To see someone who had been married 25 years amazed them.

That was already becoming a rare thing in the modern world.

Later her day of retirement became a big event for the company.

**Retirement:     Congratulations from Code-a-phone president**

## Star Wars

Coming home was an event that happened every two weeks when I trucked for North Pacific Canners and Packers. I would leave Portland every other Friday and make a 5000 mile trip. After ten days my song could have been, "Ten days on the road and I'm going to make it home tonight!"

Seldom did I go to the same place twice. Every trip was an adventure so while I was home for four days I tried to make the time interesting for the family. One trip back east I had a free evening so I went to a movie. *Charlotte's Webb* was playing and I thought it was a great family movie so when I got home I took the family to see it at a drive-in movie.

One day in 1977 when my boys were 12 and 14 I settled in for my 4 days at home and picked up The Oregonian to see what was in town. "There is a science fiction movie playing over in Beaverton that may be interesting. Shall we check it out?" The family, with no particular enthusiasm agreed. We finally found a parking spot. What was the big crowd about? We soon found out.

We had arrived with intentions of seeing the first showing but the theatre was full and a crowd was lining up for the second showing hours later. Why all this interest? *STAR WARS* was showing for the first time in Oregon. We had never heard of it but this big crowd got us curious so we decided to endure the long wait and see the show.

The excitement for this strange new movie was newsworthy. After standing in line for a while a camera crew from a local TV station showed up. In the long waiting line they zeroed in on my wife, Nell

Roy, for an interview. "Why are you making such a big effort to see this movie?"

On the late night news she was seen on TV telling how we came to see this movie. She said it would likely be interesting and exciting to our sons. And it was. We all enjoyed the show and Vincent became a big fan of the show and its sequels.

## Holdup in Gary

I had just seen the new Star Wars movie with my family in Portland, Oregon. I convinced Doc and Andrea they should see it. So after closing time we and their daughter, Tereva, went to a nearby mall in South Chicago to see Star Wars. When the car without wheels raced across the screen, wobbled a little on invisible springs as it parked and Luke Skywalker stepped out and walked away, leaving the vehicle to levitate about 2 feet above the ground, I leaned over and asked Doc, "Do you have any of those cars on your lot?"

"If I do, the first one's mine to keep."

On another visit, they had an exciting thing to tell me. It had been a cold day and all the salesmen had come off the lot to keep warm by the stove in the office. No one went out as 3 black men walked through the lot glancing at used cars. There was nothing unusual about seeing potential black customers. Gary and South Chicago was largely black. Their neighbors and customers were mostly black.

They came into the warm office and asked random questions. Too late, Andrea got suspicious and reached under her desk to get the gun from her purse. At that point they pulled their guns and got the drop on everyone. Unnoticed by anyone, 12-year-old Tereva, put her expensive ring in her mouth as they took Doc's expensive diamond ring, Andrea's wedding set and the several thousand dollars of working cash kept in the desk drawer.

When neighbors dropped by Doc told them, "Find out where these thieves are and let me know." They were determined to do just that, incensed that someone would rob their friend. "We'll find the guy behind this and cut off his head and bring it to you."

"No! No!" Andrea protested. "I don't want to see anything like that in this office."

A few days later Doc got a report. "They are in Wisconsin spending your money."

Later one of his lookouts rushed in and said the main thief was in a store parking lot down the road sitting in a car talking with Doc's friend. He would keep him there as long as possible.

Doc was sick in bed and he would be risking his life to get out. His nephew offered to take care of the thief but Doc said, "No." Doc had a friendly relation with the local police but his nephew could get in serious trouble. Doc would have liked to personally settle with this outlaw but just couldn't at this time. Reluctantly, he called the police.

The thieves were caught and sent to prison. Just don't fool with Doc James!

Doc is no longer with us. Andrea lives in Alabama with Tereva who has a pretty daughter of her own. I see them at the family home coming in Muhlenberg County, Kentucky.

With Doc James gone Gary, Indiana is not the same.

**Cancer**

We were enjoying a vacation with my folks in Kentucky when Nell Roy revealed to me that she had found a painful lump in her left breast. She was soon due back on her job so I put her on a plane for Portland. I called our family doctor in Portland and made an appointment to see him before leaving on my next truck trip.

With our visit in Butler County over, Henry, Vincent and I headed north to see my Illinois relatives before heading west.

If I didn't have relatives in Illinois I would still be drawn there to visit the place of my birth. The horse drawn farming scenes were history, the Model T Ford was gone, the old Daly farmhouse had burned down, the farm buildings had been removed but I could still drive up the lane, now used by tractors, and park where the front yard used to be, walk over and stand where the house had been and bathe in memories. It was now an open field, part of a larger farm where many hundreds of acres were consolidated into one large farm.

Standing on that black soil where, in 1925, I first saw the light of day, renewed my spirits and gave me added strength for whatever lay ahead.

My cousin, Buster Dotson was married to Bonnie who was a nurse working in a nearby nursing home. She was the first professional to reassure me about the possibly cancerous lump. "When they are painful they are usually not cancer," she said but it didn't ease my fears. I was very worried.

I was glad to get to Portland so we could get help. There had been warnings to detect signs of cancer as soon as possible. We had found the lump on July 8 and the appointment with our family doctor was on July 22.

We had used Doctor Irwin Ladd after he delivered my son Vincent. Then he and partners opened the East Rose Clinic about 100 blocks east of us. Dr. Ladd went to Japan as a medical missionary where he died of cancer. Now we used one of his partners, Dr. Howard Osborne, as our family doctor. He was a friendly man who tried trucking for a while before becoming a doctor. He always talked to me about trucking when we had an appointment.

Now he checked Nell Roy's lump and took note that it was painful. He thought it might be a bruise. "Come back later."

I suggested an x-ray. He agreed. So, because of *my* suggestion, an x-ray was taken. The zerox mammogram was taken at the clinic of Dr. Warnok. He said the x-ray showed no sign of cancer. Later the radiologist at the Kaiser Hospital read it as negative. Kaiser negligently lost the mammogram.

Through my research I knew that 15 percent of positive cancer x-rays were read as negative so I was not willing to take this as a final word.

Now what could I do?

## Trucking – A Job/A Blessing

I had limited experiences in hauling freight and they were interesting experiences but as a farm boy my heart was in hauling food. Loading in fields, canneries, frozen food lockers and food warehouses then delivering the food to distant places where it was needed was a pleasant job. In 1975, while taking a lunch break in Pocatello, Idaho I wrote a poem about hauling food.

Now my job would lead me to clues on dealing with my wife's cancer. It would give me time to think. It would lead me to the

Cleveland Clinic where I would meet one of my generation's most prestigious doctors, a modern rebel.

My first lead came from the office manager at the North Pacific Canners and Packers truck division where I got my dispatches. Bill Chaplain heard me talking about our problem. He told me his wife had breast lumps. In treating them her doctor did a needle biopsy and all of her lumps were cysts that proved to contain liquid, a sure sign that they were not cancerous. That was something for me to think about as I headed east.

When I got back home we were able to meet with Mrs. Chaplain's doctor on August 24, a month since Dr. Osborne had ordered the x-ray that had proved nothing.

Dr. McEherin was a general practitioner. He tried a needle aspiration on Nell Roy's lump. THERE WAS NO FLUID! He advised that we find a surgeon and have a surgical biopsy.

My mother-in-law, Effie White had had a growth on her cheek. Its removal would take a very skilled hand. One small bobble by the surgeon could have paralyzed the side of her face. Dr. Markee handled the surgery quite well. He sounded like the kind of doctor I wanted for my wife.

I made an appointment for Nell Roy to see him on September 1 while I was on the road and hopefully a biopsy could be scheduled while I was home the next week.

We delivered our west bound loads of meat and cheese to the Ness distribution warehouse on Swan Island in NE Portland. One of their local drivers was having the same experience that I was. The surgeons they had dealt with said they could tell that the lump in his wife's breast was not cancer without doing a biopsy.

Nell Roy's family history and her own health record did not reveal to them any reason she should have cancer. But I knew something they would not accept. Once while trucking through Spokane, Washington I practiced my habit of purchasing the local paper to read while I ate. A small item caught my eye. In England, they found that some women were developing breast cancer when using Reserpine to control their blood pressure. It was noted that it stimulated the milk glands and sometimes caused trouble. It was performing well on Nell Roy's blood pressure so I saw no need to change as long as there were no symptoms of cancer. But now there was an alarm sounding. No doctor I told this to would give any credence to the report. They didn't care about anything coming from Britain.

I wanted to see the results of a biopsy before I could relax.

## Dr. George Crile, Jr.

The evening of September 1 I called home from Toledo to see how the doctor's visit went. Did she have an appointment for a biopsy to be performed during my next layover at home? NO! I couldn't believe it. Dr. Markee didn't think the breast lump was cancer. "He said, 'Come back in 3 months.' "

"Why did you let him put you off like that?"

She said, "He told me what I wanted to hear and that is that."

Three years earlier, in 1973, Dr. George Crile, Jr. had published his book on breast cancer.   When he visited and spoke in Portland, Oregon promoting his book I noted the news and was not particularly interested in the subject at that time but did buy his book. Now I wondered what he would say about our problem. At 5 am I was unloading my Oregon food at a dock in Cleveland. After it was unloaded I drove the empty semi north to Euclid Avenue and headed east paralleling the south shore of Lake Erie. The Cleveland Clinic address was in the 9500 block of Euclid. I was watching address numbers so I wouldn't miss it. I imagined Dr. Crile as one of 3 or 4 doctors in a building about like Dr. Wan's Clinic in Morgantown. Soon I was in a huge complex of big buildings and skyscrapers. The Cleveland Clinic was some 40 buildings on 140 acres! I went 12 blocks east on Euclid before I found a parking place for my truck.

It was still early when I approached the reception desk at the main entrance. Dr. Crile was now a consultant with an office on the 8th floor of the Crile building named after his father, one of the founders of the clinic. I was soon ensconced in his reception room awaiting his arrival. He greeted me with a friendly handshake and invited me into his office where he listened to my story. The family doctor had done a mammogram at my request. It was read as negative — no cancer showing. The x-ray was read the same by a Kaiser doctor and lost. A needle biopsy had found no liquid. Now yesterday a surgeon had said come back in 3 months.

Dr. Crile said, "You have done all the right things. That lump may be cancerous. Don't let those rascals put you off." He told me that his father was a contemporary of Halsted who designed the Radical mastectomy. "But we have found that extensive mutilation is unnecessary. We either do a simple version or just a lumpectomy." He drew a triangle on a piece of paper. If a biopsy shows cancer, then in two weeks (not the next day) a 2 inch triangle is removed making a small scar.

I didn't understand the significance of his calling the Portland doctors 'those rascals' until I learned he had told them they only did the radical surgery to make big fees. They wanted to give him the bum's rush!

Back in Portland I went to Markee's office in the Lloyd Center. I said, "I want an appointment in one month, three months is too long." I said I wasn't happy about the decision at the last appointment.

"I know. You just want her cut on." The office girl sarcastically flung at me as she flounced out of the room.

We went to Nell Roy's blood pressure doctor. After his BP check we asked him what he thought of the breast lump. When he checked it he became very alarmed. He immediately got us an appointment with a surgeon we knew there at Kaiser. Two days later on September 23, we were in Dr. Troutman's office. A feisty livewire he bounced in, "What can I do for you?" Nell Roy had used Troutman before for a toe problem.

"She has a breast lump that needs a biopsy." I explained.

He exploded. "I'm the doctor here. I'll decide if we operate or not."

"I know you, Troutman. Check her out."

His conclusion: "Don't listen to him, Honey. I don't think you need an operation. Come back in a month."

As we left, Nell Roy asked, "Are you going to be satisfied now?"

"No. Markee has had his month. When I am back in ten days I have us an appointment for October 4 and I intend to be there with you."

## Unnecessary Radical Practices

Nell Roy and I were in Dr. Kent Markee's examining room on October 4, one month after his first examination and two months ahead of his suggested next call. The door was slightly ajar and I could see him studying me before coming in. How would he handle me, the persistent husband?

He made his examination and told me later that he detected change and felt surgery *was* necessary. But that is not what he told us that day. "The only way I can give you more assurance is to remove the lump." So my wife was left with the impression that she was undergoing an unnecessary operation because of me. She said that when it was over I was moving out or she would.

Two days later Dr. Markee did a physical exam. I left for my truck trip and would be back for the scheduled operation. I sincerely believed I should be in that OR with her. I sent a letter to the Providence Hospital Chief of Staff to tell him what I thought. I knew it wouldn't work but I wanted to put him on notice that some of us know how wrong they do things. There is NO MEDICAL REASON to keep loved ones out of the Operating Room. I had sent Nell Roy a card while on the road saying that if some West Coast doctor took off my wife's beautiful breast I would sue him.

October 19. I took Nell Roy to the Providence Hospital and checked her in so she could get ready for the operation the next afternoon. I strictly told the nurses that she was NOT to be shaved for a mastectomy since she was only going to have a lump removed. I went home for the night. After I had my supper I called her room and asked how things were going. "They just came in and shaved my chest, shoulder and back." She thought it didn't mean anything since she was sure she didn't have cancer so she let them prep her for a Halsted Radical mastectomy as a defiance of my request. I paced the floor in an agony of dread. I said to myself, "She is going to come home without her breast!"

The next morning I had a severe chest pain. I went to the Kaiser Hospital and the doctor said I had probably had an Angina attack. He advised I stay away from the afternoon operation. I just couldn't do that. I waited in her room.

Markee came in and told me, as I expected, that even before the lab report it was obvious to him that it was cancer. He said he wanted to talk to her without me present. Since I had been ordered out of her decision making and my heart was under strain, I muttered an O. K. and hoped she would make the right decision.

That afternoon, while still groggy from anesthesia, my wife was conned into a radical mastectomy.

October 21, 1976 an early morning operation removed my wife's left breast, the underlying chest muscles and 22 lymph nodes. No other cancer was found. Dr. Troutman at Kaiser would have done a partial if he had been shown that there was cancer.

Two days after her operation I came into her room and found her crying. I asked if she was in pain. "No. But look what they have done to me." She then begged me, "Don't sue the doctor. I take all the responsibility for what was done."

Follow up care would be cheaper at Kaiser. We kept our appointment with Dr. Troutman. He bounced into the room with his usual energy. "How are we," he greeted.

"Well it was cancer and she lost her breast." His enthusiasm wilted. He agreed to do the follow up care. As we left the room he put his arm around my shoulder and said, "You know so much about this, it scares me." Then he added, "But I'm glad you did."

After a year the Ness Company driver's wife finally got a biopsy but too late. Her cancer had spread and she died.

I sent Markee a letter saying we would never again use his services. We did not want to be exposed to the erroneous and devastating doctrine of his dope addicted "Saint" Halsted.

Wikipedia note: William Stewart Halsted (September 23, 1852 – September 7, 1922) was an American surgeon. Halsted was one of the "Big Four" founding professors at the Johns Hopkins Hospital. Throughout his professional life, he was addicted to cocaine and later also to morphine, which were not illegal during his time.

## Mount Vernon
North of Seattle, George Washington's home, Mount Vernon in Virginia inspired the name of Mount Vernon, Washington.

When I-5 bypassed the town it left a fine truck stop on the old road about a mile west of the interstate. The Crane Café was in a WWII Quonset hut. I, like many other truckers, would take the north exit, go down the old road to Crane's, have our lunch, then go a mile or so to the next ramp to continue south.

In the restaurant I would look over the menu and order one of their fine meals. Then came the good part, a delicious apple pie smothered in rum sauce!

There came a day that I was told, "No more rum sauce." Why?

A local woman was named head of the Transportation Department. She ordered the restaurant to stop serving rum sauce. She wasn't going to have those truckers dining on rum sauce then driving down the highway!

That person may have had political savvy to get elected or appointed but she was ignorant of what goes on in the kitchen.

I had acquired a large bag of old postage stamps at about face value. I would write letters and put several stamps on the envelope to equal the current postal rate. Whatever state I was in I would use appropriate commemoratives as much as possible. My brother Wayne said those stamps were causing a lot of excitement in the Morgantown post office! As I ate my apple pie, without the rum, I wrote a letter home. I thought it would be neat to use a Mount Vernon stamp and have it post marked in Mount Vernon. When the waitress came by I showed her the stamped envelope. She exclaimed, "I didn't know we had stamps like that!"

I didn't explain about George Washington's Virginia estate. Let her be happy that her home town had its name on a stamp. Everyone should be happy with their hometown.

While trucking all over the country I have experienced the hospitality of many towns and cities. I have met their people, enjoyed their food and enjoyed rest in their motels or the truck stops. I have shopped the malls and city centers. I have enjoyed Sunday meetings often and enjoyed visiting old friends I had known before. After a chance to rest, read, watch TV or write letters I have many times added that pleasant town to my "favorites" list. I adopt that pleasant place as another "Home Town." When one of them comes to mind or I see one of them in the news I can get a twinge of homesickness.

Mount Vernon, Washington is one of those memorable places.

## A Thread Through the Fabric of My Life

I never met my great Uncle Isaac Lucky Andrews. He was known as the biggest (400 pounds) Postmaster (of McAndrews, KY) in the U. S. His grave marker indicates that he was a veteran of the Spanish American War as was his brother Ollie who lived in Morgantown. His sister, Maude married John Robert Vincent in Muhlenberg County and was my Mom's mother. Mom kept up with her relatives so when the Army Air Corps sent me to Butler University in Indianapolis for 5 months in 1944 she told me that Uncle Lucky's 2 daughters lived in Indianapolis and I should look them up.

Hazel was married to Stanton Montague who was chief deputy sheriff of Marion County. Their 18 year old daughter, Norma was my companion during my free time. We explored the town. Her Dad let me ride with a deputy on police business.

In 1945 while stationed at San Marcos, Texas as a pilot for the Navigator's school all the planes were evacuated north to escape a threatening storm. I chose Indianapolis and spent 2 days with the Montagues. I met Norma's fiancé, Norman Baxter who was a Captain in the Air Corps.

In 1973 while visiting Mom in Butler County she told me that Norma now lived in Houston, Texas and should look her up if trucking that way. I later did and met her son and daughter. I got her daughter's address and phone number. Later I was trucking east across Kansas and listening to two disc jockeys play songs and talk on an all-night radio station in Oklahoma City, One asked the other if he had seen the cover on their new phone directory. "It's beautiful. It was designed by that famous Houston artist, Norman Baxter."

I sent Norma's daughter a card telling what I had heard about her Dad. The next time through Houston I called her and asked if she got the card. In her Texas drawl she replied, "Yes and it just bluuuu my mind."

Norma's brother, Ronald Montague had formed an agency furnishing detectives to stores to catch shop lifters. He made his home in Minneapolis. I had a load of Flavor-Pac food to unload at a warehouse in Golden Valley, a suburb of Minneapolis. I called Ron's wife and said that if her 17 year old son could come over I would hire him to help me unload the truck. He hurried right over and brought a friend. I hired them both and talked while they worked.

I told him that his great grandfather and my grandmother were brother and sister. Once when they were just small children they were at a family gathering. Lucky climbed a tree and a limb broke off. He lay on the ground not moving. Little Maude went in the house wandering among the adults saying over and over, "Lucky's dead. Lucky's dead."

Finally someone noticed and sounded the alarm. "We had better go see about Lucky."

I said to my young cousin, "Lucky came to, but if he had really been dead you wouldn't be here."

He straightened up and his eyes widened. "Say, that's right!"

Before I left Oregon I called Norma's Houston number. Her son answered. His Mom had died from cancer a few months earlier.

My Mom is no longer with us. She had hardly ever left Butler County after moving there in 1934. From her home on Logansport Road she had, like a master weaver, through the fabric of my life, directed threads that followed me. The weaver is gone and some of the threads have played out to their end. They can only linger for a while in my memory and find a home in my stories. How strange the patterns that shape our lives and build our memories. Interesting or dull, happy or tragic, they can never be matched in the imagination of the fiction writers.

## Oshkosh

I overheard the boss and dispatcher discussing their problem. A company truck had turned over and they were trying to get the various orders reloaded for their destinations. Two pallets of potato salad were for a restaurant at the Spokane World's Fair. I studied my dispatch. I suggested that my load had room for those two pallets. If they were loaded on the back of my trailer I could go north from Kennewick Friday evening, drop the two pallets then route myself south for Sikeston, Missouri. Saturday morning I dropped the two pallets at the German restaurant, adjusted the bill for the damaged cartons and headed east across northern Idaho and Montana. I studied the Atlas for roads going south that could get me from I-90 to I-80 where I was supposed to be. I saw a state route going south across Nebraska that looked promising. There, just north of I-80, was a town named Oshkosh. That cinched it! If I pushed right along and then called in a little late, I could report in from Oshkosh on Monday.

It was 9am when I called in. Carol took my call. "This is Charlie in Oshkosh."

"Ok. Hold the phone. Hokie wants to talk to you about the potato salad." As she put me on 'hold' she looked at the others in the office. "What is Charlie doing in Oshkosh?" That was a puzzlement to all of them. "I know he likes to visit his cousins but going to Oshkosh, Wisconsin on the way to Missouri is ridiculous." Carol leaned through the office door and in a hoarse whisper informed Hokie, "Charlie's in Oshkosh." Everyone gathered around the door to hear the fireworks.

I told him about the eight damaged cartons that had been turned down. Then he gave me full attention and with very pointed emphasis asked, "Where did you say you were?"

"Oshkosh."

"OSHKOSH?"

Now I knew I had gone far enough with this straitlaced Swede, conditional friend and great boss of mine. "Yes. Oshkosh, Nebraska."

A much tamer voice asked, "Oh! There's one there, Huynh?"

Carol told me that the high expectations of the office crew wilted. The firecracker fizzled.

Two weeks later I called from Kansas from one of the 350 Stuckey's stores that line the tourist routes. "This is Charlie at Stuckey's." Carol acknowledged my report. "Aren't you going to ask me which Stuckey's?" I asked.

"I'm not asking you anything since Oshkosh."

## Divorce

A month after we were married the romance had worn out for her. Never again would I hear, "I love you." My hugs and kisses were accepted passively but never again would I be given one.

On the way to Oregon she worried that I didn't have a job. That did not seem rational to me. I hadn't yet arrived where I could get a job.

It was a long time before I learned enough to sort out a reason for her way of thinking.

She had an older brother, Garland, and he was not a good brother. If there was a difference between them the parents always let him have his way. They asked Nell Roy to give in so he wouldn't make a big fuss. "Humor him because of his 'nervous condition.' "

Mrs. White must have had some sympathy for her. She urged her to get a business education so she could be independent and 'not be beholden to any man.' She told her she could come back home any time. This was not good advice for making a firm commitment in marriage.

In Pampa, my friend Molly McGee was a friend of the Whites. She had noted the strong attachment between the mother and daughter. Her neighbor came by while I was visiting. As he left to do some handyman work for her she told me of his experience.

He married a girl from downstate Lubbock. Every weekend she would go home to spend two days with her mother. Finally she called and told him she couldn't come back to him. Dear Abby called this abnormal attachment to one's mother, a steel wire umbilical cord. I learned that Effie had strong ties with her mother and for a while it seemed that our daughter might be a fourth generation with Mommyitis but I think that Charla is too much like me for Nell Roy to bond that closely with her.

Men can get Mommyitis also. A lady in Portland, Oregon told me that her husband couldn't stand to be away from his mother. When his mother died he visited her grave every day. On the first anniversary of her death he didn't come home. They found him lying across her grave where he had committed suicide.

So I got 2 women when I married, Nell Roy and her mother, Effie.

When my two sisters teamed together I learned to be a good loner. The experience came in handy. My marriage looked good as long as I was the invisible man. Sometime I would get in the way and be threatened with divorce. A trucker friend said, "You can't win this one. You may as well give up." But since I had been given lemons I made a lot of sweet lemonade!

I have said a marriage is a good one if it produces fine children. I have three.

After 34 years when I was served divorce papers the second time I accepted the inevitable and got divorced so Effie could live her last two years with her daughter. Someone said, "You should have done this a long time ago."

"No. I'm like the guy applying for a job. The prospective boss asked what his qualifications were. He said he had been fired fifteen times. Astonished, the boss asked, 'How does that qualify you to work for me?'"

"I'm no quitter."

## 35 Years

WWII GI home loans were about to expire. I found a 3 bedroom home for sale about 10 blocks from Lincoln Street. I had been sleeping in the travel trailer on my 4 days between truck trips. Nell was threatening to charge me rent if I didn't get it out of _her_ driveway. I delayed the final date of our divorce until after our next anniversary on July 7. Thirty-five years seemed like a nice round figure to end our marriage.

I papered Vince's room with a space mural and furnished it with a Star Wars theme. While sitting on his bed Vince appeared to be sitting on the moon.

Eighteen year old Henry had his own bedroom. I was too busy with the ashes of our 35 year marriage to notice that Mt. St. Helens, 40 miles to our north was about to fill the sky with ash. I was driving out Powell Boulevard ignoring the radio but Henry was listening. He caught my attention when he said, "That's the end of old Harry Truman." Old man Truman had refused to evacuate his home on Mt. St. Helens as the eruption became imminent. When we got to our newly acquired house on 89th Ave we climbed up on the shed in the back yard and watched the ash cloud climb high into the sky. The prevailing winds carried the ash eastward. When I was picking up my next truckload in Kennewick on Friday evening the air was clear since the ash cloud was staying north toward Spokane. But just before the last few feet of my trailer were filled the loaders were ordered to hurry and get the plants doors shut tight. The winds had shifted and the air would soon be full of volcanic ash. I headed north and east through roads deep in ash. The next day I drove through a moonscape where all the greenery had been covered in grey ash. It lasted across Washington and Idaho and on into Montana. The world had become a gloomy grey as had my life. I couldn't know that in less than a year I would experience the happiest, most beautiful period of my life.

**BOOK 7**

**Libby Jane**

### J. J. Forester

John Jasper Forester was born in 1854 in Jasper County, Missouri only 6 years before the beginning of the Civil War. After the war he grew up as a contemporary of the James brothers, the outlaws. He was 23 when Custer was killed by the Indians at the Battle of the Little Bighorn. Photos show that JJ would have been a fitting rival of his contemporary, Bat Masterson, for Masterson's title as Best Dressed Man in the West.

J.J. made his home in St.

James, Missouri not far from the resort town of Rolla. His first wife was the beautiful Malinda Senne, of part Cherokee ancestry. They had 2 sons and a daughter. Malinda encouraged their daughter, Ola, to study music and she had the talent and discipline to become an exceptional musician. In turn Ola's daughter became a concert pianist. Ola married Walbridge Powell who owned a prominent lumber business with yards throughout Missouri. JJ worked for the Powell Lumber Company but eventually built a business for himself. He dealt in used furniture and when he sold a piano or an organ he would load the instrument on a wagon, deliver it to a distant farm or town, then stay with the family 3 days to teach them the rudimentary skills for using their new family treasure.

He was a man who wore many hats so he used another talent and teamed with his son, Earl, to build houses. They were beautiful homes, traditional of the times. He wrote articles and poems for the local paper and served a term as mayor of St. James. His wife, Malinda Jane died. He remarried a society minded lady from Rolla but that lasted only a year.

In the meantime over in East St. Louis, Illinois, Lillian Alta McMickel married George Good and in quick succession, beginning in 1901, gave birth to their three daughters, Edith, Alta, and Mary. Then George died. While being tended by their grandmother or boarding in a Catholic Church Home, their mother supported them by working as a bookkeeper. She acquired the qualifications of Matron and was offered a job with the Old Soldiers Home in St. James, Missouri. Lillian could now keep her girls with her. The young girls were teenagers when JJ started courting their mother. As John Jasper and Lillian Alta, in her white matron's uniform, walked the streets of St.

J. J. Forester in 1914 with home he built

James, people would say, "There goes JJ with his white swan."

When JJ and Lillian married they lived in the nice house built by him and Earl. JJ is now in his 60s and no longer working. They sold the home and acquired one on the edge of town where they could work together raising chickens. In harmony with his innovative ideas JJ was the first in the area to extend the laying hours of hens with electric lights. A milk cow kept them in butter, cream, milk, buttermilk and clabbered milk; a truck garden served their table and filled the basement with quarts and quarts of canned fruits and vegetables.

It was here that their son, Miskel Coyle was born, he with the blond hair and the good looks of his Scotch-Irish ancestors but a rapscallion nature. He would be a bane for his ageing parents and harasser and mean tease to his sister. What sister?

A scant year after Miskel, JJ and Lillian had another child, the fifth and last for each of them. The midwife was an African American freed from slavery by Abraham Lincoln's Emancipation Proclamation. The United States entered WWI in 1917. Their daughter was a war baby born on July 14, 1917, the famous French holiday, Bastille Day. JJ was 63 years old. They named her Libby Jane. She was destined to live history and make history. Her father, who seemed more like a grandfather, loved his 'Darling Libby Jane'. Her harried, hard working mother had little time for her except to wield a switch for 'Lady Jane' for every minor infraction of the rules. Sometimes one of Miskel's teachers would be invited for Sunday dinner so Libby Jane would see dining room etiquette with white table cloth and napkins and family dining.

A music teacher was hired for Miskel. Libby Jane would listen from the other room and after the teacher left, she would go to the piano and practice the lesson. When her aptitude for music was noticed they bought lessons for her also.

## Atlasta

A movie house was built for St. James. It would soon have the grand opening and they needed a name for the new enterprise. They had a contest and Libby Jane, about 8 years old, entered. A boy's entry, the name "ATLASTA" won for him 3 years of free movies. Libby Jane's entry, a runner up, won for her free movies for a year. By the time she was 12 she was an accomplished piano player and when the regular musician was not available the manager would call for Libby Jane to spend the evening playing music to fit the tempo and mood of the silent movie on the screen above the piano. It was a historic period that ended with the arrival of 'talkie' movies.

Libby Jane's older half-sister, Alta had trained as a nurse and was working for a hospital in California. She shared a home with her sister Edith. While home on vacation a pilot was selling airplane rides in a nearby field. Alta took 8 year old Libby Jane and a niece, 15 year old Mary Ola Forester, with her to watch the show. She bought a 15 minute ride. Then she bought the $5.00 ride for Libby Jane and her niece. The two girls rode together in the front seat. Out of curiosity Alta asked the pilot his name which meant nothing to them at the time. In 1927 just two years later he flew solo across the Atlantic Ocean and the whole world knew him. His plane, the Spirit of St. Louis, was shipped back to New York and he flew it into St. Louis just one month after he had left. Charles A. Lindbergh was greeted by thousands of fans and he stayed a week.

When Libby Jane rode with him in 1925 I was entering the world about 200 miles away in Tazewell County, Illinois. The day I was born two threads materialized that would weave through the fabric of my life: Libby Jane was one, and aviation, abetted by Charles A. Lindbergh, was the other. It would be twenty years before I would meet Libby Jane but Lindbergh came close much sooner. The night that I was one year and three months old a mail plane was droning through the sky, carrying mail from St. Louis for Chicago, when the engine quit. The pilot, Lindbergh, bailed out. In the dark he parachuted into one farmer's field and his plane crashed in another field nearby just ten miles from where I was sleeping.

Another notable birth took place in the Forester home in St. James. Lillian's daughter, Mary had married Eugene Hasler. When she gave birth to Charlie in the Forester home Miskel said the baby belonged to his family. He was convinced that an airplane had dropped the baby in the Gorge Hollow behind their property and he was theirs. But when the Haslers moved to California Charlie went with them and during WWII he became one of the Flying Tigers in the Pacific theater of war and a worldwide TWA pilot after the war. This Flying Tiger became my nephew by marriage. The aviation thread became a long one in the tapestry of my life.

In 1930 Lillian Alta Forester's over worked and overweight body suffered a painful heart attack. Alta's brother, Stewart McMickel, brought his Christian Science Reader from St. Louis and they shooed everyone out of the room while they were trying to show the power of their religion to save her life. After a half hour they came out to say she had died. JJ felt cheated when he learned he wouldn't be with his beloved Swan in her final moments.

Thirteen year old, Libby Jane, who had been spending her nights sleeping with her mother, would not grieve for long. It was decided that she would live with Alta and Edith in California. After the funeral, they spent a month packing two trunks: one for Alta with her mother's things and one for Libby Jane. They were shipped to Edith's home in LA. They boarded the train for St. Louis at the St. James station. In St.

Louis they boarded the west bound bus. A spectacle of exotic scenery paraded past the view as the bus rolled westward but this change of scenery was minor compared to the momentous changes and exciting times and trials that lay waiting in Libby Jane's future.

## Los Angeles and San Bernardino

They shared the home with Edith, only moving to a larger house when Edith married George Susa. George was a compassionate and discerning man. He rented a piano and saw that Libby Jane continued her music lessons. On a vacation trip to St. James, Libby Jane, wearing a yellow taffeta dress made by Alta, played the piano in a recital. JJ was so proud of his talented Darling Libby Jane. Living in East Hollywood they lived the heyday of Hollywood's glory days. They went to shows, sometimes premier showings of movies in the nearby Egyptian Theater or Grauman's Chinese Theatre. Libby Jane became a walking encyclopedia of old movies and movie stars.

After three years, a doctor in San Bernardino offered Alta a job. They would live in a nearby house owned by the doctor. This would be Libby Jane's home for her three years attending the San Bernardino High School, graduating in 1935.

Alta proved to be a good substitute for Libby Jane's mother. Because of her nurse training she taught her young sister meticulously healthy hygiene and housekeeping. Like many other teenagers, she sought what she thought would be the freedom of an adult by an ill-advised marriage to a handsome neighbor boy who had a wonderful Italian Mama. In her senior year, she became Mrs. Howard Davis but kept it secret and graduated as Libby Jane Forester. The marriage didn't last. She got experience as a carhop and worked a telephone switchboard for some time. She was living with her brother Miskel in San Raphael when she entered the wartime workforce, not as Rosie the riveter, but as Janie the welder in a shipyard, building Liberty ships.

Soon she was noticed by a one year veteran of the job, Burl Borden, and soon they were eating lunch side by side. They were a good match and were married just before Burl went on active duty and shipped out for Europe on the QE2. When he was on the way home she learned he was on one of the old slow Liberty ships. She hoped the welding held the ship together long enough to get him home. Jane just loved Joan, Burl's young daughter by his previous marriage. To avoid a possible custody battle they quietly left California and in March 1947 moved into a trailer park just a half block from where I was building our house.

Jane and Burl became good friends of my in-laws, Roy and Effie White. I was around of course and I found them to be very likable neighbors. Burl had poor health and jobs for him were scarce. He used the GI bill to study radio broadcasting and had some success with that. I was glad to call him a friend. I saw Jane as a very supportive wife and diligent housekeeper. We kept up our friendship when they moved across town and when they moved to Hillsboro where Jane once more was a telephone switchboard operator. Our daughter, Charla Kay, was born in the Immanuel hospital in 1949. Jane's daughter Melinda was born in 1950 in the Adventist hospital about 30 blocks from our home. I am listed as one of her visitors when she was one day old. When they moved to Phoenix, Arizona we lost touch for a few years.

In 1973 I was home between truck trips and spending the day alone when the phone rang. It was Jane Borden. Burl had died in 1970, now 3 years later, she took her vacation from her job at Honeywell in Phoenix to come to Oregon to visit old friends. While staying with friends south of Portland she had time on her hands as they worked their day jobs so she got the telephone directory and called those she remembered, hence my phone call. We chatted, catching up on the news of the last few years.

I mentioned that I enjoyed trucking to the Midwest since I would really like to move to Kentucky but my wife, Nell Roy, wouldn't consider moving away from her mother in Oregon. As an expression of disapproval for that wifely attitude, Libby Jane said, "I would move to Kentucky with you." That was not considered even a remote possibility but I never forgot that statement. I took her address and phone number in case my truck dispatches ever took me through Phoenix.

In 1974 I pulled in to a Phoenix truck stop and called, "Would you like to come down to the truck stop and have breakfast with me?" The answer was negative. It was just 2 hours until time to go to work and my early morning call had interrupted the last hour of her much needed sleep. She had been going to work with a sad face, still missing her dear husband, Burl. But this morning a fellow worker saw a big change. "Why are you so cheerful this morning?" she asked.

"I got a call from an old friend and he reminded me that I had many memories of happy times with Burl. He gave me reasons to cheer up."

Six more years pass. I send Jane Borden a letter with news of family and friends.

She wrote a friendly letter telling me the latest in her life. She would be 64 on her next birthday. She had a HUD apartment where she expected to spend the rest of her life. My next 'friendly' letter raised alarm bells. She said she enjoyed hearing from me but would not write further letters unless I assured her it was OK with my wife. It was time to let her know I was now single!

Thus began an old fashioned courtship with love letters filled with poems. I wanted a lot of letters before starting phone calls and when they did start there were some large phone bills.

My poetic urges had been on hold during my 35 years of bad marriage. Now they became full blown. Janie responded in kind. She, who had never written a poem before, began writing beautiful poems in answer to mine. One day as I was trucking east I realized that her apartment number was the same as my truck number. I grabbed my pen and as I drove along I jotted down the words of a new poem titled "28."

How neat to spy that you and I
Both have the same address.
It caught my eyes with great surprise,
Coincidence I guess.
But your 28 is sitting sedate
Where the evening shadow steals.
While my 28 is rolling late
On 18 big truck wheels.

Number 28 became our special number.

## I Meet Vivian

I had not seen Janie since she moved to Phoenix 25 years ago. Now we had been writing letters and finally talking on the phone for a few weeks when I had an opportunity to meet her in person. I had loaded in Texas and was trucking west on I-40 that would take me through Flagstaff, Arizona. I called Janie. Yes, she could meet me in Flagstaff for breakfast. In answer to my question she said she did not have a camera. At a truck stop I bought her a Polaroid camera as a gift.

The Little America in Flagstaff caters to the numerous truckers driving through. For a reasonable price truckers could spend the night in a comfortable room instead of the truck. I rented a luxurious room. It was large with a writing table, TV and other luxuries in a rich finish. After a good night's sleep I was awaiting my breakfast guests from Phoenix. Janie was bringing a longtime friend, Vivian Murphy as our chaperon. We were having an old fashioned courtship.

We had not seen each other for decades so she had asked me on the phone what would be my first words to her. I said I would probably say what Adam said when meeting Eve, "At last." A call on the house phone informed me they had arrived. I told Janie my room number and told her to come on up. Vivian gave us 5 minutes!

I waited a few feet from the door. When she pushed the door open and stepped in my first words were, "Will you marry me?" Her answer? "Yes, yes, yes!" as she flew into my arms.

At breakfast I met Vivian for the first time. Janie's friend was a gracious lady. She would become my friend also. After an all too short a visit they headed back to Phoenix and I headed for Oregon through a snow storm as I drove through Reno.

Vivian missed our reception that was held in Phoenix. She was visiting her relatives in Kentucky. The ride she depended on refused to return a few days early so she could be with us.

## Melinda

Janie's daughter, Melinda was married to David Wilkinson. She was fascinated by her mother's late life courtship. Her reaction? "Don't let that man get away!" So I had an ally in my courting. My name in her hospital guest book proves that I have known her she since she was one day old.

They talked and raised questions. "What will he think when he learns that you are 8 years older?" Janie didn't remember that she had mentioned her age in her first letter to me. "Will he not like your name Libby when he learns about your first name?" She didn't know that a return address sticker on one of her letters revealed her full name to me some time ago. Later I wrote a song using her poetic name and because of me she learned to love her name even as I did. "Mom, his first wife was beautiful." As a photographer and artist I was aware that Nell Roy had a glamorous beauty but from photos I knew that Janie had a lovely beauty of her own and a superior soft personality. So, all of Janie's and Melinda's concerns evaporated. We planned a wedding for May.

## Romantic Poets

In 1934, a neighbor, Raleigh Beliles became my friend. He was a poet and soon had me writing poems which I continued all through high school. During WWI Raleigh had met a girl in France. They corresponded for some time and their letters were always in the form of a poem. I was fascinated by the book of poems he had printed from those letters.

During my first marriage any romantic interests were suppressed. Now as I wrote to Janie the poet in me came alive. Janie responded in kind. She, who had never before in her 64 years, written a poem, sent me a fine one showing great talent in the use of words. Trucks were no longer a noisy nuisance. Her thoughts were with her Charlie who was guiding his 'great ship' in a useful and very necessary service.

The poems were soon flying to and from Phoenix. Maybe I will publish a book like Raleigh's someday.

A Sound of Night by Libby Jane Borden

What's this I hear in sleepless night?
When daytime birds have gone to rest
And sounds of silence creeping in
To help me get my peaceful rest?

Through my window, far away,
It sings a song that sounds so near
But not for all to listen to
Like an echo, loud and clear.

And as I listen attentively,
I identify this sound.
It's the wheels of trucks that carry far
Their heavy load from town to town.

The whining wheels, the change of gears,
These sounds do not disturb me now
For they bring a message clear,
That I have figured out somehow.

Ah, yes! It's very clear to me,
They help the trucks that roll and roll
Bringing us the many things
That we all know that we need so.

I think about the one who sits,
In command of this great ship
Such great satisfaction brings
To him – he never quits.

There are many things inside that cab
To keep him busy company,
A tape, a phone, a song or two,
And "Breaker 1-9" on his CB.

Now as I sink in sweet repose,
And get back to my dreamy dreaming,
Happy and content, for now I know
These sounds, and revel in their meaning.

## Wedding 1981

Between Phoenix and Portland the logical place to meet for the marriage was Las Vegas. In Portland I came in from my truck trip, and the next morning I dressed up and went by Flav-R-Pac to get my check. From the office Hokie the boss said, "Why is Charlie so dressed up?"

Carol said, "He is flying to Las Vegas to marry a lady from Phoenix."

He then asked, "When did we ever send him to Phoenix?" I headed to the airport.

Melinda and her daughter, Sunny, drove with Janie from Phoenix. They got the marriage license, reserved the chapel and met my plane. After the ceremony we had dinner and retired to our hotel. I had reserved rooms in the Circus Circus. The next day we saw Melinda and Sunny off for their home. Our brief honeymoon continued.

I had reservations for the Engelburt Humperdinck show at the Hilton. We dressed up for the show. We were in the middle of a long line waiting for the door to open for the theatre. The line formed along 2 sides of the huge room. A woman employee came walking across the large room on her way to the other side of the line. Everyone was watching as she walked and walked and walked across the wide empty center of the room. She zeroed in on our spot to cross the line. As she crossed in front of us she quietly said, "You two are really something."

It would not be the last time we would be told that we were an outstanding couple. I was sure proud of my lovely bride.

We got back to Portland in time for my next truck trip. Soon, on a Portland layover, we would go to Phoenix for a beautiful reception. I wrote a song telling our story. I called it:

# Our Love Story

A man can get lonely in rainy old Portland trying to live all alone.
The house is so empty with no wife to live here and children all grown up and gone.
Keeping house for me and no one else but me and cooking is no fun alone.
A man needs a helpmate, a sweet loving life-mate, one he can call all his own.

Janie was living in Phoenix, Arizona where the desert sun shines so hot.
Her doctor said. "Janie, you must find some weather that's cooler than Phoenix has got."
"But Doctor," she cried, "I'm sure I would die if I must live up north all alone.
"Oh why can't there be a Prince Charming for me? Oh where have all of them gone?"

The postman delivered a letter from Charlie, a friend from a Long time ago.
Her answer was casual, she thought he was married, a friend she was so glad to know.
But when he informed her that he was now single, she accepted his wooing with joy.
And, my! What a romance! With flowers and presents and phone calls from her lover boy.

With love songs and poems and words of affection, he told her he loved her so dear.
He told her how empty his home was without her and how that he wanted her near.
They planned a big wedding for late in the summer but they had waited so many long years,
They eloped to Las Vegas where Janie in springtime was a bride with sweet happy tears.

Their first home together in the old Circus Circus made memories they love to recall.
Melinda and Sunny were so delighted to have a new dad and grandpa.
He took her out dining in style at the Hilton and my, oh my, what a night,
With Englebert singing her sweet favorite love songs, and her new husband holding her tight.

Their reception in Phoenix is one they'll remember for many and many a year.
It was presented with love and affection by those whom Janie holds dear.
With music by Danny and his fine musicians, refreshments and presents galore,
With Janie so happy, her heart filled with gladness, what bride could ever want more?

·Now Charlie and Janie are happy together in their home way out in the west.

Their romance continues and even gets better with mini vacations for zest.

Whenever they travel to faraway places they're thankful to God up above.

That they have a home they can live in together, one that is filled with LOVE.

Libby Jane brought love and music into my home.

## A Freightliner Built for Two

My trucking career continued with my new partner. On our first trip together I routed through her old hometown of St. James, Missouri. An older gentleman in a real estate office remembered Janie's father. He told her where her old grade school teacher, Mr. Cahill, lived and let us use his car to go see him.

The truck, number 28, was our magic carpet to adventure. We rode

a streetcar in Detroit. In Spearfish, South Dakota we visited a friend of Janie's whom she had not seen for years since she had moved from Phoenix. We spent the night and they had a great visit. We had a midnight dinner with old friends in Sauk Centre, Minnesota and learned they were moving back to Portland and didn't know where they would stay until they settled. We gave them a key to our house in case they arrived there when we were gone. The nation was our playground. When the winter blizzards crossed the country, so did we. When Michigan woods took on their fall colors, we were there. I wrote a song about our magic carpet: a parody of the old song, *A Bicycle Built for Two*, taking a little liberty on weaving the story.

Now Charlie is a trucker who drives the nation wide.
He longs to have his Janie sitting by his side.
The road is long and lonesome; he longs to have her near
So when he got his big rig home, he said to her, "My dear."

    Chorus:
    Janie, Janie, give me your answer, do.
    I'm half zany over my love for you.
    It won't be a stylish marriage, I can't afford a carriage,
    But, you'll sure look sweet upon the seat
    Of a Freightliner built for two.

But Janie was reluctant, she said, "I have my home
"And I should raise some little ones before I start to roam."
So Charlie said, "I'll go along and help you have your dream,
"Then some day when they're grown up
"Then we'll become a team."

    Chorus
Now Charlie's daughter's married to a trucker on the road.
And Charlie's son named Henry is hauling his own load.
Now Charlie's not lonesome anymore, his dream has now come true.
His Janie is his partner in their Freightliner built for two.

For fun I deliberately misread billboards that we passed. Janie began to think she had married nearsighted Mr. McGoo! After stopping at several toll booths in Chicago, I stopped to tend a matter. While I was gone a few minutes Janie got curious about the writing on an envelope lying on the doghouse. It said *I toll you.* "Can't he spell?" was her first thought. Curious, she peeped to see what was in the envelope. Just toll tickets! 'Toll' identified the contents; the other two words were my doodling. One night traveling down I-55 from St. Louis in powdery snow, when I met a truck the snow whirling up behind him had me driving blind for a few yards. Janie said, "That is so scary when you meet another truck I shut my eyes."

"Me too."

"Don't say that!"

Trucking east from Spokane, Washington we came to a Montana tourist attraction called *The Snake Pit*. We stopped to see the snakes on display. We walked down a long row of glass cages reading the legends of each snake. At the end of the room we turned back, studying the creatures along the other aisle. I was reading the posted stories and Janie got ahead of me. When I caught up with her I put my arms around her and dragged my toe up the far side of her leg. She tore away from me and ran the rest of the length of the exhibit room and through the gift shop and didn't stop until she was outside with the truck!

Back home in Oregon we went to a movie in Gresham. We sat in the front row of the balcony. During intermission I got real lovey dovey. My shy Janie pushed me away in alarm as she glanced over her shoulder to see who was watching. No one was there. I had made sure of that before putting on the smooching act. At Knott's Berry Farm and Disney land a ride through the dark tunnel in the mine car had her brushing away spider webs that were not there and a tap tap on her back in The Haunted House caused an alarmed look over her shoulder. Janie would tell her friends about the tricks her husband had up his sleeve and a poem in our book of poetry saved the memory of these events.

### You'd Better Watch Out for Charlie

When you go down to Disneyland,
And go to the Haunted House,
You don't have to worry about scary things,
There's no real ghost or mouse.
So, when you feel a spider web
Clinging to your face
It cannot be a real one there.
There's none in the whole darn place.

So what's this that's brushing you
    In the dark where you can't see?
Never fear a spider, Dear,
    But, you'd better watch out for Charlie!

What's this tap tap on your back,
Demanding your attention?
You shiver, quiver, quake, and shake
In great apprehension.
You turn around with frightened eyes,
But, there is no one there.
"Just where is this awful thing
That gave me such a scare?"

Oh, you'd better watch out for Charlie.
   You'd better watch out for Charlie.
There's no such thing as a real ghost here,
   But you'd better watch out for Charlie.

You travel 'cross the country,
Stop in at a zoo.
They've got a lot of snakes here.
You want to see a few.
You are very safe, my Dear,
With each locked in his cage.
But, what's that crazy thing you feel
A crawling up your leg?

Oh, you'd better watch out for Charlie,
   You'd better watch out for Charlie.
Where is Charlie's toe? — Uh oh!
   You'd better watch out for Charlie.

Charlie buys a ticket.
He takes you to a show.
You settle down to see it,
The things that thrill you so.
Charlie's hands are busy.
"No! no! Charlie, no!
"Charlie, you can't do that here.
"No! I told you. No!"

You'd better watch out for Charlie!
   You'd better watch out for Charlie!
When you go to the picture show
   You'd better watch out for Charlie!

## The Hearst Castle

Libby Jane and I took a mini-vacation down the coast of California. We stopped to tour the Hearst Castle. We secured the Buick in the parking lot and waited our turn for the shuttle bus to take us up the hill to the castle. The surf (Big Sur) was pounding the coast line below us to the west.

We arrived at the castle and Janie headed for the entrance. As she looked back at the camera she shaded her eyes from the bright sun. Ahead of her was the entrance whose doors and iron gates came from a monastery in Spain. High above were 2 round towers from a Muslim castle in Europe. How could the architect logically feature these 2 cultures on the same building? Our tour guide explained.

Above Janie, stretching across the building is a frieze, a wood carving of a battle scene of soldiers and horses. The guide said that scene represented Charles Martel defeating the Muslim army in 732 at Tours, France.

That was the decisive battle that kept Europe from being Muslim. They continued to hold their conquest in Spain for 7 centuries until driven from their last strongholds in western Spain. King Ferdinand and Queen Isabelle drove them back into Africa in 1492, just a few months before financing Columbus in his exploratory voyage that discovered America.

Charles Martel's grandson, Charles the Great (Charlemagne), on Christmas day in 800 AD was crowned by the Pope as the first emperor of what became known as the Holy Roman Empire. It lasted 1000 years until 1815 when Napoleon crowned himself.

Muslims continue to dominate northern Africa. France's liberal immigration laws have resulted in the largest population of Muslims of any European nation. They may be looking for another Charles Martel soon.

Janie and I got a good reminder of our High School history lessons the day we visited the Hearst Castle near San Simeon California.

## Jack London and Me

In High School I spent a lot of time in Jack London's literary world but knew little of his real life. In 1973 I entered that part of Jack's life when my friend, Albert Soen, took me and my sons to visit the ruins of London's Wolf House in Napa Valley. There was to be a lot more.

In 1984 Janie and I took a vacation trip to California with a special goal of San Francisco, a favorite city of mine. We parked our car in a public lot in East Oakland and caught a Bay Area Rapid Transit (BART) train to downtown 'Frisco. At Powell and Market we transferred to the Cable Car. We clung to the side like veteran commuters and headed for Fisherman's Wharf. At the end of the line we hired a rickshaw. We were excited when our vehicle was Number 28. Just 3 years earlier when we were courting I was driving out of Portland in truck number 28 while she was living in Phoenix in Apartment number 28.

Since 1997 we have shared the same address: Box 11**28** in Morgantown, Kentucky.

Arriving at Number 9, Fisherman's Wharf, my favorite restaurant for eating oysters, we were soon seated in a window overlooking the fishing boats at their dock. Janie ordered fish. She doesn't share my appetite for oysters.

I had been here 21 years earlier when Henry was a few weeks old baby. This restaurant was so crowded that we went across the street to Joe DiMaggio's restaurant. I sat Henry in his baby carrier on a ledge in the window while his mother and I dined.

After Janie and I left the restaurant we went down the street to the big brick building known as The Cannery. What a busy place it must have been in the old days when tons of fish were brought in for canning. Now it was full of little shops of all kinds. In the courtyard was a young troubadour offering a dollar if you could name the next song he played. Janie won his dollar. She lived in LA and also just North of San Francisco when she was young and Hollywood was in its heyday and she is a walking encyclopedia of music and songs.

Riding back to our car in Oakland I saw directions to Jack London Square. I had to see it. I rung the buzzer and we exited. Soon we were exploring and Janie took my picture standing by the small cabin, a replica of Jack's home the winter he spent in the Yukon.

In a nearby tavern we sat at a table that tilted. The floor had been left tilted after the great San Francisco earthquake of 1906. With our soft drinks leaning precariously we listened as the bartender told tales of Jack London and Robert Louis Stevenson sitting at this very table exchanging yarns of their adventures.

This area was home to Jack London. Much of his writing was done here after returning from distant adventures. The setting for his novel, "The Valley of the Moon" is here. The couple in the story leave the graphically described labor strife in this area and walk North a ways to farm. Was this the Napa Valley where Jack himself built his Wolf House? On their farm was a secluded valley called The Valley of the Moon from which the book gets its name. His fiction life and real life sure mixes a lot. The spirit of his life and writings permeates this Oakland area.

Jack London's 40 short years of life left a big footprint here and in the world and in the life of a boy from Butler County, Kentucky.

The holidays were coming up and Janie and I had an empty trailer and no dispatch was available for a westbound load. The boss asked me to check with the local brokers for a possible Oregon load. One broker had a load of grapefruit waiting in McAllen, Texas – destination: Oregon. That was a long way from Missouri but Janie and I were soon on our way.

The dock workers were charmed by my 65 year old bride. The manager loaded a box with choice grapefruit for our personal use. Our load and destination were interesting. Hundreds of boxes with postal labels affixed were filled with two, four or more grapefruit. The boxes were addressed to Dr. So and So and numerous other private individuals. They were Christmas presents. I took the load to the central Portland, Oregon Post Office where half was unloaded. Then I parked in the home lot and another driver was scheduled to take the rest of the load to the Seattle, Washington Post Office. It was an interesting collaboration between the US Postal Service and private trucking.

Riding in a truck is a brutal experience. Even though I paid hundreds of dollars for an air ride seat for Janie I could see it was hard on her body. She would stay home every other trip to recover. Truck #28 had been our magic carpet for seeing the country. I had been trucking 14 years and now I considered making a change. I gave my notice and took off on my last trip. The on-board computer recorded every minute of it: my speed for every minute, every time I touched the brakes, every minute I was stopped or shut down. My last trip! I could relax. Why worry about my record. It was over for me. Yet my pride in my skill kept me on the ball. When I got back to the office 10 days and 5000 miles later Bill Chaplain downloaded and printed the thick record of the trip. Bill studied each record to see if there was a way to perform better for economy. The boss wanted us to stay under 60 MPH to save fuel. Bill called me into the office. Uh oh?

"Charlie, this is a text book performance. You touched 60 MPH only once – for less than a minute." He gave me a copy of the printout for a souvenir.

## Our Swiss Holiday

There's nothing like the mountains
For a mini-holiday.
I like to take my Janie
To the mountains far away.
There I can call her
With a Yodel le de A
And she can be my Swiss miss
On our blissful holiday.

We went to the mountains
In the state of Washington.
The Alpine town of Leavenworth
Was really lots of fun.
They call its style Bavarian
Or German if you may.
For us it was a perfect town
For our Swiss holiday.

We stayed in the Edelweis
We got a room for two.
We browsed the shops for souvenirs
Where we bought quite a few.
We dressed up in antique clothes
And had our picture 'took'.
My Swiss Miss was sweet to kiss
With her 1880 look.

The Autumn leaves were falling
When we took our holiday.
It was a time of festival
And artwork on display.
I'll go again when on the town
The snow has worked its charm
And my Swiss Miss will hug me tight
To keep her body warm.

# BOOK 8

# School Busses

## Arthur L. Williams

Now that I was no longer a trucker what would I do? Irv Yeats, a Regional Vice President with A. L. Williams, introduced me to the company. The concept of replacing Whole Life Insurance with cheaper Term Insurance and investing the savings in mutual funds made sense. I soon earned my insurance license and a license to sell securities. I had a measure of success and I am glad I helped some families with their finances. I am pleased that I contributed a small part in making Art Williams a billionaire. He did a great service to the country. But I am not a good salesman. If an offer that is good for the client is presented and they want to think about it, a good salesman would come back as many times as necessary to help the client make up his mind. My attitude was, 'take it or leave it — now.' I value what I learned from my excursion into the world of insurance and securities but I missed having my hands on a steering wheel.

## School Bus Services

Nine miles east of my southeast Portland home, in the town of Gresham, Lee Larson had built a variety business with school buses. I applied for a job with his company. Would I like driving school buses? The management even considered whether I was overqualified for the job. The modest name of the company didn't immediately reveal the diversity of the company. The next few years would prove to be one of the most interesting of my careers.

The core of the business was to furnish, under contract, transportation for students in various school districts throughout Oregon and Washington and even in a large district in Texas. Each district was a separate company division with its own bus yard, office and manager. The Gresham depot hosted the corporate headquarters where Mr. Larson had his office. All of my duties would be assigned from this division.

School requirements had us driving regular bus routes, Special Needs van routes, field trips, special events and transporting Ski Clubs for a long day and evening on Mt. Hood. SBS was a private company so the buses could be used for other purposes. Lee Larson was a dealer for Thomas Buses. We would get assignments to pick up or deliver new and uses buses. Sometimes there would be needed a whole caravan of buses with drivers. Events, such as the Billy Graham Crusade would require several buses to provide rides from several locations, to and from the main event. Charter trips were fun. Fire fighters would need buses and drivers for days or weeks. A real plum of an assignment was driving one of the two buses leased by the Steens Mountain High Altitude Running Camp for two weeks every summer.

As Annie said as she saw her new home, "I think I'm going to like it here."

After being hired by School Bus Services I observed that Application forms and other business forms had been copied so much that they were faded and parts almost faded out. I am not a typist so I proceeded to restore the forms with a pen. I consider that as my small beginning into desk top publishing. Before I left SBS I would become a full-fledged editor and publisher with great modern tools.

## Happy Noise

I have a considerable tolerance for noise. Some school bus drivers work hard at having a disciplined and quiet bus. My passengers soon learned that I didn't mind the noise so a lot of happy chatter filled the bus. But it had to be happy noise. If rowdiness or angry words marred the scene they quickly learned that I had a voice that could override the noisiest crowd, especially through the microphone.

One day as the bus got loaded at the South Middle School the principal tried to get my attention and tell me to quiet the kids. I drove off without noticing him. Angered, he called the office and told them he never wanted to see me at that school again. That made some of the drivers angry. I laughed it off and said another route was alright with me. A short time later I reported for work and was told to take my bus and go to the South Middle School. The driver of the lead bus had not made it to work. I said, "I'm not supposed to go to that school."

"Forget that. Just go."

When I arrived at the loading zone the other 4 or 5 buses were hanging back waiting for my number one bus to park at the head of the line. If we loaded in the wrong order the kids would be confused as to which one was their bus.

When I got past the other buses and was ready to pull into the number one loading spot, there was a car already parked there. I set the brake and stepped out of the bus. I asked the waiting crowd, "Whose car is that."

It was the principal's!

I hurried to the door and down the hall to the principal's office. He was sitting at his desk. Startled, he looked up at my abrupt entrance. "Your car is in the bus loading zone." He was out of the door in a flash. He moved his car, I parked the bus, the other buses pulled up into position behind my bus and we opened the doors for a crowd of homeward bound schoolkids. The principal isn't in sight as the noisy number one bus leads the parade out of the parking lot.

## Anna - A little blind orphan

Annetta drove the school van that took little 5 year old Anna home from Elementary school. Annetta was computer literate so they needed her in the office of School Bus Services in Gresham. Thus I inherited the duty of taking this little blind orphan girl to her foster home each afternoon.

I parked at the loading zone behind the school and the teacher brought Anna out to meet her new driver.

"This is Charlie."

Anna was having none of that. My name was from then and always "Not-Annetta"

Annetta told me that Anna sat quietly in her own silent world except sometimes she would say, "Gresham Base" in imitation of the two-way radio call so I knew she could talk.

Every day I talked the route as I drove it.

"Now we are going through the parking lot past the big school buses. Now we turn right on street 232. Now we turn right and go fast on Highway 212. Wow! Here's where we turn left on 242 and go to Anna's street. Turn right on Hoffmeister and immediately right again into Anna's driveway."

Right away she was saying the name of the streets after me.

Soon she would name the entire route without my help. One day she waited a while after I turned a corner. I thought she had forgotten so I named the street we were on. This brought a shouted reprimand, "NO!" She knew where she was and would name the street when *she* was ready.

Another day I turned on 242nd and said, "Oh no. I have forgotten Anna's street. What *is* that street Anna lives on?"

"HOFFMEISTER" she yelled at that dummy in the driver's seat!

One day when the foster mother met the bus to help Anna into the house she had something to tell me. The case worker had been by for a routine check on Anna. After a while she exclaimed, "Anna has become so lively and alert since the last visit. What caused this big change?"

"Well, you see, Anna has this school bus driver that has taught her the route. Now when we are out driving she tells us what street we are on. If it is a new street that is not on her route she wants to know what it is."

The case worker was astounded. "That driver opened up the world to this little girl."

Authorities say that eyes that can't see still play a part in direction orientation. I hope no one for cosmetic reason or otherwise ever removes Anna's precious eyes. Her ability to learn was an inspiration for me.

Anna, I'll never forget you!

## Heard on the School Bus

Little 6-year-old Amanda was the last one on the school bus. Sitting right behind me she says, "Charlie, would you turn the heaters off?" I looked over at the panel of switches.

"Amanda, the heaters are not turned on."

"Oh, well, I guess I'm just having another hot flash."

Little Jerry was so disruptive he had to be sent 20 miles from Gresham to a special school in SE Portland. One day I was dispatched to pick him up in a boxy old van. After he was seated and his seat belt secured I headed east on Woodstock to take him home. Right away he was out of his seat. I pulled over to the curb and said, "Jerry, get your seat belt on so we can go home." Soon I had to repeat the whole procedure.

Finally, a considerable period of time went by when all was quiet. I got curious. What is he up to? I raised my eyes to the passenger mirror. I saw him seated and shaking his little finger at me and demanding;

"Keep your eyes on the road!"

I was subbing a new route. At the intersection I didn't know whether to turn right or left. I appealed to my passengers. About half were yelling, "Turn right." The other half was advising, "Turn left." Then one little voice piped up and straightened things out. "No, Charlie, you turn straight."

I got our imagination going one day. "Be careful about that puddle. I think I saw a shark cruising in it." One of the kids was sure he saw a lion lurking in a bush near the bus stop. A girl in the back of the bus contributed to the game when she reported a rhinoceros chasing the bus. "Someone yelled, "Don't hit that zebra"

One by one the kids got off until one little boy remained. I opened the door at his stop but he didn't move. I looked over at him and he said, "I'm scared."

I turned left and drove to the middle of the block and stopped in front of his door. "We got away from them didn't we?" He smiled a big smile and agreed with me then he ran for the safety of his front door!

Be careful when it is raining cats and dogs. You might step in a poodle!

## Chocolate Cake

As a Thomas Bus Company dealer, Lee Larson sold a new bus to a Medford, Oregon school and I was given the assignment to deliver it. Janie rode with me as I drove the modern bus south. Beth, our chase driver followed in her car.

After delivering the new school bus Janie and I, along with our chase driver, had a nice lunch at the hotel in Wolf Creek. Janie ordered dessert: Chocolate cake. Wow–did she get chocolate cake! It was a slice big enough to cover a dinner plate. She boxed most of it to take home.

It reminded me of another chocolate cake I met in Iowa.

I was travelling west on Interstate 80 when I stopped for lunch at a truck stop in a rural location. A trucker's lunchtime may occur at any time 24/7. This stop was not at a usual lunchtime and there were only two other diners. I took a booth on the east side of the room. The other truckers were on the south side and one soon left.

The waitress came over from behind the counter to take my order. She was an older lady, stiff and formal, dressed in grey to match her hair that was put up in an old fashioned bun. Did she belong in one of the stately old farm homes that dotted the Iowa landscape? Was she a widow, having to work to keep her home?

She took my order and I was soon dining on that good Midwest cooking.

Looming high in a glass pantry behind the counter was a cake stand displaying a tempting chocolate cake. Those were the good old days when I could eat a meal *and* a dessert so I decided I just had to have some chocolate cake. The lady was clearing a table on the south side and had her back to the counter. When I said I would have cake for dessert she acknowledged my request with a nod. She continued to clear the table and I added, "Since you have only one piece left I may as well eat it."

She stopped working and stared at the wall for a few seconds then turned rather quickly to look at the cake. Just as she thought–there remained a fourth of the large cake good for at least 3 good sized servings!

"Sir!" she exclaimed, "How big is your appetite?"

I started laughing. The other trucker laughed. Her face brightened into a happy smile when she realized this silly trucker was kidding with her.

Maybe, just maybe, she was living a longtime dream to get out of the house and work in public. Maybe it was a satisfying activity and not a necessity for her. I do hope so and maybe my little joke added joy to her day.

For any of us it can make a better day when we have a little humor and lots of chocolate cake.

## Bali

Lee Larson, the owner, had his office in the Gresham depot just 9 miles east of my home on the east edge of Portland. When Susan Retter was the manager in the mid 80's I was invited to produce a newsletter for that division.

In addition to publishing the monthly "BUS BIZ" I drove school routes, special needs vans and for 2 one week sessions each August I drove the leased bus for the Steen's Mountain High Altitude Running Camp in southeastern Oregon.

I sometimes delivered modern new school buses with push button gear shifts to school districts who ordered them from Lee's "Thomas Bus" dealership. Or I would pick up or deliver used buses that had been bought or sold. If multiple buses were involved, I would lead a convoy.

A memorable trip was when I and a second driver delivered 2 used buses to a client in the San Francisco, California area. We left the yard at midnight, delivered the buses that afternoon, caught the plane that night and were met at Portland (PDX) by the other driver's wife. I picked up my car at the bus yard at midnight!

One driver resigned and rented a U-Haul truck to move to Phoenix, Arizona. He wanted an experienced driver to assist him. He paid me $100, bought my meals and gave me a plane ticket to return home. In Phoenix I spent the night with Janie's daughter, Melinda and her family and they took me to the airport the next day.

Charter trips were interesting. I took 3 people to Mount Hood one day. The couple was teasing the old country boy type unmercifully. I ask where they were from. This humble man said, "I am from Bali. Do you know where Bali is?"

"Yes I do." I replied, "You go east in Indonesia to the end of Java and there is Bali across that bit of ocean. We have a movie you should see called South Pacific and it has a song called Bali Hai." His self-esteem soared when this Oregon bus driver proved his homeland was an important well known place.

The teasing stopped.

## The Khyber Pass
Driving a chartered van, I had a most astounding and far reaching experience. Two couples from Pakistan paid for a van to take them to the Mt. Hood area. I drove east in the scenic Columbia River Gorge. At Hood River I turned south skirting the east side of Mt. Hood. I turned right on Route 26 for Portland then right away took a spur to the right up the mountain to Timberline Lodge. After I parked one couple hurried up the lot toward the lodge. The other couple strolled along with me. They explained that the others lived in hot weather near India and were in a hurry to see the August snow behind and above the lodge.

"But we live in NW Pakistan in the mountains."

"Then you must be near the Khyber Pass," I said.

"Yes, we are only 30 miles from the pass."

"Then you are not far from where Alexander the Great had his easternmost camp."

"Yes, I've been to that site," the man said.

Wow! I've been to these faraway places by reading lots of books but here is someone who has physically been there!

Now fast forward to 1997. I move back to Morgantown. My oldest son, Henry Kent is with a crew in Portland, programming for the Marsh Company in New York. Their manager has moved to New York and she wants the rest of the crew to move there also. Four times in two years Henry has spent a week with his boss on floor 96 of the Twin Towers skyscraper. Now she wants the whole Portland crew to move to New York. Henry puts his home up for sale. The first plane hit Floor 96 and Henry's boss and job were vaporized. The Marsh Company could not replace, in New York, their forty floors of rented offices lost in the Towers. Henry's job went to India and Osama Ben Laden went to Pakistan.

Henry's job is still in India but one night US stealth helicopters flew through the Khyber Pass into NW Pakistan and the Navy Seals took Ben Laden out.

Henry now lives in Morgantown, Kentucky and has an 8 hour a day job here. His wife, Griselda, from Ecuador, with her fluent Spanish and English, is an asset to our Head Start Program. My

Granddaughter, Vania is growing into a tall slim Spanish beauty. Her personable younger brother, Isaac, with his South American Indian and Spanish heritage prominent in his features, is a delight to his teachers and others. I am proud of him.

It is amazing how faraway places and faraway people and long ago events now seem so close to home!

PS Alexander the Great didn't make it back home. In Babylon he got pneumonia and died. He made Greek the universal language of the world of that time. That's why the New Testament was written in Greek. While in NY, Henry was learning Greek, but when he married Griselda he had good reason to make his second language Spanish. He's quite good at it.

## Two Tonys

One was English. One was Irish. Francis (Tony) Parsons and Anthony (Tony) Ryan pooled their skills and resources to build a large machine shop in NW Gresham. With contracts from Boeing and other companies big and small, and a loyal workforce that work together like a family, they have prospered.

These 2 great guys have as strong a family sentiment for their wives and families as I have ever seen. I, who have English and Irish blood, with some Scotch and German mixed in, took an immediate liking to these two entrepreneurs.

They called School Bus Services. They wanted to hire a bus and driver for a night on the town as a treat for their workers. I got the assignment. I reported to the pick-up point then drove to a few homes to gather up the rest of the party participants. For fun I negotiated the curves in East Multnomah County with a little emphasis to sharp turns and soon had the laughing passengers calling me Mario!

The bosses were treating their American employees to a Pub Crawl in the Irish and English tradition. The first stop was The Refectory, named for the dining quarters of monasteries and Fraternity houses. It was known in Portland for great steaks. Some of the fellows came out with part of their drinks still in the glasses. I have 2 in my kitchen cabinet. They have Libby brand on the bottom. They are not cut glass; neither are they cheap. I have drunk many a glass of milk or water from them to remind me of my friends in Oregon.

After several stops as designated driver, I took this well-behaved group of gentlemen home. I was pleased when they agreed to ask for me the next time they needed a driver.

Janie and I visited Tony Parson's beautiful home once. I told him I enjoyed being his chauffeur and if he ever needed a butler I would like to have the job! I called his company recently and told his secretary I was checking about the job!

Sadly, I learned that the Refectory had closed. The land owner could get more rent from a Dollar Store. Thirty-five years of loyal rental meant nothing to him, nor the fate of 30 employees, 15 of whom had been with the restaurant from the beginning.

## Oregon's Pacific Coast

One of the most memorable assignments was on Saturday, July 16, 1988. Tony Parsons called to reserve a bus for that weekend. The company personnel were to be taken on a deep sea fishing trip. I was requested to be the driver. This was exciting for me. I had made trips to Victoria, Canada on ships that cruise coastal routes. This would be my first and only trip out into the Pacific Ocean beyond the sight of land.

After the plant closed on Friday evening I arrived to load the passengers for the trip to the coast. Motel rooms had been reserved so we would be there for an early start on Saturday morning. In about 4 hours we pulled into Newport. There was a room reserved for me but I was the taxi for the evening. Each guy had his favorite restaurant or bar to visit. I would drop them off and asked when they wanted to be picked up. This was before cell phones! I finally got to bed at 2am with a wake-up call for 4am. I had to see that all were awake and breakfasted in time to leave for the boat dock. We were to head out to sea about daybreak. The

Newport Tradewinds Deep Sea Fishing charter service was engaged by the Pro-Met crew for a day of fishing.

I dropped the guys off and parked the bus in an all-day lot. Then I went aboard the fishing boat. I was a paid customer, guest of Pro-Met. Soon we were chugging out to sea with numerous other fishing boats following in our wake. The morning sun highlighted Tony Parson's face as we headed out to sea. The morning mist made an eerie scene as we were leaving the bay, going under the Highway 101 bridge, passing the last pier and seeing nothing ahead but open water.

Ocean fishing was sure different from running a trotline in Green River. You didn't pick a spot and wait for the fish. The captain hunted them. The fishing boats were equipped with things like echo sounders and sonar. When the captain found a school of fish on the screen he stopped and everyone manned the fishing poles and hoped to catch one. When no fish were biting we hooked the bait and hook on the reel and went on the hunt again. We could

see other boats parked or cruising around doing the same thing. Fishing boats were on the horizon but no land was in sight.

I didn't always man my line. Part of the time I was inside sitting at a table holding my tummy to hold it down. The sea was rocking the boat with a constant rhythm. Six times there was a swish, swish, swish, swish, swish, swish then the seventh one was a big swoo-o-o-sh. It was exactly the same over and over. You wanted to scream for it to stop. I never got used to it but managed it, barely. We had cruised 2 hours to get to the fishing grounds. We were going to fish 4 hours before heading back.

I, who had never been airsick from flying barely coped as mild seasickness plagued me on this fishing trip. Tony Parsons had noticed my struggle and told me, "For a while I thought we were going to lose you." I was glad to see the shoreline ahead. Tony Ryan relaxes as we enter the bay and head for the dock.

I had caught 4 red snappers, a tasty ocean fish. Some of the fellows had caught several fish and tossed a few of them in my bucket so I would be taking home a good supply of fish for the freezer.

We were not fishing for salmon but 3 were caught. This was a bonanza for those who caught them. Cannery people were waiting at the dock to pay a good price for any they could buy. Also waiting for us on the dock were entrepreneurs who would clean and fillet your fish for a price. We all bought the service. Then with coolers and buckets full of fish we loaded the bus and headed for home.

**Bus Biz is Born**
The morning runs were over and I was lounging in the driver's room basking in the banter and buzz of my School Bus Services family. Sandy, our present office manager, was moping. It was her 40th birthday and she was sure she was 'over the hill'. I, who was already in my 60s said, "I like to see those birthdays roll around."

She stopped pacing and stared at me in astonishment, "You do?!"

"Yes," I replied. "What worries me is when they stop." I'm not sure that made her feel any better.

Susan Retter became our office manager. We had gathered in the driver's room for a monthly driver's meeting. At the end of the meeting she suggested that if anyone had a suggestion for something that would help the company she would be glad to hear it. After the meeting I told her if the company ever considered a newsletter I would like to be involved.

A few weeks later Susan appointed one of her office staff to organize a newsletter. "Check with Charles Romans." Under the supervision of the manager I soon had the project under way. A contest for a name was won by the owner, Lee Larson. We all agreed that Bus Biz was the best name. The newsletter was a hit with Corporate (our reference to the owner and management) and later a companywide Bus Biz newsletter was started so I named our local publication, Bus Biz Gresham.

As of 1990 I was producing a monthly publication. That lasted until 1997 when I moved back to Butler County, Kentucky. It was a great experience. The most popular feature was the section called ATTA BOY/GIRL. One liners gave "thanks" and "congratulations" to and from numerous drivers and managers. Events were announced or reported on. For sale items were advertised. Safety articles were listed. Cartoons were enjoyed.

A lot of cut and paste work went into the early editions. I bought a word processor to speed up my work. I would not get a computer until much later. It was a big help when Lee Larson bought me a laser printer. Printers are cheap now but that reliable old HP4P cost $1000 at that time. Puzzles were popular. I made original crossword puzzles for Bus Biz so I became a Cruciverbalist. As a faithful subscriber to my hometown newspaper I sometimes found an interesting item to share with my Oregon audience. This puzzler was in the May 1, 1991 issue of The Green River Republican.

CAN YOU IDENTIFY THESE OLD FOLK SAYINGS COUCHED IN THE LANGUAGE OF SOME POLITITIONS?

Precipitancy creates prodigality.

Compute not your immature gallinaceans prior to their being produced.

Failure to be present causes the vital organ to become more enamored.

You cannot estimate the value of the contents of a bound, printed narrative from its exterior vesture.

Socially oriented individuals tend to congregate in gregarious homogenous groupings.

A rotating lithoidal fragment never accrues lichen.

The individual of the Class Aves, arriving before the appointed time, seizes the invertebrate of the Group Vermes.

## Mt. Hood Ski Trips

A ski run, driving one of the schools' Ski Clubs to Mt. Hood for a day of skiing was sometimes challenging and always fun. On a cold sunny day I was following a Raz Transportation bus east on route 26 headed for Mt. Hood. Our destination was Timberline Lodge. We went on past the ski area at Government Camp which was mostly for less experienced skiers. A little farther up the mountain we turned left on a spur that took us to Timberline. Timberline Lodge was built by the WPA, a program under President Franklin Roosevelt. Because of the growth in popularity of skiing a large concrete building was added a block or so down the parking lot from the lodge to accommodate the skiers. A good restaurant was included leaving the restaurant in the lodge for the tourist. Below this new building was a large parking lot for buses and overflow from the parking lot in front of the lodge.

There is no road to go farther up the mountain. From this 6000-foot level you can ride the chairlift one mile up to the 7000-foot level or skiers can grab the rope tow to go up for another run.

At the top of the lift a shelter was built. It's named the Silcox Hut. The south wall is open. The seats on the chairlift enter the open side, ride around the big flat overhead wheel and proceed downhill without stopping. If you have just arrived, you jump off the slow moving seat onto the wooden floor and let the chair pass you. If you are going down, you step in front of an empty seat and fall backwards into the seat for a downhill ride to Timberline lodge. You swing several feet above the snow in the 2 passenger porch swing without a porch.

On the way to the mountain I got the attention of my passengers. "See the slogan on our competitor's bus?" There is was on the back of the bus we were following: *We go the extra mile.* "It ought to be interesting, to see him drive that bus a mile past Timberline Lodge and up to the Silcox Hut!"

## Mount Hood Meadows
While waiting for my load of skiers at Timberline Lodge I would take advantage of a writing nook with seat and table to read or write. The day would pass with naps and meals or enjoying the fireplaces with the lodge mascot, a big friendly laid back Saint Bernard dog.

A competitor to the Timberline Lodge ski resort was founded on the east slope of the mountain. Most of my runs were to Mount Hood Meadows. On one trip a young skier broke her leg. She was stabilized in the first aid building and kept comfortable until a few hours later when it was time to load for home. On a stretcher she was loaded through the left side emergency door and placed across two seats. Her father met us with a pickup at the town of Sandy a few miles east of Gresham.

Another trip was plagued by wet weather. Of course at the lodge level the snow was dry. But when it was time to drive home I was soon in the area of wet snow. As I negotiated the slushy pavement and dark curves the left windshield wiper fell off. As the wet snowflakes kept sliding down the windshield I weaved my face back and forth and got an adequate view to keep moving. It got better when a lower altitude turned the precipitation to rain. At Sandy I borrowed a screwdriver from the store and put the right windshield wiper on the left side. It fit at a crazy angle but it worked while I took the ski club members to their destination west of Portland. My skill and experience had delivered the kids safely home without a long wait on the mountain for a mechanic with a windshield wiper.

One evening, an hour or so before closing time, I was surprised to find my youngest son, Vincent, among the skiers. I told him I wanted to watch him ski down the slope. As we looked at the little figures coming down the lighted slope high above us he said, "You couldn't tell me from the others."

"Oh yes I could. The wildest one will be you."

Sure enough, a little later I could see one of the little figures speeding and zig zagging down the mountain. As he entered the flat area ending at the finish line near where I was standing, he leaped into the air, turned and slid in backwards.

I never took up skiing. With my family and job obligations I didn't want to risk a broken leg. After Vince became a family man he too gave up the risky sport.

After I moved back to Kentucky Vince brought his family for a visit. We rented a boat. As his wife, Danielle, sat behind him he showed his son Chris how to steer the boat. As we zipped past Turkey Rock on Green River, our experience on that cold mountain at the far end of the continent seemed to be in another galaxy, long ago and far away.

### The Basque

I first heard of a Basque at the Portland Boxing Club. I was the photographer for the owner, Tom Moyer. I overheard a discussion about a heavyweight from the past who was a Basque. They were referring to Paulino Uzcudun. He was the champ in Europe when he retired. He came out of retirement to fight Joe Louis in Madison Square Garden on December 13, 1935. Joe Louis won in the 4th round and that ended the quite long and outstanding career of Basque boxer, Paulino Uzcudun. Three years after that, in 1938, I was visiting relatives in Muhlenberg County where I listened on the radio as Joe Louis won over Max Schmeling. Then in the 1960s I met Joe Louis who was visiting the Portland Boxing Club. What interesting threads weave through the tapestries of our lives! That was the last contact I had with Joe Louis but I wasn't through with the Basque.

Homeland for the beautiful Basque people is a territory that straddles the border between Spain and France. Theirs is not one of the romance languages of Europe. Their unique language is older.

On a sales trip I learned that Elko, Nevada was one of many towns where Basque festivals are held. In Winnemucca, Nevada I stayed in a

Basque hotel where the dining room door is opened at the traditional 6:15pm and the guests file in and sit at long tables and dine family style. The main occupation for Basque men was sheep herding. Nevada was a prime destination for migrants from Europe but they can be found throughout the Americas. Later when trucking through Las Vegas I would stop at the Showboat where I learned to love lamb chops. I was learning to love Basque food, history and ways. When I went to work at School Bus Services I was set to meet a great friend and associate and experience the Basque presence in Eastern Oregon.

Harland Yriarte was the grandson of a Basque who herded sheep on Steen's Mountain in Southeastern Oregon. Harland's parents own a hotel in Burns, Oregon. Harland owns a ranch in that area. He became the athletic director for the Lane Community College in Eugene. Knowing the value to athletes to train in high altitude he used his familiar home territory to arrange a place for athletes from all over the world to get that experience. He founded the Steen's Mountain High Altitude Running Camp. The small beginning grew fast. He drove the bus at

Harland Yriarte and Charlie Romans

first. As growth made more responsibilities he had to hire a driver.

The mountain is dangerous and must be respected. Each one-week session includes a day of races at Wild Horse lake located at the bottom of a volcanic crater at the Steen's Mountain peak. The South wall of the crater was blown away by a long ago eruption. The bus dropped the runners off on a plateau and after a mile or so of walking to the rim of the crater they followed a steep trail down the north wall to the small grassy plain around the lake. As the session neared its end half of the class headed up the steep slope. At the top the bus was still a mile or so away. A sudden mountain storm rapidly developed. As the driver ran across the open space for the bus he was killed by lightening. The group in the bottom of the crater had hunkered in a fetal position to be a smaller target for the lightning. After the front passed a runner came back down the trail to tell them their driver was lost.

Eventually I was the driver who took his place for 10 years. I would see the genius of Harland Yriarte, the founder of an outstanding training camp.

## Faux Greyhound Bus Driver

They came from far and wide; these were young athletes who wanted to hone their skills and develop the capacity of their lungs and heart in the high altitude. They came to Oregon. It was my duty to get them to the camp.

City bus drivers drive a lot but don't get anywhere much. About 1947 Vern Albers quit Portland Traction Company and made driving city to city for Greyhound his lifetime work. His older brother stayed with the city buses until they added light rail. He thought it would be great to be in streetcars again. The busy times of seven-minute intervals on the old 1940s street cars were pure leisure compared to the on-the-minute time points and electronic signals that made for a lot of tension for an old street car operator. He could hardly wait for the next run signup so he could go back to his bus route.

I had quit the city buses in 1967 and now in the 1980s I was driving school buses all over the western states. In 1987 when I began driving for the Steen's Mountain High Altitude Running Camp it was the nearest thing to a Greyhound run I would ever do.

Early on Sunday morning I would check my bus and leave the Gresham yard. My first stop was the Trailways Bus Terminal across the street from the Portland Railroad Station. Here the campers who had paid for a ride to camp, loaded their baggage and climbed aboard. Some fifty miles south I picked up the second group at the Salem bus station. When I got to Eugene I used the angled parking slot to nose up to the bus depot door like a veteran Greyhound driver. I opened the baggage doors under the side of the bus and hurried to the men's room to make room for a quick cup of coffee.

Now we left the Willamette Valley and headed east. We crossed the Cascade Mountains, drove through the lava beds and entered Oregon's high desert. As I drove on the road that had been built on the lava that had cooled centuries ago I told my passengers that I was glad the lava didn't get over the road! The Bend bus depot was a storefront office with a large dusty lot out front. I parked and while my passengers stretched their legs the new campers loaded their gear. Now we headed for Burns. It was a long monotonous drive. As I

**Greyhound Bus Depot in Bend, Oregon**
**Steen's Mountain camp bus loading**

approached Burns most of my passengers were dozing. I now did what would become a regular trick on my future trips. I yelled, "Hey!" I pointed off to the right. Some even stood up to see what the excitement was about. Sure enough, there spread out in a big rancher's field, were many bales of hay. There was amusement at my wake-up call and the next expectation was mealtime. I parked at the Hotel owned by Harland's parents. While pickups and other vehicles retrieved the baggage and headed for camp we went inside where Harland and Jan Yriarte soon checked the camper's names off and collected the balance of the camper's fees. I fueled the bus at a local gas station before joining the crowd for a delicious spaghetti dinner that had been prepared for us.

## Steen's Mountain High Altitude Running Camp

Day was not over. We loaded and I drove south to French Glen. Most of the trip was in the dark. Turning left at French Glen I drove up the mountain to the camp. We were met with lanterns and each camper searched through the mounds of baggage for his or her gear and checked in at the assigned tent to rest for tomorrow's strenuous training. I slept in the bus and the next morning I scouted the area and, in a quiet place yards above the camp, I set up my dome tent where I would have quiet and seclusion for reading and napping in my time off. I would later regret my decision.

The day started with a meeting in the Corral. After a talk about the day's activities the runners made a short run to get the heart pumping higher. Then back in the Corral we would see if our pulse was back to normal in one minute. I say 'we' because I made that run with the athletes and until I moved away at the age of 72 my heart passed the one minute test. It was a great mountain vacation with pay. I would be on call to drive the campers to various training areas when needed. On the big day I would drop them off far up the mountain then drive a few

miles down to a parking spot where they would come out of the last canyon. If anyone was sick or injured they could take a shortcut to the waiting bus. In late afternoon, the hardiest runners arrived at the bus. Some of these superb athletes would rest a bit, refill their water bottles and run the last few miles to the camp. On August 13, 1991, on one of these long days of standby, I wrote the Steen's camp song. On the internet, you can see that a lively modern pop song has replaced my ballad like song.

One day when returning from a practice the route took me across a plateau that dropped off steeply and suddenly. The almost cliff like slope was on our left as we descended. Far below us a herd of cattle grazed in a pasture. The looked so small but your reasoning told you they were normal size. I took advantage of the illusion; I spun a yarn for my passengers.

"This rancher raised these miniature cattle for an experiment. These cattle are only one foot tall and a few were put in a space capsule and were put in orbit for a trip around the earth. They became known as *The herd shot 'round the world.* The passengers stared in awe. Then an amazing thing happened. The farther down the hill I got, the more those cattle grew. When I descended to their level they were full sized cattle!

Our mountains and plains give us majestic vistas and even magical illusions. A tenderfoot from back east checked in at a resort. The next morning he went for a walk. A distant formation caught his eye and didn't seem too far away. He walked toward it until he was exhausted and it didn't seem any closer. I search party found him and leading him back to the lodge explained to him, "In the mountains something that seems near may be miles away." They came to a 3 foot wide stream and the tourist sat and started taking off his shoes and socks. "What are you doing?"

"I'm getting ready to swim this river."

It was true. Wild Horse Lake was a long way down the wall of the volcanic crater. I parked the bus about a mile from the lip of the crater. After I secured it I followed the crowd that was almost to the top. When I got there I followed the trail down the steep inside and was soon with the crowd preparing for their timed runs. On this first time here on my new job I heard one of the runners ask another, "How is that old man going to get out of here?" Well on my last year on the job when I was 72 I was still going down to Wild Horse Lake and climbing back out.

On Saturday morning I would load the campers and return them to their bus depots. Then on Sunday morning I would repeat the routine for the runners signed up for the second week session.

## History's Black Marks

It has been observed that the human brain is the crowning achievement of Jehovah's material creation. A rival miraculous gift is our ability to produce more humans so God's purpose to populate the earth can be fulfilled. He is rightfully hurt and angered when he sees this marvelous gift misused.

On one of my first trips to California as a trucker on Homer Wood's Exley Company truck, he pointed out to me a Texaco Truck Stop that was notorious as a hangout for prostitutes. I made it a point to never use that truck stop.

With a load for Phoenix, Arizona we were approaching Las Vegas, Nevada from the north. Homer pointed out to me a side road leading out into the desert. Down that road a ways was the Cottontail Ranch, a legal brothel. In a similar business near this location recently a talented young man added illegal drugs into the mix and almost died. You have seen the extensive news.

While Homer and I were having lunch at a truck stop I heard old cigar smoking, Fred, declare, "If my wife won't give me satisfaction at home, I'll get it down the road." Sometime later I heard he drove down that sandy road north of Las Vegas and got stuck. The towing bill for pulling him out of the sand to the road was a hefty bill but he did not dare turn in that road expense to the office.

While driving the bus for the Steen's Mountain Running Camp I often drove past a meadow called Whorehouse Meadow. Wikipedia says the meadow earned its name in the days of the Old West when females from Vale, Oregon set up camp here. Steen's Mountain was a lively place in those days.

French Glen was the turning off place to go up the mountain to the camp. From the camp French Glen about 16 miles away was the closest telephone for any homesick campers. It was from that phone I ordered my first computer. It was a Leading Edge made in Korea. It had a whopping 750 kilobytes of space on the hard drive! Now I have 2 hard drives with a terabyte of memory on each one.

Peter French had acquired about 2000 acres by often crooked ways. The Paiute and Bannock Indians took umbrage at his stealing their ancestral lands and during the summer of 1878 they burned buildings and ran off cattle and horses. French survived that onslaught but when he, on horseback, had a confrontation with a former employee and took his whip to him he got shot out of the saddle. The remains of his empire are his name on the town, the chimney and foundation of his burned out home and the round barn he invented. The barn's inside perimeter next to the outer wall was a clear runway for exercising and training hundreds of mules and horses during the winter weather.

Steens Mountain is a large mountain some 50 miles long north to south. It runs about 4000 feet high and where the Running Camp is located on the south end it reaches a summit elevation of 9,733 feet. It is another world from the Willamette Valley where Portland is located.

Like the rest of the world, it has been marred by violence, greed and immorality. That will soon end. Keep praying, "Thy will be done, in earth as it is in heaven."

## Mountain Storm

It was peaceful for reading and quiet for sleeping where I had set up my personal tent on the slope above the running camp; one night something hit the tent with a loud *whomp*. Then it hit again and again. The plastic ribs of the tent could not stand the strain and snapped like the crack of a rifle. The tent was lying flat on me as I lay on my back and put my feet strait up to pull on my boots. That flattened undulating tent was what my two rescuers saw in the light of their flashlights. A sudden mountain storm had killed a previous driver. Now one was after me.

They helped me get separated from my tent and we struggled against the wind as we made our way down to the bus. The campers had abandoned the battered army tents and were in the bus, pick-ups and other vehicles. That's where we spent the rest of the night. In future sessions I would set my tent under a tree about 10 feet or less from the door of the bus. In case of another storm I was prepared to be the first one in the bus!

The camp was in tatters. Harland hurriedly arranged to spend the rest of the session in the old CCC buildings located farther down the mountain. The buildings were not occupied at the time and the barracks like buildings had many beds with springs without bedding. On them we installed our sleeping bags and made ourselves at home.

There was a hill nearby that resembled a miniature of Australia's Ayer's rock. This furnished a steep slope for training in addition to the usual places back up by and above the old tattered camp. I transported them as usual. With a lot of work the camp would be restored for the next week's session.

On my last season with the camp, a room in a building became available. Someone made a fancy sign saying 'Charlie's Bunkhouse' and posted it to the left of the door. So this cowboy with a big yellow horse slept in a bunkhouse!

This area in southeast Oregon was Harland Yriarte's home territory. Only he could build this renowned camp that benefited thousands of young runners. I saw how he had the connections to keep it running in the face of disaster.

This great recreation area is reasonably safe for tourists. But a tenderfoot without savvy of the mountains can, unwittingly, expose himself to serious danger. One time as I took a bus load of campers to the top of Steens, there, just before the top over on the left at the brink of the steep drop a family had set up their tent and spent the night. A storm such as I had been through would have tossed them over the brink and scattered them on the rocks hundreds of feet below.

I was getting smarter. I learned to sleep close to the bus!

## The Big Day

On the Big Day I had 12 hours to wait; I could read, nap, take short hikes staying in sight of the bus and write. After two or three years of learning the routine and philosophy of the camp I spent this 12 hour wait to compose a song that became our camp song. A verse of the song says:

> We'll be glad when the Wild Horse Canyon
> And the Cross Canyon runs are done.
> We'll board the bus for Denio, Nevada
> And one last day of fun.

As the roster grew, a second bus and SBS driver was added. Matt Anderson joined the crew. He brought Michelle and her two children with him. They were good company.

Saturday the campers would load for the Greyhound bus depots where they would meet their families or buses for their rides home. But Friday evening was a time to relax and have fun after 5 tough days of training. Each tent group had prepared a skit. Records were announced and awards handed out. For a period of years this evening was spent several miles south at Denio, Nevada.

## Denio, Nevada

After setting up our sleeping bag camp in a park and being fed by the cook we spent the waning hours of the day by driving a few miles South and West to the Hot Springs. What a delightful way to end a lively, eventful week.

One such evening found 2 older gentlemen had parked their 2 pickup campers in the little park by the Hot Springs. One was a police chief in California. The other lived in Nevada. These two old friends got together here to watch the desert stars and talk over old times. Imagine their surprise when out of the deserted desert Matt and I unloaded 2 bus loads of shouting, diving, splashing youngsters in front of their camp! No complaints though. They thought that these lively young people in their swimsuits made a good show, especially the girls!

## Saturday Morning

We rendezvoused at the hotel in Burns. Everyone ate and prepared for the long trip west. A contribution I had made to the camp was, with my new computer, to make color-coded baggage tags. The last color stuffed in the baggage space under the bus would be the first off in Bend. We boarded and I prepared to start the bus. Where are the keys? We searched my pockets, the bus, the hotel and the grounds. Time was wasting. I finally gave up and called a local locksmith. With sympathy for the young passengers they made me a set of keys without charge. What a relief to be on our way, even an hour late. After a while, I felt the need for a peanut. To keep myself alert while driving I often shucked an unshelled peanut and nibbled. We were about an hour down the road when I reached for a peanut in the brown bag sitting on the tray. I grasped something and instead of a peanut, I pulled out the bus keys!

After a good laugh, someone asked me to sing a song.

"Any requests? Any one except 'Waltzing Matilda'."

"Why not Waltzing Matilda?"

"Never mind. You've been warned. Just don't ask for Waltzing Matilda."

Of course someone soon did. The steering wheel whipped back and forth. Then to a rousing 'Waltzing Matilda, Waltzing Matilda' the bus maintained a straight path but tossed right and left like a boat riding waves in a violent storm. The passengers thought it was a hilarious show.

That night the last passengers got off in Portland and I parked the bus at the Gresham lot and went home for a short night's sleep. The next morning the mechanic met me to service the bus and adjust the brakes. He came out from under the bus surprised that after a week in the mountains the brakes needed no adjustment! I was ready to take the next class for a week at the Steen's Mountain High Altitude Running Camp.

I did not know I was making an impression. I did not know I was a role model as I used my stamina to climb the steep trails or gathered skunk cabbage with everyone else for the turkey roasting pit. I wasn't competing with anyone but myself. I was enjoying myself but I *was* just the bus driver. I marveled at the performance and dedication of these young athletes I was chauffeuring but I did not know they were impressed by my meager participation, or my song writing and singing or my skillful handling of a bus on jeep trails. I was practicing my philosophy: Only work at what you can do well and be the best. Only work at what you enjoy. Enjoy the work you do. By having fun for 10 years this Old Man of the Mountain had become a legend!

## Portland, Oregon to Portland, Maine

My goal of returning to Kentucky seemed to be more and more practical. My three children were growing up and the housing market was good for selling. In two years, we could do it. Then we could explore the east coast as we had the west coast. I told Libby Jane that we may be too old and our health may limit our activities after 1997 when we expected to move. "We should have a good vacation in 1995 while the schools are out." So after the Steen's mountain stint was over in August we headed east. To fulfill a wish to drive from Portland, OR to Portland, ME we would make our first major stop in Maine. On the way we did spend 2 nights in Buffalo, NY to do laundry and explore Niagara Falls. We arrived in Portland in the afternoon then continued down the coast to York Harbor where we had reservations at the historic York Harbor Inn.

Our reservation was for room # 1 on the second floor. Directly below us was the dining room. To get to it we went down the stairs and through a room with smoke darkened beams. This had been a seine drying room for fishermen in the 1600s. It had been moved here from an island way out in the Atlantic and the hotel built around it. In the dining room I fulfilled another wish by eating a Maine lobster in Maine.

Danbury, Connecticut was our next stop. Commuter trains took locals from here to Manhattan every day. The Bob Evans restaurant by our motel was my introduction to this restaurant chain. This was our base to go west into upstate NY to visit the Watchtower farm and printery at Wallkill. The next day we toured the newly opened Education Center at Patterson, NY. Sunday morning found us entering Manhattan from the north, driving along Central Park. Our reservation was in the Ramada Inn in lower Manhattan. The *Phantom of the Opera* was playing on the ground floor but when Janie learned that her favorite singer was not in this performance we traded our tickets in for *Cats* a short walk north in the Winter Garden Theatre.

While Janie stayed in the room for a day of rest, I walked to the east side of Manhattan and took pictures of the United Nations building. Next, I was on the sightseeing floor of the Empire State building. I walked into one of the Twin Towers and in a deep *deep* level boarded the Path Train for New Jersey. There I visited the grand Stanley Theatre fully restored by Jehovah's Witnesses. A mother & daughter and I were the only ones on the next tour. The guide showed us, among other features, the women's rest room that had 40 stalls!

After a tour of the Watchtower Headquarters and factory we drove south to Boston. As I drove uptown to see the Old North Church I got caught in an Irish parade until a Paddy stepped forward and made us a path out of our trap. On our way south we had a blowout and bought new tires. Still north of Washington, while stopped in traffic a driver raced from behind and swerved into the left turn lane as he intended to do but left our rear exposed to the speeding driver that was pacing him. She slammed into the back of our car. There was no visible damage so we continued. Washington was mostly closed on Sunday so we looked at the sights as we drove on through and got a room for the night in Manassas, Virginia. The next morning, at a breakfast counter, a local policeman told me all about the Civil War battle of Manassas.

We almost made it to my mom's in Morgantown, KY but near Leitchfield the car went dead. I raised the hood. The battery case was warped forward and the spinning alternator had ground a hole in the battery. The acid killed the alternator. It was years later before I connected that damage with the accident 2 days earlier. Yep, I'm a slow thinker! Since this was before cell phones, I thumbed a ride to a public phone where I called a tow truck.

### El Paso, Phoenix and Home

In Morgantown I bought a new battery. I went to the Napa auto parts store and traded in the alternator and replaced the voltage regulator. The voltage regulator lasted until we got into Missouri where we spent the rest of the night in the car until we could get another one. The alternator lasted until we got to El Paso, Texas where we had reservations.

We left the car at the local Ford Dealer's and caught a bus to do some sightseeing and shopping in Juarez, Mexico. We caught a bus to go back to El Paso and after a while figured out that we were headed south. We got off and crossed the street to catch a northbound bus. We enjoyed our room one more night and prepared to leave for Phoenix the next day.

We left the Ford dealer's shop and headed for the highway. The Ford would not shift out of low gear unless I revved the motor and hit 40 MPH. We go back to the Ford dealer. After checking, the manager said the transmission was bad and it could be fixed in 2 days for 2000 dollars. No. Thanks. We would try for Phoenix. When we arrived at Melinda and David's she sent us to their mechanic. He raised the hood, looked on the back of the engine and re-hooked a linkage someone had disconnected. He charged $10, a big difference from the $2000 quoted in El Paso. Our home in Portland, OR really looked good after the long days on the road but we had made great memories. I took the bad alternator to Morgantown, KY when we moved 2 years later. I was given only a core deposit price for it.

### A Steen's Mountain Farewell

1997 was my tenth and last season as their bus driver. At the last Friday night skits I sang my Steen's Mountain song as usual. I walked over to Matt Anderson and handed him my pith helmet. "Matt, I am passing the hat to you. Now you are the senior driver." Then as a completely unexpected surprise, I became the star of the show. I was presented with a rich, woolen Indian blanket. Then there was a coffee cup with a picture of me on the rim above Wild Horse Lake.

I was invited to sit. For a week the camp had been involved in writing a poem about me. It had been a well-kept secret. I sat in awe and heartfelt love as the words of my Steen's mountain family were read to me and a copy handed to me with all their signatures.

## Charlie

The skies above Steens Mountain
Have witnessed courageous deeds,
The hardy souls who come here
Are a tough and noble breed.
From the Rooster Combs to the Blitzen
They're here to do or die,
But getting them to the starting line
Requires a special kind of guy.
Charlie takes the yellow bus
Where most people can't take their cars.
And he carries campers and water jugs, dirty socks
and Power bars.

When the road was closed at Jackman Park
To bury a cattle guard
Charlie powered his way around the pit –
He drives that yellow bus hard.
He drives like the pioneer pilot he was
In that old Stearman double-wing
And if you've been here on Awards night
You know that man can sing.

We've seen them all here – Stars of road and track,
Men and women who can really fly.
But we all know that the real hero in life
Is the big-hearted stand–up guy.

We can only dream of the deeds we'll do,
Only imagine the things we'll see.
But we need look no farther than Charlie
To see what we hope to be.

Now Charlie was born in the flatlands
And to Kentucky he's bound to roam,
But we hope that in some corner of his heart
Steens Mountain will always be home.

How can I ever forget the Steen's Mountain High Altitude Running Camp?

## Transporting Fire Fighters

Circumstances in August 1997 gave me the opportunity to see the life of fire fighters first hand. My Oregon home was up for sale. I did not renew my Oregon school bus driver's license so I wasn't available to help start the school year that fall. I still had my chauffer's license and the fire fighters needed 2 more buses for the Towers Fire burning south of Pendleton. So on Friday, August 30 Matt Anderson and I took two school buses and headed east. We had lunch at Biggs then hurried on to get registered for duty. We wanted to find out our next day assignments before dark. As we approached Ukiah we could see east of us smoke rising like a mushroom cloud reaching into the sky.

The camp was huge with a population of 1200 and across the road was another camp of 550 Marines there to fight the fire.

As the breezes lessened of an evening and the setting sun withdrew its heat we would load the firefighters in the waiting buses and go to camp for the night. After washing up they went down the chow line for their choice of food. I had thought I was fed the best as a pilot in the Army Air Corps and I had to pay for it but I never saw anything like that food at the firefighter's camp. There for the taking was your choice of steaks, shrimp, Prime Rib, salad bar, you name it. As their bus driver I was part of the crew. I dined with Indians from New Mexico, Inuits from Alaska, professional firefighters gathered from all over.

They were a serious lot. One evening I couldn't resist telling my favorite fireman story to those at my table.

*"Several barrels of oil in a lot behind a small town service station caught fire. A crowd gathered. Someone told the owner that he was fortunate that the famous fire fighter, Red Adair, was staying in a local motel and here he comes now. But he declined to help. He said he put out big fires like oil well fires in Kuwait. He said their local volunteer firefighters would do fine on this fire."*

*The alarm had been sounded and here came the fire truck lickety split with volunteers hanging on the sides. It plowed right into the center of the burning barrels. The men leaped off and fought fiercely and put out the fire. Adair said, "I am impressed. You did a very efficient job."*

*Someone said, "You guys will get the fifty dollar award for outstanding service."*

*Someone else asked the chief, "What are you going to do with that award money?"*

*"Well, first, we are going to get the darn brakes fixed on that fire truck."*

Some laughed. The rest of the evening was free time. In a big white tent a movie could be seen but the lights went out at 10pm. Rest was needed for a hard day tomorrow. So it was off to tent city and to bed.

My bed was in the bus. My mother had sewed a blanket from some soft fuzzy remnants. That topped my cozy bed across two seats. With a big cooler filling the aisle between the seats I was ready for a good night's sleep. Good food and a long day made sleep come fast. I *fell* asleep. The firefighters were sleeping. The day's heat had subsided. The breezes had quieted down. The fires were marking time. Comes dawn and refreshed firemen would be ready for another long day of trying to contain the fire, man's friend turned enemy. Beginning the next day I would transport my crew to a point a mile from the fire line and they would walk to where they would work all day. I would wait where I unloaded them. I would be there when they were ready to go back to the camp or sooner in case of emergency.

On the way to the work area I drove through miles of burned over forest. Animal trails were exposed where the forest critters traveled to food and water. Where were they now? Forest fires are terrible for people and animals.

When Matt Anderson and I checked in for duty at the Eastern Oregon wildfire camp it was reminiscent of the time in 1943 when I reported in at Jefferson Barracks, MO for duty in the Army Air Corps. Matt and I went to the supply tent and were issued fire resistant clothing. Anyone caught not wearing them on the grounds or on duty in the fire zone would be discharged and sent packing for home.

But there was a problem. They were out of pants that would fit me so I continued to wear the short pants I came with.

Every day I would drive my dozen firefighters 12 miles to a designated spot along the road and they would walk to my right to the fire containment zone about a quarter mile away. I would read, nap and watch the helicopters pass just ahead as they carried big buckets of water to dump on the fire.

In case the wind changed and the fire got out of control I had on my fire resistant clothing (except the pants) and kept an emergency aluminum cloth tent to hunker under and would hope the fire would pass over and not roast me alive. A stream ran through a thicket about 100 yards to my left. I imagined it would be a good place to lie under my little tent if the fire came my way. That cool water was sure inviting and 2 different days I stripped off and had a refreshing bath in that ankle deep water.

Then one day a dozen cattle came through and were herded right through that thicket by 2 cowboys and a COWGIRL! No more baths in that thicket!

One day, with my safety tent on my belt, I took my camera and walked about 3 miles back up the road to photograph the devastation of tree skeletons where the fire had already burned. Soon a green Forestry Service pickup screeched to a stop. The guy got out and said, "I've been working fires for 19 years and I have never seen anyone in the fire zone wearing shorts!"

So I said, "Now that you are stopped, take my picture," and handed him my camera.

In the year, 2012 the United States broke a 118-year heat record in July. That year's wildfire burn was nearly 8 million acres at the end of August, about the time that the budget allocated to fight them ran dry. The firefighters have a tough and dangerous business – even the ones who fly the aircraft. Once when I was Public Relations rep for the *Oregon Aircraft Owners and Pilots Association* we had a meeting scheduled in Klamath Falls, Oregon. I hitched a ride with a Portland pilot in his business plane, a Piper. Klamath Falls is rather remote and as we arrived I spotted a coyote atop a mound watching us land. Our meeting was in a room with large windows looking out on passenger planes just outside the window. During the meeting a call came in. One of our members was on call and lightening had set fire to a dead tree in a nearby valley and needed a water drop quickly. He told us he would be right back. A local mechanic went along for the ride. He dropped the water but the old WWII airplane couldn't clear the ridge. Someone came to tell us he would not be coming back.

Dawn each morning at the camp found a bee hive of activity. There were sinks, running water and paper towels for washing up and shaving. Inside the semi-trailer buildings were showers.

At the cooks trailer with the sides opened the cooks were ready to serve a hearty breakfast to be eaten at the tables in the large dining room tent nearby. Sack lunches were supplied to take along for the noon meal.

A long line of parked buses were waiting. Matt and I had to stow away our bedding, give the buses a thorough pre-trip inspection and have the motors running when our passengers came with their gear ready to be taken to various places on the perimeter of the fire.

My responsibility was to transport a team from Minnesota. One morning I got them well awake by picking up the mike and singing:

Matt Anderson

Oh listen to the rattle
As this old bus comes alive.
We're headed down the highway
In old Five-Eighty-Five

We came from Minnesota
In answer to the call
Now we are headed for the Tower fire
In the Roman Cannon Fireball!

After 12 days the Tower fire in Oregon was under control. After one last breakfast I loaded my Minnesota team and drove them to Pendleton. They boarded a commuter plane for the first leg of their trip back home.

## SBS to Ryder

Loose-Wiles Biscuit Company became Sunshine Biscuits. The Damascus Milk Company became Carnation. The California company that owned Portland Traction sold it to the city of Portland and it became Rose City Transit. Now it happened to my place of employment again. Lee Larson sells School Bus Services to the Ryder Company and SBS becomes Ryder Student Transportation.

Lee arranged for a party to say "Goodbye and thanks," to all the SBS personnel and assure them he had negotiated a sale that protected their interest. What a party it was! Lee secured the ballroom atop one of downtown Portland's tall buildings for this unforgettable event. Dad's brother, Bill, always claimed the whole nation celebrated his birthday. He was born on July 4! Since I would be leaving Oregon later that year, I would love to call this great party my goodbye party! The dinner was the best. This was Lee Larson's party. It was a party for all of SBS. Everyone was enjoying the food, the awards, the games and the speeches.

By prearrangement, I had something to present to the audience. Matt Anderson and I, the two Steen's Mountain Running Camp drivers spent a Friday evening at the Awards and Skits program. "As the party continued we slipped away, along with Michelle and the 2 children. We needed to rest for the long drive to Portland the next day. At the bunkhouse in Crane, Oregon we decided to take a dip in the swimming pool before retiring. After a while, Michelle said, 'Charlie, I want to sing you a song.' There in the moonlight, below a star-studded dome, her beautiful voice sang a song that seemed to have been composed just for me. So you can share that magical moment, Michelle will sing that song for us."

Here is the chorus.

Eighteen wheels and a dozen roses,
One more day on his 4 day run,
A few more songs on the all night radio
Then he'll spend the rest of his life
With the one he loves.

Janie sat in happy surprise. She had not been told ahead of time. The audience showed their appreciation with loud and sustained applause.

I presented Lee with an award certificate for providing me with a decade of most enjoyable experience to top off over a half century in transportation and photography.

**BOOK 9**

**Back To Kentucky**

## Our Old Kentucky Home

I want to move back home to old Kentucky
And take my darling Janie by the hand,
And show her all the places of my childhood,
And enjoy the finest food in all the land.
I want to hear the Whip-Poor-Will at sunset
And roosters crow to wake me up at dawn,
And redbirds singing lively in the woodland
While the mocking bird tunes in to sing along.

I like to drive this great big 18 wheeler
Across the land and see the distant scenes
But I'll be glad when I can take my boots off
And put my work shoes on to hoe the beans.
I'll steal a kiss from Janie in the kitchen
Where she is cooking dinner with the wood.
And, I'll be glad that I won't have to leave her,
Since I've retired and parked the truck for good.

I want to put a line in old Green River,
And catch a mess of catfish for the pan.
I'll take that old rifle from the closet
And get a squirrel or rabbit if I can.
I'll gather sweet persimmons after frost time,
And pick up hickory nuts beneath the tree.
While Janie makes sweet jam from all the berries,
I'll dig some root to make some sassafras tea.

The cantaloupe will ripen in the garden.
The truck patch will be full of beans and corn.
The good fresh country air will make us healthy,
So that we will thank the day that we were born.
While the garden grows we will take a journey,
And maybe see that famous Mammoth Cave.
Or, maybe we will go down to Nashville
And see The Grand Old Opry's latest rave.

We'll not have much use for that old rocker;
Our children are not babies, don't you see?
We'll be too busy staying young and healthy
To sit around a' staring at TV.
We'll find time to walk down through the timber,
To swim the river or to climb a hill.
The things that God put here for our enjoyment
Are the main things we enjoy, and always will.

We'll dress up in fine clothes and go to meeting
And learn things from God's word, and how to teach.
We'll hold hands and learn these things together,
And then go out and practice what we preach.
We'll show our love for all of our good neighbors,
By telling them about the things we've heard.
Our life together will be long and happy,
By living it according to God's word.

## Me and Reeta

Butler County has been blessed with the talents of several fine artists. To mention a few that comes to mind, there was David Coats, my dad's grandfather, a photographer. Ruey Annis and her daughter, Alma Mildred, Dad's cousins who made beautiful oil paintings. George Dabbs was our home town photographer and artist who preserved the steamboats and other long gone scenes in his paintings. Now we have Reeta Burden, painter and singer and player of Old Time Country and Gospel music on 2 popular DVDs. Reeta became a valuable thread in the fabric of our life.

When Libby Jane and I arrived in Morgantown in 1997 we could not find property or homes available anywhere. Mayor Charlie Black was enjoying fresh air in front of City Hall. I introduced him to Janie whose father had been a mayor of St. James, Missouri and we told him of our dilemma. He told me that Reeta Burden had some property on Sawmill Road that she might sell. She would, and that is how I met Reeta. Reeta's prolific scenic paintings adorn offices and homes throughout Butler County and beyond. Some portray scenes of Butler County's past that I knew when I was in school. One shows the Walnut Grove church where my Dad's parents are buried.

We almost lost her talent to diseases that were a real curse at that time. But let her tell us about it in this excerpt from her Memoir, used by permission.

~

## Eden's Child by Reeta Burden

My earliest memories are of lying in bed with a brace on my leg, visits from the health department and quarantine sign on our front door. Polio was my rude awakening to a world filled with sickness and uncertainty. A four year old child doesn't realize at the time what has happened to her, but as time goes by, it becomes apparent. By degrees an extreme inferiority complex is developed, as the child enters school and sees others are not afflicted as she is and that she cannot run and play as they do. The atmosphere at home seems to be friendly and her place there is not at all unpleasant. In fact more attention is given to the unfortunate one in order to make amends for something for which no one is to blame, but for which everyone feels a measure of guilt. Even the crippled child feels guilty because she does not measure up.

Fortunately, I have never experienced much ridicule because of my condition. Most people have been sympathetic or just unconcerned. I just hate for someone to ask me about my limp. It is embarrassing when someone stares at me but it is usually for just a moment, then they accept me as I am. Although I am truly blessed that I have only a slight limp, it is difficult to adjust in a society in which excellence is held so high. If I had done what I felt like I would have shut myself up at home where it was safe and secure and never spent a day in school; however I did develop a stiff upper lip and tried to convince myself that I was as good as anyone else.

When I began school, things went along rather uneventfully until I reached the age of ten years. I then experienced my second trauma which was a broken arm while on stilts. Of course a child without all her faculties should not try to walk on stilts; nevertheless, I did try, the result being a compound fracture. My doctor failed to give me the tetanus shot and tetanus developed. I went into convulsions and ultimately coma. I remember being placed on a stretcher to go to the hospital with no room in my mouth for my tongue. My doctor said there was no hope for me. Another doctor was called in who said I had a fifty-fifty chance if they got me to the hospital quickly. My dad lay by my side in the hospital room for twenty-one days, during which time I was unconscious and subject to repeated convulsions. I was given all the penicillin my body could take. The doctor said no more could be done, it was up to me.

The firsts thing I remember when I regained consciousness was a door slamming across the hall and the reaction by my body of another convulsion. During that time my arm was re-broken in the cast. Not wanting to subject me to any more suffering and believing that I would not survive, nothing was done. My arm grew back crooked and shorter. Nevertheless, by all rights and assumptions I should not have lived through that ordeal. Before penicillin, people just did not live through tetanus as a rule. I have often wondered why I was allowed to live after coming so close to death. It would have been so easy to slip on over. Being a person who tries to see a purpose in everything, I have to believe there was a purpose in this suffering that I was allowed to endure. Over the years I have come to see the light.

∼

## Driving again – School Buses and Lawn Mowers

With a half-acre lot on Sawmill Road we soon bought a manufactured home to meet a goal of having a home on Sawmill Road that had a garbage disposal and sewer hookup. Our next goal ran into a hitch. We had sold our car in Portland and had come here in the U-Haul truck. I had no trouble buying the Crown Victoria Ford as I planned. I had Allstate insurance in Oregon but when I, a Master Driver with SBS, tried to get insured in Kentucky, some idiot at Allstate decided to get rid of a 72 year old liability and my agent could not get them to renew my insurance. Other companies made the same decision. Finally, Gene Kelley, the State Farm agent, got me insured. Years later I reminded him that he was the only one to get me insured when I moved here. He said he was pleased to have us with State Farm. I said I had even driven the school buses here for 3 years. "Yes I rode with you once." I had not recognized him when he went with the kids on a field trip. "I expect to see you driving when you are 100." That was a nice vote of confidence from my insurance agent.

My Teamster's retirement was small so being a substitute school bus driver made a nice supplement to my Social Security. The biggest benefit was a chance to learn Butler County as I had never learned it as a schoolboy. The numerous curves and blind hilltops were a challenge. The rural scenes were a delight. "Look! That cloud fell out of the sky last night." The kids would look in silent wonderment at the fog in the valley, awed by this strange perspective. A usual response was, "Cool."

A black cat was seen racing across the barnyard. "Look! That white cat got in the soot." The bus was quiet as the kids watched the kitty run away all covered in black.

My silly tricks got me in trouble with some of the regular drivers. "Charlie, you spoiled my kids. They don't want me anymore. They want you to be their driver." Actually having different loads each day was easier. I could use the same jokes over and over. As we passed a field I yelled, "Hay." The bus quieted and the kids looked where I was pointing. Sure enough, the field was full of bales of hay. Two days later I subbed the same route. Little Brittany sat behind me. "Charlie, I liked your joke about hay."

"You did?"

"Yes. I played it on my mother."

"What happened?"

"She slammed on the brakes, stopped and slapped me."

I had no trouble with the routes. On my computer I made some official looking *Back Seat Driver's Licenses.* I would go to the first address on the route and give the first student to board the bus a license. They were very conscientious in telling me where to turn and where to expect to see a rider waiting to board or come running out of a home.

A friend was mowing lawns and one lawn had a steep bank. He was afraid of turning over on it. He asked me if I would take it over. I liked it. It was healthy to ride a while then walk while trimming the perimeter, sidewalks and flower beds. I quit driving school buses at the age of 75 and soon had the few lawns I needed to supplement my income. I met interesting people. I went up to Mayor Charles Black's door one day and said, "I don't think your lawn needs mowing today."

"You decide," he said. Mary Alice was at the door with him. "We are just leaving to go to the doctor's."

"It doesn't do any good for me to go to the doctor," I said. "They don't have a pill for my problem."

"What's your problem?"

"I've been tested positive for the age virus."

He popped to attention and spat out, "What's that?"

"The age virus..."

"Oh! Get out of here."

When I mowed for Lenora McCoy her pay often included a fried apple pie like Mom used to put in my school lunch. After she passed away her son, Alan Shields, who lived in Indiana, had me continue caring for her place until he sold it. When my mother at the rest home was sick all night my sister, Wanda Smith, and her husband J. T., came from Owensboro to sit with her all night. I went by the next morning, talked with them a while and kissed Mom goodbye and left. I met up with Alan Shields and he bought my breakfast at the Farm Boy Restaurant. While mowing a lawn later that day, Libby Jane called me on the cell phone to tell me Mom had passed away. She had lived to the ripe old age of 87. At the end of the season in 2015 my 90 year old body could no longer take the rough ride on the mower. My last call from Alan was that he had sold Lenora's home. So I did not have to find him someone to replace me. For 15 years Lenora McCoy and Alan Shields had been a happy thread through the fabric of my life.

After my mother died, my sister Velma, in settling her estate, sold her home to Lannie and Anne Scott next door. So when I mowed the

Scott property I mowed the lawn at Mom's last private home also. I am truly at home in Butler County.

## Digital Photography

I had no intention of pursuing a photography career in Kentucky. I was disillusioned with the inks used in the printers. They deteriorated rapidly in sunlight. The industry was working hard to change that. Finally Hewlett Packard claimed that photos with their inks would last 200 years. I bought a HP commercial printer that used 8 ink cartridges. I wanted any pictures I made to have the quality of the pictures I had made for 50 years using chemicals in the darkroom or printed by the color labs. Soon I was making 13x19 borderless color enhanced prints of Reeta's paintings. Many more prints of her paintings were sold from her shop on Main Street.

Some of Butler county history was fading away. I made an album of Mayor Charles Black's final days in Office. Another album saved the memory of Dr. Richard Wan's Clinic before it became a branch of the Graves Gilbert clinic. Cindy Black's Halloween decorations made her a **Boo Boo Book**.

Old historical scenes were gone and the pictures of them had almost faded away. I restored the faded photos to their former luster good for another 200 years.

## Indians in Butler County

Green River bordered the back of our 60 acres on Logansport Road. It included Turkey Rock and the Old Swimming Hole. Green River banks are usually slick mud but this one spot had a sloping shale rock 'beach' making an ideal spot to park one's clothes and wade in for a swim.

I once found an arrowhead among the flat rocks so I knew we were not the first to use this swimming hole. How many Native American children played here while the adults did other things like carving the intriguing designs on Turkey rock about 100 yards downstream?

Descendants of Noah's 3 sons populated the earth. Shem's stayed in western Asia – Israelites and Arabs mainly. Ham's had white and black descendants. The whites were Canaanites and the blacks settled Africa. Japheth's descendants went west as Europeans and east to populate Asia and the Americas.

When their European cousins came across the Atlantic with superior weapons and devastating diseases they wrested the land from its first inhabitants. Just because God foretold the outcome in Daniel and Revelation doesn't mean he approved of the brutal methods. Nyla Morgan filled me in on the shameful "Trail of Tears" that brought the displaced Cherokees across Kentucky.

But *we* have become more civilized and now treat our native citizens with more respect.

Mom's Uncle, Ollie Andrews was married to Aunt Mamie, an Indian woman. Uncle Ollie was a cantankerous old Spanish American war veteran. If I had a bad day and acted stubborn about something I was sometimes called 'Uncle Ollie'. Aunt Mamie finally had enough and took Ollie Junior and went to Arkansas. Mom kept in touch and remained friends with her. Ollie Newman Jr. became a deputy sheriff in Little Rock about 30 miles south of Aunt Mamie's home. Aunt Mamie married again and her son by that marriage was an official in a local bank. Her daughter, Virginia Couch, looked very promising to be my brother Duane's wife but he died before that happened.

Virginia married Coy Fortson from Michigan. I was visiting Mom once when Coy's mother, Coy and Virginia and their 2 sons came by for a visit. When trucking through Michigan I stopped to visit them a number of times. I was talking with Mayor Charlie Black one day. He told me how most of his projects for Morgantown, no matter how good they were, had opposers. So I told him about Coy in Michigan. Coy worked for Maytag. The company wanted to do things for the community. They would maybe buy vacant land and want to put in a playground at no expense to the community. Opposers would try to stop the project. I told Charlie I had a name for them. He asked me what it was. I said, "I call them 'agin'ers."

Charlie poked his finger in the air for emphasis and said, "You've GOT IT!"

And so it goes. The Indians in our midst are married into our families or running their businesses or playing the politics of their Indian Nations. Governor Patton declared November 1998 Native

American Indian Month in honor of their contribution to our society. A word of warning: If you are on vacation and come across one of their legal gambling casinos you'd better not go in. You may get your wallet and bank account scalped!

## Janie's Ch... Ch... Cha...

Janie's 99 years weigh heavily on her much of the time and she has very little energy. Her 12 year long digestive disease, undiagnosed and untreated by our broken medical establishment, supresses her appitite most of the time. She prepares her own tolerated meals most of the time. But when she has one of those rare moments of feeling better and tells me she is hungry for one of my special ham and cheese sandwiches, it's time for her Chief Chef Charlie to spring into action.

I set my induction cook top at 275 degress and place, in the skillet, 2 slices of rosemary bread. As one side warms moderately I use a spoon and shave thin layers of whipped butter to rub into the up side of the bread. This will help brown the outside of the sandwich. I lay the 2 slices on a plate. Then I sizzle the water out of 3 thin slices of deli honey-roasted ham. I coat a slice of the bread with honey mustard and lay the ham on it. I cut 2 thick slices of rare and delicious Tillamook cheese from the small dairy region of the Oregon coast. These I put in the skillet and melt a little on each side. With a thin spatula I lift the 'fried' cheese onto the still warm ham and cover with the other slice of rosmary bread. I gently place the complete sandwich, buttered side down, into the skillet. After each side is lightly browned I put the sandwich on a small Royal Albert plate featuring the Jubilee Rose and cut it in half and serve it to my princess Janie. Janie grabs a half while the other half, oozing delicious melted Tillamook cheese, awaits its turn.

Old age offers a lot of discomforts and few pleasures. This is one small pleasure I am pleased to provide my Janie from her Chief Chef Charlie! Thanks, to my mother, for teaching me to cook when I was a teenager.

My comfort food is still a plate full of beans and cornbread. I use a smaller plate now. I can no longer handle a big meal as I did as a trucker. I like beans and cornbread with green or sliced onions. I like beans and cornbread with dill or sweet pickles. I like beans and cornbread with pepper sauce. You can see I like variety in my diet! Recently I discovered a condiment that is proving to be my favorite.

At Billy White's Boogie Barn on Old Ferry Road I found home canned green tomato relish. It is the most delishous condiment for my beans and cornbread I have ever found. It is produced on site in an efficient commercial kitchen. I hope Mr. White never runs out of green tomatoes. When I sit down to a plate full of beans and cornbread, enhanced with green tomato relish, and downed with a glass of whole milk, it is my Kentucky moment.

## Memory and Old Age

### Memory Box
On March 21, Carol Hill of Fort Worth, Texas bought a little chest on eBay to hold stereoviews, those 3D pictures on 3.5 x 7 cards. It was her first eBay purchase and it was from my friend, Jerry Dean who now lives in Columbia, east of Bowling Green.

Carol made her second purchase on April 2 when she bid on a stereoscope and 25 stereoviews that I had listed on eBay. With 3000 stereoscope related listings on eBay it is an astonishing coincidence that a newcomer would make her first and second purchases from Jerry and me.

I saw Jerry recently as we were both picking up supplies at Staples in Bowling Green. I should have asked him if he had another 'Memory Box' for sale, one that would fit in my brain!

They say that age wrecks short term memory. You can't remember much about yesterday but long ago memories remain sharp. When I moved back to Butler County in 1997 I told Dr. James Carver that his name as Superintendent of schools should be Louis Arnold. Mr. Arnold signed my grade school Diploma on June 1, 1939 and mailed it to me on June 8 in a three cent stamped envelope to the farm on Logansport road. He was still superintendent when I graduated from High school in 1943.

Our county agent was Sam Kent. His wife, Dorothy Moore was Postmaster. I should know our present Postmaster, Mr. Chris Chiles just as well. He has guided me in packaging and mailing eBay sales and hired me to make a group picture of the employees as well as mowing the PO property for a few years *but* I got his name wrong in a recent article.

I have been aware of Joe Louis for over half a century but something made my fingers type Lewis. Most embarrassing is that these slips glare at you when they are in the large print title as was the Khyber Pass article without the h.

Errors can be amusing as well as irritating. When I worked with one company an associate, Robert Safford, ordered business cards. The 1000 cards arrived with the name, Robert Stafford. He sent them back and asked that the superfluous t be left out. The next 1000 cards came to Rober Stafford!

Names of people and names of things suffer the most in the memory bank. I have said for some time that Janie and I are concerned about the hereafter. We go into the next room and look around and ask, "What am I here after?"

It has been observed that short term memory is lost but long term memory can be at its best in old age. That's why it is best to wait until you are 90 to write your memoirs. I heard that there are 3 signs of old age. One of them is loss of memory and the other two are… er, ah. "Oh shucks. I forgot what those other two are."

### 1914 – 2014

Featured in the news: It has been 100 years since the beginning of the Great War, a.k.a. WWI.

It has been 99 years since the United States entered that war. My wife, Libby Jane has lived every one of those 99 years. Born on July 14, 1917 in St. James, Missouri, she was delivered by a midwife who was an ex-slave. On May 11, 1981 I joined her for the latest 35 years of her trek through history.

Although ravaged for over a dozen years by a debilitating digestive problem, undiagnosed by an inept medical profession her mind is sharp and she soaks up knowledge like a sponge. I keep her supplied with magazines, The Daily News where she quickly works the crossword puzzle and a steady flow of items I print from the Internet. We read the Bible daily. WWI history is of special interest to us.

On Saturday, August 2 the Syndicated Columnist, Cal Thomas discussed WWI in his column printed in the Bowling Green Daily News.

He draws much of his comments from Max Hastings' book, Catastrophe 1914. Through my years of study I can understand his comments and could even contribute to them. He says, "Of all the wars, this one may have been the least predictable." The world was caught completely by surprise by the rapidly escalating war. But it need not have been. For some 4 decades a group of Bible students had been warning that Daniel's prophecy had indicated 1914 as a time for great change. That fall one newspaper even said this group could say, "I told you so."

Jesus disciples knowing his presence in the last days would be invisible, asked what sign we, at this time, could see as evidence. He said there would have been wars and rumors of wars but now it would be 'nation against nation, kingdom against kingdom'. In other words it would be a world war. Of all 900 major wars from 500 BCE until 1914, WWI was 7 times more destructive than all of them put together. What stronger sign could we expect? See Mathew Chapter 24.

In Revelation Jesus revealed the cause of the war. There would be a war in heaven and Satan thereafter would be confined to the vicinity of the earth. "The Devil will come down to you having great wrath, knowing he has a short period of time."

Cal Thomas wrote: Hastings quotes the Fabian Society's Beatrice Webb who was offended by what she called "the disgusting misuse of religion" to stimulate patriotism.

Thomas wrote of a lasting revulsion when the merits of the allied cause became tarnished by the baroque language and spurious religiosity with which it was marketed.

WWI was fought by 'Christian' nations and when the preachers on both sides blessed the cause and armaments of their respective sides they lost credibility.

Janie and I may be close to the limit of life allowed imperfect descendants of Adam but as we see the world descend into ever increasing moral and political decadence we may see the fulfillment of "Thy kingdom come" yet. God would not destroy the Canaanites until their wickedness justified his doing so.

We are getting there.

## Backing up? Watch out!

In the Beverly Hillbillies TV show the doorbell was featured in some very funny scenes. The bell would chime for several seconds and instead of answering the door they would wonder where the music was coming from. Jed, Jethro, Elly Mae and Granny would frantically search around the room looking for the source of the sound. Jethro observed that after the music a visitor always knocked on the door. Sure enough an impatient visitor would decide the doorbell wasn't working and knock. I recently had a similar experience. Read on.

Backing up can be a hazardous experience for anyone behind the vehicle. The driver of a big rig can't see what is centered behind his trailer. While backing into a parking spot at a truck stop I have climbed down from the seat a dozen or more times to see if I was staying centered. When backing in a jackknife configuration the rear view mirrors are useless.

While I was the editor of Bus Biz, the monthly newsletter for School Bus Services, I featured a safety article about backing up a school bus. If you back in too close and pull up to reposition don't steer too sharply or the long overhang behind the rear wheels will swing into the vehicle beside you. It's called tail swing.

Many modern buses and trucks feature a sound when the vehicle is in reverse. If you hear that distinctive dee dah, dee dah, dee dah, you had better see who is backing up.

Recently I heard that distinctive sound. I was in my home so why would there be a truck backing up in here? After about ten double beeps it stopped. I passed it off as probably something on TV. The next day I heard this warning again. This time I was in the bedroom so it couldn't be the TV. The weather radio wasn't on so it couldn't be giving an emergency warning. It stopped without me figuring it out. The next day when the warning sounded again, I hurried from one end of the house to the other. It was just as loud in one place as another. Was it coming from outside? No trucks or buses were around. I noticed it was 8:30 am. Why that was the same time every morning. So at that time the next morning I alerted Janie to listen for it. She didn't hear anything until I moved close to her. She said, "It seems to be coming from you." That gave me a clue.

The next morning I got in a confined place and the signal was loud and clear. It was from my pacemaker! Early last Monday I was at the VA medical center in Nashville. I was at the Check-In desk at 8:30 and told them to listen. When they heard the sound they called my device manager and told her to check me. She wirelessly tuned in my pacemaker and checked its recorded message. It was telling me that my heart was intermittently going in and out of rhythm. Nothing serious. She didn't shut it off; she just reprogrammed it to go off if something more serious occurred.

I jokingly told them, "That was a mean trick to play on an old trucker, making me think a truck was backing up on me.

### The Toughest Job
Mr. Shepherd lived in a notorious town in eastern Kentucky. He was into bootlegging and other less than honorable pursuits when his

brother got elected sheriff. So as not to be an embarrassment to his brother he moved to Oregon.

I was managing the photo lab and photographing for Dee's Distinguished Photographs on the main street which was also highway 26 that goes through Gresham, Oregon when I heard that we had a new manager at the Texaco Station down the street and he was from Kentucky. I went by and got acquainted with Mr. Shepherd.

One day he told me that he had been cleaning the windshield for a customer. He said that he had seen so much in his life that nothing could shock or embarrass him. But as he wiped the windshield on the driver's side he couldn't believe what he had seen. He wiped across the window once more and looked again. Sure enough. The female driver had her coat laid open and there was nothing underneath!

That's how Mr. Shepherd learned that not far away there in east Multnomah County there was a nudist colony.

Sometime later Mr. Shepherd got a job on a road crew as a flagger on road repair and road building projects. One day he couldn't work the job so they hired his son for the day. I later talked to the young man about it. He said, "I have a lot more respect for my old man since that day. I thought he had a soft, goof off job but that was the toughest job I ever did. I thought the day would never end."

Recently as Morgantown's Main Street which is Highway 231, was being repaved they had four flaggers directing the traffic safely through the project, Linda, April, Heather and Michaela. I talked to Michaela Woodcock about her job. She verified everything young Mr. Shepherd had told me. The job is demanding and impatient drivers make it worse. They become rude and insulting.

I have noticed that when I wave and smile at the flaggers I get a big smile in return. If you show that you appreciate their keeping you safe they will show that they appreciate you for making their day a friendly one.

## Once Upon A Time – ONCE

Miss Bessie Romans, Dad's first cousin, was our home room teacher. Her brother Orville was coaching a basketball game in the gym when the ball was tossed to me as I was running away from the basket. I sort of twisted and tossed the ball and made a perfect throw through the hoop. The next time I got close to Orville he quietly said, "You can't do that again." I agreed. That was my one and only professional performance.

Swimming was the only sport that interested me. Down by Turkey Rock on Dad's farm I once swam back and forth across Green River 10 times and quit because I was bored. When the Army Air Corps sent me to Butler U. in Indianapolis our "barracks" was the Hinkle Field House. On my first free time I swam the length of the Olympic sized swimming pool 100 laps in about 3 hours. My group wanted me to represent them in an upcoming swim meet. I said, "Anybody can swim faster than I can. I have endurance but no speed." They insisted so I represented my outfit. I came in last and they cheered that I had stayed the course in my one and only public swim performance.

Uncle Tyler Dockery here in Morgantown made his own violin. I thought that was a neat accomplishment. In Oregon my friend, Percy Cornwell, had a friend in North Portland that made violins. Percy invited me to go over there with him one evening. The basement workshop walls displayed several violins made of rosewood and other exotic woods. They were soon playing duets. Then they asked me if I could sing. I knew a few songs so I named one. They started playing and I guessed as to when to start singing. I know absolutely nothing about music except I like to listen to it. On the way home Percy asked if I had ever had singing lessons. I hadn't. He said, "You started your song at exactly the right time." Wow. I had guessed right for the one and only time I ever sang solo to music!

In the A. L. Williams Insurance business I sold Insurance and Securities in Vice President Irv Yeats group. At the company picnic in Troutdale Park just east of Portland we challenged the Jim Myers group to a baseball game. I was playing outfield when a high fly was batted my direction. I got under it and easily fielded it bare handed and threw it back into the game. The first chance he got Jim Myers said, "That was a good catch." My one and only claim to baseball fame!

My wife and I were sleeping in one Saturday. We called to 5 year old Charla Kay to join us. She was delighted. She was soon between us chattering and giggling. The radio was on the floor beside my side of the bed. It was tuned to a request program. I had mailed a postcard in. I guessed it was about time for my request to be played. I said to the radio, "For Charla Kay Romans play 'Chocolate Ice Cream Cone' by Jimmy Roberts."

The very next words from the radio were, "For Charla Kay Romans the next request is 'Chocolate Ice cream Cone' by Jimmy Roberts.

Charla listened quietly as her favorite song came over the radio just for her. What would she say when it was over? Her next words were:

"Play me another one." Oops!

When I lived in Oregon and my dad lived here in Kentucky I came for a visit every 2 to 5 years. My son Henry lives here now. Daughter Charla has visited and calls for a chat every week. When Vincent brought his family for a visit I rented a boat and we enjoyed the Swimming hole without negotiating the steep trail. Chris enjoyed his boat driving lesson as his mother, Danielle rode along in back. The Mt. Hood ski slope seemed long ago and far away.

## Golden Years

In old age our memories are often more golden than our day by day realities. I am weaving the final fringe on my tapestry of life and memory. Some threads through the fabric of memories can be detected through the whole length of my life. Others singly and in groups appear for a while making a separate book to hold ones attention, a distinctive picture before blending into the background after leading us into the next book of memory.

I am comfortable and pleased to be back in Kentucky. For the last few years I have been a correspondent for the Butler County Banner. Every week I have shared my stories. My Butler County neighbors have enjoyed seeing how a native son spent over a half century having many adventures in distant places.

But I have left a big hole in the story. My experience with the medical profession is a book in itself and I hope I live long enough to write it. I was disappointed, shocked and enraged at the ignorance, the animosity and the dangerous attitudes I encountered in dealing with health problems. If you can learn my story you may understand my conclusion: The medical school training destroys the humanity in men more than any other profession I know. When you find a doctor who still has his common sense and empathy treat him well; he is a golden apple in the rotten barrel.

## Veterans Affairs Medical

Here in my golden years I do have a golden experience of great life giving benefit. I first used the VA health care in Portland, Oregon. Here in South Central Kentucky I leaned toward the culture of Tennessee rather than Louisville so I checked in with the Nashville VA rather than Fort Knox.

The Bowling Green Clinic took care of minor problems and on a routine 6 month checkup the nurse asked, "Do you know that you have a heart problem?" I didn't so she immediately set up an appointment with the Nashville VA hospital.

The Nashville facility has the unique advantage of being back to back with the Vanderbilt University Medical Center, a teaching hospital. They can use their doctors. Dr. Henry Ooi, at Vanderbilt can go out the back door, cross the lot and enter the back door of the VA facility where he can go down the hall and up the elevator to the 2nd floor Heart Clinic. He examined me and checked my lab report and gave me serious news. My heart was very weak. It could fail anytime. A possible knee replacement was pending. Unless my heart was strengthened an operation could not be considered. Dr. Ooi immediately authorized the implanting of a pacemaker with a defibrillator. For the rest of my life I will be keeping an appointment at the device clinic every six months and, to keep a fresh battery, a replacement of the device every 5 years; that has happened once already. With all the nationwide criticism of the VA I am happy that I have been able to tell positive stories of the outstanding performance and friendly people at this facility. They have saved my life and are keeping me alive so I can care for my beloved Libby Jane and write my story. They are truly a rich part of my golden years. They know me when they see me coming and expect to receive copies of my latest Butler County Banner Column. So I'll end my panoramic tapestry with one of those stories.

## A Visit to the Veteran's Health Care Center Nashville

I left Morgantown early for my appointment at the Veteran's Hospital and Clinic in Nashville. I went to downtown Nashville and drove south on Broadway. About 20 blocks south I angled left to go in front of Vanderbilt. Since the VA is behind Vandy 2 right turns put me to the parking lot. Lots of parking spaces this morning so I am soon in a corridor on my way to my first appointment.

Instructions said, "No food or drink after midnight" so I ignored the Starbucks coffee as I went by. On my way I met Ms. Linda Howerton, the RN who is my coach for managing my heart treatment. She explained to the nurse with her that here was a patient who was a photographer and writer and restorer of old photos. I saw a victim for my old trucker's joke so I told the new nurse that we were exploring a possible knee replacement and if I needed a brain transplant I wanted a trucker's brain. They say they have never been used,

Ms. Howerton spoke up and said, "I would want one like yours." Linda says the nicest things! I proceeded to the blood drawing lab. Every time I go to Nashville they draw a lot of blood. Then they say I am anemic!

Next stop is the Dental Clinic. Dr. Durick was a naval aviator. He is a real artist when it comes to repairing teeth. We discussed the large gap where I lost a molar. It had opened a hole up into my sinuses. The two dentists who had pulled the teeth were shining a light and seeing it come out the other end. I was hoping it wasn't my ears they were looking through. I made arrangements for dental work with Dr. Durick and proceeded to my next appointment.

Dr. Bernui outlined a need for building up my blood. I asked him about his name. His father was from Peru. Had he ever been there? Yes, twice. Did he see those ruins up in the mountains? Machu Piccu.

Yes. He had been there. Wow! We are talking of a place I know from pictures and stories and now I am talking to someone who has been there!

Now I go to the basement where I will see the gym for the vital exercises needed if I get the knee surgery. I browse the magazines as I wait. A National Geographic has a photo article about Machu Piccu! I get permission to take it upstairs to Dr. Bernui's receptionist. He called me at home the next day to thank me for that random act of kindness!

I go back to the basement where I'm soon being interviewed about my medical history by a nurse who strongly resembled a certain movie star. Soon she paused and said, "and my name is Karen," I think she said.

"Oh! I thought it was Meryl Streep."

"I wish! But your next stop is the eye clinic!"

Now it's to the Heart Station on the 2nd floor.

The waiting room is full and one gentleman in a wheelchair was reading an aviation journal. I moved over to see if he was an Air Corp Vet as I was. He was. We were soon talking about the dihedral of wings, etc. He said it was sure good to talk to someone who knew the language! He started to tell me something but it slipped his mind. He is deep in thought trying to recall what it was. He was hard of hearing so in a loud voice in that quiet room I told him, "The hereafter has me and my wife worried. We go in the other room and look around and say, 'What am I here after?'" The whole room of old folks broke into laughter.

I was laughing, too, as I was called into the device room where I sat in a chair and a nearby computer read the information my pacemaker had recorded. I assured the technician that the defibrillator had caused me no trouble but I was being very careful not to tell a fib.

Now, it's time for a final session with Linda Howerton. She has NR after her name and some other impressive letters but no DR, so I can't call her a pill doctor but she sure has me on a lot of pills. She works closely under Dr. Ooi, a senior heart specialist from Vanderbilt next door. Their performance is excellent and I try hard to follow the doctor's orders.

One last stop before I leave Tennessee. The cafeteria serves real down south southern cooking with friendly servers to dish it up!

It's been a long time since midnight.

As I drive north for Morgantown, I think what fine friendly personnel and patients we have at our Veteran's Healthcare Center in Nashville where they take care of our wounds and illnesses.

**Treasures and Memories**

Memories can be great and even better when we can share. I was so pleased to get my sons to Pampa, Texas to meet my dear friend from WWII before she died. Marie (Molly) McGee was so happy to meet the grandsons of her old friends, the Roy Whites. We got a picture with Vince standing behind her and Henry Kent behind me. She was truly a treasured friend.

When our treasure becomes a memory, our memory becomes our treasure. My treasure chest is truly running over.

**Tapestry Complete**

My tapestry of memories is almost complete. The final fringe is being woven. Am I ready to sit in my rocker and look back. Should I let these memories form my dreams and stir my sleep at night? No! In 2017 the 40 year old Steens Mountain High Altitude Running Camp is having a reunion of all past associates who wish to come. I plan to be there. Portland beckons me to see the modern metropolis they have become and tell them about the old days I lived there.

I want to see Pampa, Texas again and show them a book of memories, mine and theirs. Has San Angelo forgotten the old bi-planes? I would like to bring them some memories. Would San Antonio like to be reminded of the cadets who walked their parks in 1944 and meet one who fell in love with their town?

I tell my doctors in Nashville to keep me alive until I can write the story of my experiences, good and bad, with the medical establishment and how I helped change some things for the better.

And a book of those beautiful poems that Libby Jane and I wrote while courting could show this new generation that making a commitment can be a beautiful thing.

Over 9 decades ago I was born with a curiosity that still makes me want to see what is around the next corner and what I can do with it.

### Janie's Country Boy

I am just an old hillbilly from the hills of old Kentucky
And I'll always have the country in my soul.
My girl is from a small town, a sophisticated lady
And why she loves this farm boy I don't know.
In the hills of Butler County I was a farmer's son
And I read a book a day when times were slow.
So when Old Uncle Sugar needed pilots for his airplanes
This old country boy was set to go.

Over in Saint James, Missouri Janie's father was the mayor
And he showed her what a good man ought to be.
Then she moved to California where she grew to be a lady
And her Daddy's hills became a memory.
Came the war and Uncle Sam needed welders in the shipyard
And that is where she worked to end the strife.
That is why this country bumpkin found out on the west coast
A lovely lady to become his wife.

I am just an old hillbilly from the hills of Old Kentucky
And I'll never be a slick big city man.
But I'll always love my Janie from the hills of Old Missouri
And I'll always make her happy if I can.
I have been a coal miner in the hills of Butler County
And I've farmed in the fields of Illinois.
But my Janie doesn't mind it if I'm rough around the edges
Because — she loves her country boy!

What better place to contemplate the tapestry of my memories than on the Romans Bluff below the hill where my home stood on Logansport Road. Below me at the bottom of the 100 foot cliff the trail continues down the rocky, tree covered hillside to the banks of Green River at the swimming hole. The echo of the steamboats that roiled her waters is only in my mind. Push back the past. It is back, way back. It has been a great pilgrimage. Now the future is here. I am ready to live it. The best is yet to come.

The nation has been my playground. My playground is being torn apart. Every terrorist attack seems to be where I had been. Jesus said the last days of this system would be marked by unprecedented troubles. We are there. (Matthew 24). There will be a resurrection. In his sermon on the mount at Matt. 5:5 Jesus said the meek ones will inherit the earth. What a privilege it will be to have a part in rebuilding our everlasting home, the paradise that Adam lost.

Dear reader, I'll see you there

Notes:

Made in the USA
Lexington, KY
18 May 2019